Fall Protection
and
Scaffolding
Safety

4/21

An Illustrated Guide.........

Grace Drennan Gagnet, CSP

Michael Drennan, Illustrator

Government Institutes
Rockville, Maryland

Government Institutes, a Division of ABS Group Inc.
4 Research Place, Rockville, Maryland 20850, USA
Phone: (301) 921-2300
Fax: (301) 921-0373
Email: giinfo@govinst.com
Internet: http://www.govinst.com

04 03 02 01 00   5   4   3   2   1

Library of Congress Cataloging-in-Publication Data

Gagnet, Grace Drennan.
     Fall protection and scaffolding safety: an illustrated guide / Grace Drennan Gagnet,
Michael Drennan, illustrator.
     p.cm.
     Includes bibliographical references and index.

     ISBN 0-86587-692-4 (soft)

     1. Scaffolding—Safety measures. 2. Falls (Accidents)—Prevention. I. Title.

TH5281 .G34 2000
690'.22—dc21

                                          00-021214

Printed in the United States of America

Summary Contents

Contents

Chapter 3 **Principles of Fall Protection** **39**

Chapter 4 **Prevention of Falls and Falling Objects** **49**

Chapter 6   **Scaffolds** **101**

Chapter 9   **Special Applications** **173**

Grace Drennan Gagnet is a Certified Safety Professional who specializes in the development of occupational safety and health training programs. She and her brother—**Michael Drennan**, illustrator—have been working together since 1994 under their company name, AFA (Accident Free Advantage) Safety Services, Inc. Most of their training courses are designed to be delivered in sessions lasting from one to eight hours. This textbook combines the content of several courses. AFA designs courses both for instructor-led classes and for self-instruction on the Internet or on a company intranet.

Grace worked for electrical utility companies in Florida for 12 years before moving to Dallas, Texas, to work as a safety consultant. Michael worked for 30 years as a draftsman for a public facility and two private companies before collaborating with his sister on safety and health courses.

Although they now live thousands of miles apart, they stay in touch on a daily basis with postcards, other correspondence, and phone calls.

Concept for Book

Most safety professionals will readily admit that they rely upon a lot of the same sources of information to develop training materials: U.S. DOL-OSHA regulations, consensus standards, government-sponsored research publications, books offered by the National Safety Council and American Society of Safety Engineers, trade magazines, and internet sites, among others.

However, regulations and standards have page after page of fine print that is hard to read and understand. Illustrations are few and far between. It takes a strong will and determination to learn how to comply with OSHA regulations, even for the most dedicated safety professional or supervisor.

Through experience and because of my brother's talent as an illustrator who can draw almost anything, we have found that people in our safety classes respond best to simple, clear drawings. Photos are good, but they often have too much detail that is visually confusing, or they don't exactly show what you are trying to convey. Magazines and publications often have good photos, but they do not reproduce well when you want to use them as handouts in a training session.

What you will see in this book are many drawings that were prepared especially to explain the text. The text often consists of the very same rules and regulations that were published by OSHA, but you only need to look at the pictures and the captions to really understand what they mean. And we want you to understand these rules and regulations; it could save your life someday, or the life of a co-worker.

Look at the pictures and you will know what to avoid and how to apply the safe work practices that are recommended in this book.

Fall Protection Course

This book can also be used as a self-study guide, reference, or textbook to learn about the scope and range of fall hazards and prevailing standards that are designed to mitigate them.

If you are a safety trainer and you would like to order a CD with electronic files of Power Point™ presentations that correspond to each of the chapters of this book, call AFA Safety Services at 1-888-627-0099 or visit our website at http://www.afasafety.com.

Key Learning Objectives

The goal of this book is to prepare you to prevent injuries and deaths due to falls and falling objects. The key learning objectives are as follows:

◆ To determine by visual inspection whether an open-sided floor, platform, or elevated walkway is equipped with proper guardrails and whether toeboards are required or not.

◆ To understand and be able to apply safety rules for elevated storage of materials and protection against falling objects.

◆ To select effective fall protection system components for various exposures to falls.

◆ To be able to identify and correct mistakes in the selection of components or rigging of personal fall arrest systems.

◆ To understand and be able to plan and execute a safe rescue for a person who has fallen but is suspended by fall arrest equipment.

◆ To determine by visual inspection whether or not a supported or suspended scaffold has been properly erected and whether or not it has safe access.

◆ To be able to properly set up and secure a mobile ladder or a portable ladder under a variety of working conditions.

◆ To be able to distinguish between safe and unsafe practices related to elevation of personnel on manlifts, aerial lifts, and personnel platforms lifted by forklifts or cranes.

◆ To understand and be able to apply safety requirements for work on roofs and leading edges of new construction, including options to prevent falls through roof openings and falling objects or materials from falling onto persons below.

◆ To understand and be able to recommend safe work practices for steel erection that will prevent injuries due to falls and falling objects.

Trend Analysis

Falls from elevated locations result in a high number of fatal and disabling injuries each year, especially in the construction industry. It has been an emphasis area for enforcement of OSHA standards. There have even been some criminal prosecutions of management representatives in companies where OSHA had evidence that the company knew of fall hazards and willfully disregarded them.

OVERVIEW

Whenever we begin to study any subject related to accident prevention, it is important to focus our attention first on major problem areas, then on control methods.

For a safety professional, major problem areas are usually catastrophes like fatalities and disabling injuries, or situations that have the potential to result in the worst kinds of accidents or expensive fines from regulatory agencies. It is not that we are naturally pessimists, thinking that the worst things imaginable are going to occur. It is the cumulative experience we have had when making proactive recommendations after surveying a work location or (worse) after investigating an accident, and our suggestions are met with the argument from someone who is in charge or the senior person on site who says, "I've been here X (number of) years and it has never happened before."

It is never a good idea to wait until disaster strikes before you decide something is important enough to do. It is always a good idea to find out in advance all the bad things that could go wrong, in order to recognize when something like that may occur and to take timely steps to head off disaster.

In this chapter we will look at some reliable studies about the causes of fatal and disabling falls, in order to orient our thinking to priorities for fall prevention and protection, and to help instill in each of us the motivation to pay attention and learn what we have to do.

Some very good data analysis has been done on falls by the Texas Workers' Compensation Commission and, of course, by the U.S. Department of Labor, Bureau of Labor Statistics (BLS) and Occupational Safety and Health Administration (OSHA). In addition, some in-depth research into factors that contribute to fatal or seriously disabling falls has been done by the U.S. Department of Health, Education and Welfare, National Institute of Occupational Safety and Health (NIOSH).

We are also going to review the most commonly cited OSHA standards that are related to this subject, since the fear of thousands of dollars in fines for serious or willful violations is very often effective in motivating someone in a supervisory capacity to take an interest in the subject of fall prevention and fall protection.

FATAL INJURIES CAUSED BY FALLS IN TEXAS

According to the Texas Workers' Compensation Commission, falls to a lower level accounted for 8% (36) of the fatal occupational injuries in Texas in 1997, 9% (45) in 1996, 11% (52) in 1995 and (48) in 1994, and 9% (48) in 1993.

The TWCC's 1997 report on fatalities stated, "There were 471 fatal occupational injuries in construction from 1993 through 1997—the most of any industry. Falls accounted for the highest number of fatal work injuries in construction over that period (28%), followed by electrocutions."[1]

The TWCC once did a more detailed analysis of fatal falls in construction, and concluded, "Falls from roofs accounted for nearly one-third of all fatal falls in construction between 1991 and 1994. Falls from scaffolding resulted in the second highest number of falls."[2]

The same study indicated that many fatal falls also occurred from building girders or structural steel (11%) and ladders (9%).

Disproportionate Number of Fatalities among Hispanic Laborers

The *Dallas Morning News* of December 2, 1996 contained a report that stated the following:

"Fatal injuries among construction workers in Texas tend to occur among young, unskilled Hispanic laborers.... [L]aborers accounted for 100 out of 378 construction workers who died from on-the-job injuries. This figure is notably higher than the proportion of laborers at job sites. Roofers had the second highest number of construction deaths, with 24.

"Laborers do not have a trade like carpenters or electricians, but are general workers at construction sites....A full two-thirds of the laborers who died were Hispanic, even though Hispanics make up less than half of that workforce....Many Hispanic workers in Texas might not speak enough English to understand detailed instructions."[3]

DISABLING INJURY DATA ON FALLS

TWCC data[4] show that about one third or more of disabling injuries in Texas involved 31 days or more lost days in a five-year period:

- 1996 - 35.5% of 6,711 lost-time injuries

- 1995 - 36% of 6,430 lost-time injuries

- 1994 - 30% of 8,632 lost-time injuries

- 1993 - 32% of 6,435 lost-time injuries

- 1992 - 39% of 7,472 lost-time injuries.

The median number of days away from work ranged from 10 to 26 in this same 5-year period.

Disabling Injuries Caused by Falls in the U.S.

The U.S. Bureau of Labor Statistics publishes data on events or exposures involved in disabling injuries, although there is usually a time lag of 2 or 3 years after the end of a calendar year to compile the data. Following are some highlights on disabling falls for the years 1994, 1995, and 1996.[5]

- Total lost-time injuries from falls to a lower level
  - 111,308 in 1994
  - 104,801 in 1995
  - 98,544 in 1996

- Lost-time injuries from falls down stairs or steps
  - 25,823 in 1994
  - 26,391 in 1995
  - 22,712 in 1996

- Lost-time injuries due to falls from ladders
  - 25,794 in 1994
  - 24,034 in 1995
  - 25,383 in 1996

- Lost-time injuries due to falls from nonmoving vehicle
  - 19,692 in 1994
  - 20,811 in 1995
  - 19,204 in 1996

- Lost-time injuries due to falls from scaffold, staging
  - 5,268 in 1994
  - 4,601 in 1995
  - 4,376 in 1996

- Lost-time injuries due to falls from roof
  - 4,398 in 1994
  - 3,843 in 1995
  - 3,129 in 1996

Industries with Highest Incidence of Disabling Falls

According to BLS data, the incidence rate of disabling falls to a lower level for the years 1992 through 1994 was 14 or 15 cases per 10,000 workers.[6] A disproportionate number of cases occurred in two industries:

- Roofing, siding, sheet metal work—113 cases per 10,000

- Masonry, stonework, plastering—81 cases per 10,000.

OSHA STUDY ON FALLS IN THE CONSTRUCTION INDUSTRY

Prior to issuing new fall protection standards for the construction industry, OSHA did an in-depth study of fatalities over a five-year period (1985–1989).[7] Some of their observations related to falls are quoted below:

- Falls from elevation represent the largest cause, 33 percent, of all construction fatalities. [p. vi]

- Approximately 40 percent of the fatalities due to falls from elevation involved falls from elevations of greater than 30 feet. Twenty-five percent of the fatalities occurred from falls from elevations between 11 and 20 feet, and a similar percentage from 21 to 30 feet. [p. vii]

- Roofs and scaffolds are the major locations of fatalities due to falls from elevation. [p. vii]

Most Frequently Cited OSHA Standards Related to Fall Prevention in the Construction Industry

Aggregated data from January 1, 1990 through April 1, 1996 on the 50 most frequently cited OSHA standards for the construction industry include various provisions related to fall protection or fall prevention:

- Guardrails must be provided on open-sided floors, floor holes, and runways. (#2)

- Tubular welded scaffolds must have proper bracing, mud sills, guardrails, and toeboards. (#5)

- Manually propelled scaffolds must have tight planking, secured platforms, ladder or stairway, suitable footing, plumb stance, wheels locked, guardrails, and toeboards. (#11)

- Stair rail and handrail must be provided along each unprotected edge of stairs. (#13)

- Scaffolding must have safe access by ladder or equivalent. (#16)

- Scaffolding shall have guardrails and toeboards when more than 10 feet high or when 4–10 feet high with less than 45 inches of workspace. (#20)

- Reinforcing steel onto which employees could fall shall be guarded. (#23)

- Portable ladder side rails must extend at least 3 feet or be secured at top. (#24)

- Workplaces more than 25 feet above the ground or water shall have safety nets when ladders, safety lines/belts, temporary floors, scaffolds, or catch platform are not practical. (#35)

- Scaffold footing or anchorage shall be sound, rigid, and capable of carrying the maximum intended load. (#40)

- Ladder and stairway training shall be provided. (#41)

- Wall opening shall be guarded. (#42)

- When working from an aerial lift, a body belt and lanyard shall be attached to the boom or basket. (#44)

- Guardrails, safety nets, or personal fall arrest systems shall be used at heights of 6 feet or more. (#45)

- Scaffold planking shall extend over the end supports not less than 6 inches and not more than 12 inches. (#46)

Preamble to OSHA's Fall Protection Standards for Construction

In its preamble to the new fall protection standards that OSHA issued for the construction industry (January 26, 1995), various trends and observations about fall injuries were summarized:

- A NIOSH analysis of death certificates from work related injuries over a 10-year period has made it clear that falls are the leading cause of work related injury death among construction workers....

- An OSHA study involving 99 fall-related fatalities... suggests that virtually all of those deaths could have been prevented by the use of guardrails, body belts, body harnesses, safety nets, covers, or other means which would reduce employee exposure to the fall hazard.

Preamble to OSHA's Scaffold Standards

The preamble to the new scaffold standards that OSHA issued for construction (August 30, 1996) contained additional observations on trends related to fall injuries:

- Seventy-two percent of the workers injured in scaffold accidents covered by the BLS study attributed the accident either to the planking or support giving way, or to the employee slipping, or being struck by a falling object. Plank slippage was the most commonly cited cause.

- About 70 percent of the workers learned of the safety requirements for installing work platforms, assembling scaffolds, and inspecting scaffolds through on-the-job training. Approximately 25 percent had no training in these areas.

- Only 33 percent of scaffolds were equipped with a guardrail.

NIOSH Alert on Falls from Suspension Scaffolds

NIOSH issued an alert in August 1992, on deaths from suspension scaffolds.

- Fatal falls from scaffolds during the period 1980–1985 accounted for 17% of all falls from elevations (461 of 2,705) and were second only to falls from buildings....

- Falls from scaffolds accounted for 21% (82 of 386 incidents and 86 deaths) of fatal falls from working surfaces reported for the period 1974 to 1978 [OSHA 1979].ßΣ

- Suspension scaffolds were involved in 30% (25 of 82 incidents and 27 deaths) of the falls from scaffolds.

- Of the 25 falls from suspension scaffolds, 68% (17) involved scaffold equipment failure.

- Personal fall protection equipment was used in only three of these incidents, but it was used improperly in each case. In one incident, a worker fell out of his improperly fastened safety belt; in the other two incidents, excessively long lanyards broke or separated after victims fell 30 feet.[8]

NIOSH Study on Falls through Skylights and Roof Openings

A NIOSH Alert published in December 1989, focused attention on eight fatal accidents involving falls through skylights and roof openings.

- The NIOSH National Traumatic Occupational Fatality (NTOF) data base indicates that during the period 1980–85, falls accounted for nearly 10% (3,491 of 36,210) of all traumatic occupational deaths for which a cause was identified [NIOSH 1989a].

- Of this total, 28 deaths resulted from falls through skylights, and 39 deaths resulted from falls through roofs or roof openings.

- A NIOSH survey in seven States revealed that approximately 22% (14 of 64) of the fatal falls reported to State occupational safety and health officials occurred when workers fell through skylight openings or smoke-vent skylights (translucent plastic domes that serve as both skylights and automatic smoke vents in case of fire).[9]

"Many AC [acrylic] and CF [corrugated fiberglass] skylights have been exposed to outdoor elements for 20 to 30 years and have become brittle with age. They were never intended to support body weight and with age, they are even less capable of supporting body weight. OSHA reports detail the causes and results of falls. Usually, falls through acrylic dome skylights result from trips, slips, leaning on, sitting on, or backing into the skylight dome.

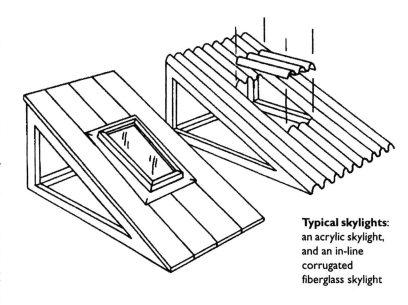

Typical skylights: an acrylic skylight, and an in-line corrugated fiberglass skylight

"The corrugated fiberglass skylights are difficult to detect because they are installed in line with the metal roof panels and can be painted over, making them indistinguishable from the surrounding roof. The usual accident causes for corrugated fiberglass sky lights are simply stepping onto them inadvertently."[10]

Preamble to Proposed Steel Erection Standards

An in-depth study of hazards related to steel erection was done by OSHA in conjunction with the Steel Erection Negotiated Rulemaking Advisory Committee (SENRAC).[11] Relevant excerpts from this analysis are included below.

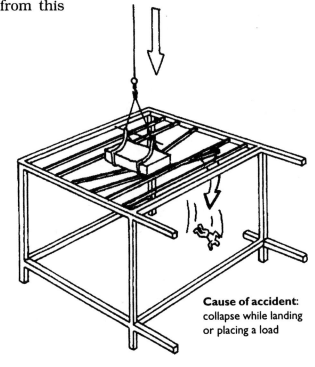

◆ The best available data are derived from NIOSH and industry studies and from the Bureau of Labor Statistics (BLS) (Ex. 9-39). During SENRAC negotiations, OSHA staff and a Committee statistical workgroup analyzed accident information derived from OSHA's IMIS system....

◆ An analysis of OSHA fatality/catastrophe data was performed by the SENRAC Statistical Workgroup which analyzed an eleven-year period (January 1984 through November 1994) and

Cause of accident: collapse while landing or placing a load

determined that 323 fatal accidents involved factors that are addressed both by OSHA's current and proposed steel erection standards....

◆ After categorizing the accidents according to primary contributing factors, the SENRAC workgroup concluded that the leading initial cause of accidents was slips (23.8%). The next highest categories were unknown (17.3%) and collapse (15.8%). Categorizing the accidents in the IMIS database by the immediate (final) cause of death, the SENRAC analysis reveals that 284 of the 323 fatalities (87.9%) involved falls from various heights where fall protection was either not provided or not used. Categorized by activity, decking was associated with the most fatalities (22.9%), followed by connecting (17.0%) and bolting (11.5%).

◆ An OSHA staff evaluation of these reports for a seven-year period (January 1984 through December 1990) revealed that fatalities associated with various types of accidents were caused by the following factors:

○ **Collapses while landing or placing a load**—most were the result of placing loads on unsecured or unbridged joists.

○ **Collapses while connecting joists or trusses**—most were the result of prematurely disconnecting the crane before the piece was secure.

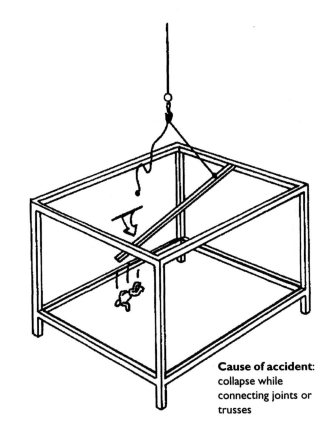

Cause of accident: collapse while connecting joints or trusses

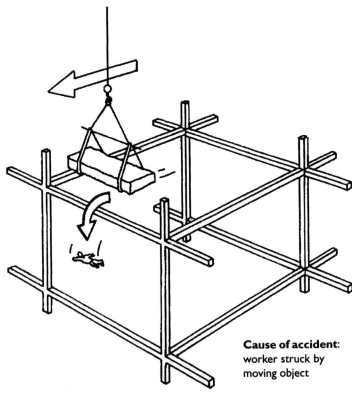

Cause of accident: worker struck by moving object

○ **Workers struck by objects during miscellaneous activities**—most were the result of walking or working under a load.

○ **Workers struck by objects and then falling**—most were the result of being struck while landing a load or making a connection, by a tool slipping, or by a piece of decking being blown off a pile when fall protection was not provided or used.

Cause of accident: unsecured or unstable decking

○ **Improper use or failure of fall protection**—most were the result of employee failure to use available fall protection systems even though the worker was wearing a belt (and in some cases lifelines were rigged).

○ **Unsecured or unstable decking**—most were the result of stepping onto or working on unsecured decking that slipped out of place when fall protection was not provided or used.

○ **Other falls during decking activities**—most were the result of stepping off the metal decking onto insulation (and then falling to the ground) during roofing operations where fall protection was not provided or used.

○ **Plumbing, bolting, welding, and cutting**—most were the result of the worker not being tied off while at the workstation (whether or not fall protection was provided).

○ **Walking/standing on the beam/joist** (i.e., moving point-to-point)—most were slips or falls where fall protection was not provided or used.

NOTE: Ironworkers or other construction personnel *should not* walk on beams that have a flange width less than 6 inches.

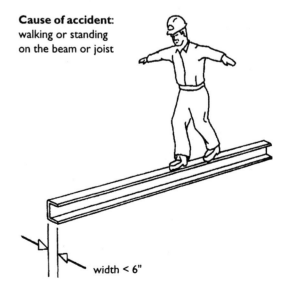

Cause of accident: walking or standing on the beam or joist

width < 6"

EMPHASIS AREAS

Data Summary

Based on the data that we have reviewed in this chapter, we should concentrate our fall prevention and fall protection efforts on high-risk exposures such as:

- Work on roofs
- Scaffolding
- Steel erection
- Work on ladders
- Construction laborers with a poor command of English
- Stairs
- Aerial lifts
- Skylights

Controls

The rest of this book will focus on controls. Engineering controls are considered the most effective, followed by administrative controls and personal protective equipment.

- We will start in Chapter 2 with a short, practical overview of OSHA standards that apply.
- In Chapter 3 we will become philosophical and try to get the "big picture" of fall protection principles.
- Chapter 4 will illustrate OSHA standards on engineering controls for guarding open-sided walking and working surfaces, and standards related to protection against falling objects, including storage of materials on elevated levels.
- Various types of personal protective equipment will be discussed in Chapter 5, including guidelines for its adjustment, use, care, and limitations.
- The next four chapters will each cover specific types of fall exposures:
  - Chapter 6: Scaffolds
  - Chapter 7: Ladders
  - Chapter 8: Elevating Personnel (elevating and rotating work platforms, personnel hoists, and personnel platforms elevated by forklifts or cranes)
  - Chapter 9: Special Applications, including:
    - Work on roofs
    - Proposed steel erection standards and
    - Elevated electrical transmission and distribution work

◆ Chapter 10 presents five different situations with fall hazards. These situations might be discussed in small groups in a classroom setting or in a safety meeting. They are intended to provoke active thinking on subjects that are not spelled out in this book.

That's right! Not all the answers are in this book. From time to time in the future you may confront a new or unusual situation that requires fall protection. Armed with the information in this book and with the help of other knowledgeable people, you can probably arrive at the best, most practical solution for any fall protection challenge that comes up.

ENDNOTES

1. TWCC, *Fatal Occupational Injuries in Texas 1997* (Austin, TX: Workers' Health and Safety Division, Sept. 1998), page 16.

2. TWCC, *Fatal Occupational Injuries in Texas 1994* (Austin, TX: Workers' Health and Safety Division, Jan. 1996), page 15.

3. "Study examines construction deaths in Texas," *Dallas Morning News*, Monday, Dec. 2, 1996, page 8D.

4. TWCC, *Occupational Injuries and Illnesses in Texas*, published annually from 1992 through 1996 (Austin, TX: Workers' Health and Safety Division).

5. BLS, *Occupational Injuries and Illnesses: Counts, Rates, and Characteristics*, published for the years 1994, 1995, and 1996 (Washington, D.C.: USGPO, Apr. 1997).

6. *Ibid.*, 1994 edition, pages 114–115.

7. OSHA, "Analysis of Construction Fatalities: The OSHA Data Base 1985–1989," (USDOL, Nov. 1990).

8. NIOSH, "Request for Assistance in Preventing Worker Injuries and Deaths Caused by Falls from Suspension Scaffolds" (DHHS/CDC, Aug. 1992), Publication No. 92-108, pages 1–2.

9. NIOSH, "Request for Assistance in Preventing Worker Deaths and Injuries from Falls Through Skylights and Roof Openings" (DHHS/CDC, Dec. 1989), Publication No.90-100, page 1.

10. Key Sandow, "Up on the Roof," *Occupational Health and Safety*, Oct. 1998, page 170.

11. OSHA, "Proposed Safety Standards for Steel Erection," published on Aug. 13, 1998 in the *Federal Register*, pages 43455-43456.

Overview of Applicable Regulatory Standards

OSHA has organized a special emphasis program on fall protection for the construction industry, because of the high incidence of fall-related fatalities and disabling injuries in construction work. Changing conditions and different exposures to falls related to different trades make the Construction Standards more performance oriented and flexible than the General Industry Standards. OSHA's General Industry Standards place a greater emphasis on engineering design to guard exposures of fixed locations.

For accuracy's sake, the actual wording of the OSHA standards is used in many cases in this chapter. Rewording sometimes leads to misinterpretations. Drawings have been added to clarify the meaning of the text.

OSHA'S CONSTRUCTION STANDARDS

OSHA's Construction Standards have a greater number of requirements than the General Industry Standards on subjects related to fall protection and fall prevention. The heights that trigger fall protection requirements vary from standard to standard, and this can result in confusion.

Application

Construction Standards apply to construction, renovation, alteration, large-scale painting or decorating, and major repairs or overhauls. They also apply to vendors who deliver products to construction site locations that are 6 feet or more above a lower level.[1]

Construction Standards have very specific requirements for specially designed fall protection systems that are usually temporary and require a competent person to be on site in a supervisory capacity.

Fall Protection

29 CFR 1926 Subpart M (§500 to 503, and Appendices A to E)

Some of the most important provisions of the fall protection standards that OSHA issued for the construction industry in 1995 are summarized below:

- Before work is done in an elevated location, a competent person must inspect walking/ working surfaces to ensure they are strong enough to safely support workers.

- When there is a 6-foot or greater drop from an unprotected side or edge, workers must be protected by a guardrail system, safety net system, or personal fall arrest system.

- When the use of guardrails, safety nets or a personal fall arrest system is impossible or would create a greater hazard, there must be a formal Fall Protection Plan.

- A personal fall arrest system (or covers or guardrails) must protect each employee from potential falls of 6 feet or more through a hole, skylight, or other roof or floor opening. Skylights must have covers.

- Each employee on the face of formwork or reinforcing steel shall be protected from falling 6 feet or more by a personal fall arrest system, safety net system, or positioning device system.

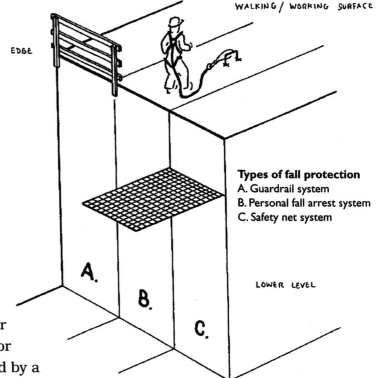

Types of fall protection
A. Guardrail system
B. Personal fall arrest system
C. Safety net system

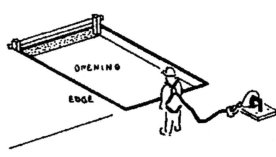

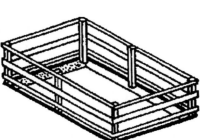

Fall protection requirements for holes, skylights, or other roof or floor openings are guardrails, personal fall arrest systems, or covers

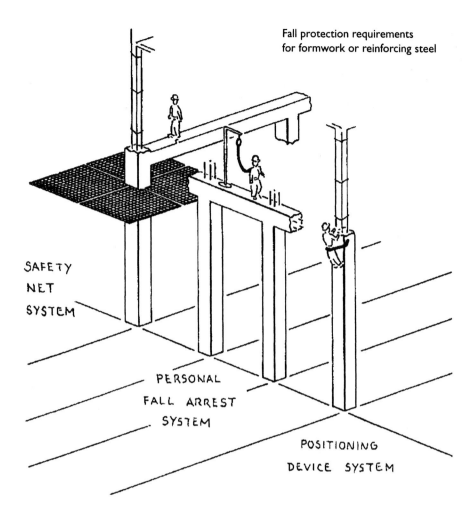

Fall protection requirements for formwork or reinforcing steel

SAFETY NET SYSTEM

PERSONAL FALL ARREST SYSTEM

POSITIONING DEVICE SYSTEM

Training Requirements of Subpart M

◆ Each employee who might be exposed to fall hazards must be trained about:

○ The nature of fall hazards in the work area and OSHA's Subpart M standards

○ Correct procedures for erecting, inspecting, and disassembling fall protection systems that are used

○ The care, use, operation, and limitations of fall protection systems and other protection used

○ The role of each employee in a safety monitoring system, when this is used

○ Limitations on the use of mechanical equipment while doing roofing work on low-sloped roofs

○ Correct procedures for handling and storage of equipment and materials and the erection of overhead protection

○ Role of employees in the Fall Protection Plan, if applicable

These rules will be discussed further in Chapters 4 and 5.

COMPARING STANDARDS

"...[T]he general industry fall protection regulations were proposed by OSHA in April 1990, but the final standard has never been published. Given the lapse of time, it is probable that the standard will need to be re-proposed. In addition, key OSHA standards officials, knowledgeable in fall protection, have retired and others may soon depart if the Department of Labor waits much longer before bringing consistency to the general industry and construction standards.

"The OSHA Fall Protection Standard for Construction was published in August 1994, and became effective in February 1995. The lack of standards conformity has produced a strange situation in the United States, especially for those who view compliance with standards as a goal rather than a minimum to be exceeded.

"Plant owners are bound by general industry requirements, yet they must administer the construction requirements to their contractors. The 1994 OSHA construction requirements are far more detailed and stringent than the existing 1971 general industry standards.

"The result of the standard's nonconformity is that while the construction regulations have moved from the belt to the harness, the body belt is still theoretically legal in general industry. In addition, the shock-absorbing lanyard is more commonly used in construction, but currently, such equipment remains a rope lanyard in general industry."[2]

Another key difference is that the Construction Standards require guarding of open sides at a height of 6 feet, and the General Industry Standards require guarding of open sides at a height of 4 feet.

OSHA'S GENERAL INDUSTRY STANDARDS

The General Industry standards apply to manufacturing operations and service industries, among other permanent places of employment.

Compared to construction standards, they place a greater emphasis on engineering design and fixed (as oppvosed to temporary) fall prevention equipment (guardrails, covers, etc.).

Walking and Working Surfaces

29 CFR 1910 Subpart D (§21–32)

1910.22(c) *Covers and guardrails.* Covers and/or guardrails shall be provided to protect personnel from the hazards of open pits, tanks, vats, ditches, etc.

1910.23(e)(7) *Cover specifications.* Floor opening covers may be of any material that meets the following strength requirements:

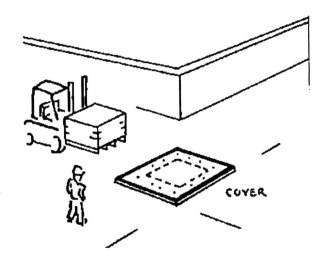

(i) Trench or conduit covers and their supports, when located in plant roadways, shall be designed to carry a truck rear-axle load of at least 20,000 pounds.

(ii) Manhole covers and their supports, when located in plant roadways, shall comply with local standard highway requirements if any; otherwise, they shall be designed to carry a truck rear-axle load of at least 20,000 pounds.

Floors, Platforms, and Runways with Open Sides

1910.23(c) Protection of open-sided floors, platforms, and runways.

1910.23(c)(1) Every open-sided floor or platform 4 feet or more above adjacent floor or ground level shall be guarded by a standard railing (or the equivalent as specified in paragraph (e)(3) of this section) on all open sides except where there is entrance to a ramp, stairway, or fixed ladder. The railing shall be provided with a toeboard wherever, beneath the open sides,

(i) Persons can pass,

(ii) There is moving machinery, or

(iii) There is equipment with which falling materials could create a hazard.

1910.23(c)(2) *Runways.* Every runway shall be guarded by a standard railing (or the equivalent as specified in paragraph (e)(3) of this section) on all open sides 4 feet or more above floor or ground level. Wherever tools, machine parts, or materials are likely to be used on the runway, a toeboard shall also be provided on each exposed side.

Runways used exclusively for special purposes (such as oiling, shafting, or filling tank cars) may have the railing on one side omitted where operating conditions

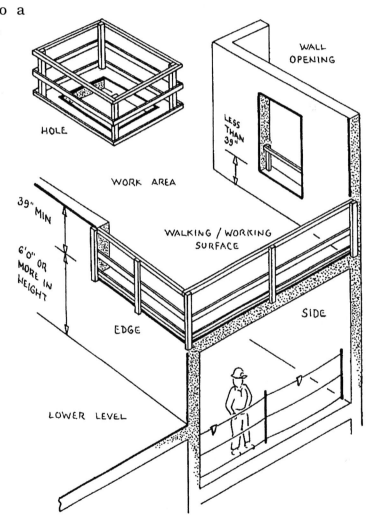

Guarding requirements for walking and working surfaces.
NOTE: OSHA's General Industry Standard requirement is 4 feet or more above adjacent floor or ground level; OSHA's Construction Standard requirement is 6 feet or more above a lower level (as indicated in this illustration).

necessitate such omission, providing the falling hazard is minimized by using a runway of not less than 18 inches wide. Where persons entering upon runways become thereby exposed to machinery, electrical equipment, or other danger not a falling hazard, additional guarding than is here specified may be essential for protection.

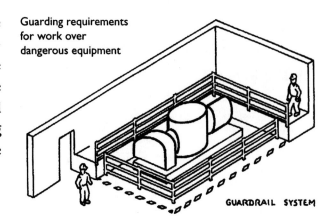

Guarding requirements for work over dangerous equipment

GUARDRAIL SYSTEM

Work over Dangerous Equipment

1910.23(c)(3)

Regardless of height, open-sided floors, walkways, platforms, or runways above or adjacent to dangerous equipment, pickling or galvanizing tanks, degreasing units, and similar hazards shall be guarded with a standard railing and toe board.

Construction Rule on Ramps and Runways

1926.502(b)(14) Guardrail systems. Guardrail systems used on ramps and runways shall be erected along each unprotected side or edge.

OSHA's Construction Standard guarding requirements for ramps and runways.

STEEL ERECTION

29 CFR 1926.750(b)

New OSHA standards for steel erection were proposed in August 1998. They have not yet been finalized, but OSHA has issued guidelines for compliance officers that dovetail with the new standards. The proposed standards will be discussed in Chapter 6.

The standards that are currently in effect are included below. The flooring standards are intended to prevent workers from falling through the floor to lower levels.

Temporary Flooring—Skeleton Steel Construction

926.750(b)(1) Temporary flooring—skeleton steel construction in tiered buildings.

(i) The derrick or erection floor shall be solidly planked or decked over its entire surface except for access openings. Planking or decking of equivalent strength, shall be of proper thickness to carry the working load. Planking shall be not less than 2 inches thick full size undressed, and shall be laid tight and secured to prevent movement.

(ii) On buildings or structures not adaptable to temporary floors, and where scaffolds are not used, safety nets shall be installed and maintained whenever the potential fall distance exceeds two stories or 25 feet. The nets shall be hung with sufficient clearance to prevent contacts with the surface of structures below.

(iii) Floor periphery-safety railing. A safety railing of 1/2-inch wire rope or equal shall be installed, approximately 42 inches high, around the periphery of all temporary-planked or temporary metal-decked floors of tier buildings and other multi-floored structures during structural steel assembly.

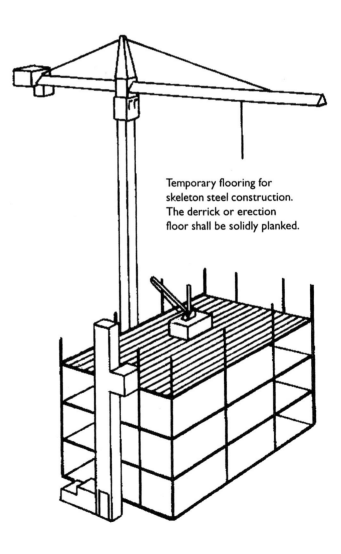

Temporary flooring for skeleton steel construction. The derrick or erection floor shall be solidly planked.

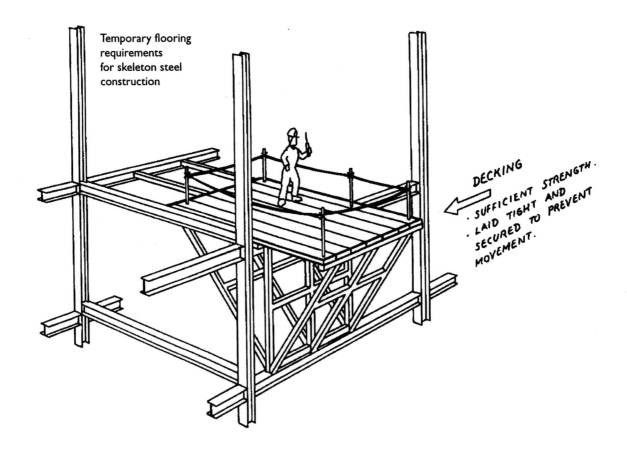

Temporary flooring requirements for skeleton steel construction

DECKING
· SUFFICIENT STRENGTH.
· LAID TIGHT AND SECURED TO PREVENT MOVEMENT.

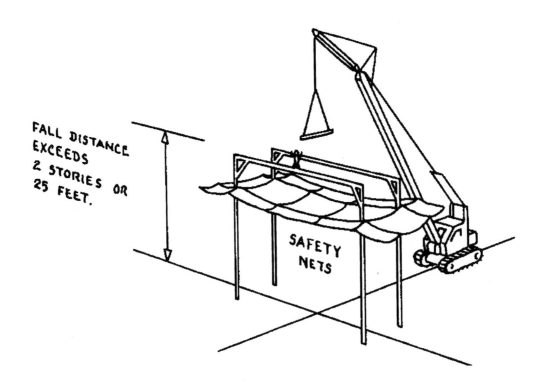

FALL DISTANCE EXCEEDS 2 STORIES OR 25 FEET.

SAFETY NETS

1926.750(b)(2)

(i) Where skeleton steel erection is being done, a tightly planked and substantial floor shall be maintained within two stories or 30 feet, whichever is less, below and directly under that portion of each tier of beams on which any work is being performed, except when gathering and stacking temporary floor planks on a lower floor, in preparation for transferring such planks for use on an upper floor. Where such a floor is not practicable, paragraph (b)(1)(ii) of this section applies. [NOTE: Paragraph (b)(1)(ii) requires installation of safety nets.]

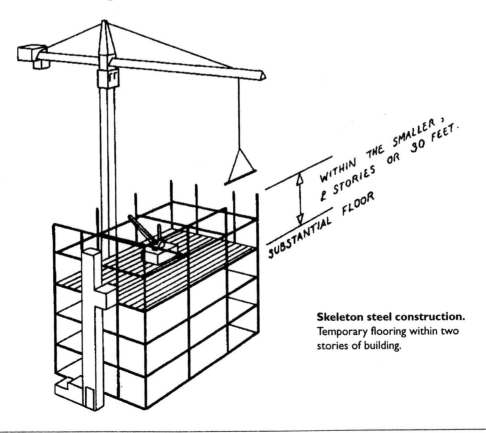

FLOOR PERIPHERY - SAFETY RAILING, ½" WIRE ROPE OR EQUIVALENT.

APPROX. 42"

Skeleton steel construction
Safety railing for floor periphery

TEMPORARY FLOORING, PLANKED OR METAL DECKED.

(ii) When gathering and stacking temporary floor planks, the planks shall be removed successively, working toward the last panel of the temporary floor so that the work is always done from the planked floor.

WITHIN THE SMALLER; 2 STORIES OR 30 FEET.

SUBSTANTIAL FLOOR

Skeleton steel construction.
Temporary flooring within two stories of building.

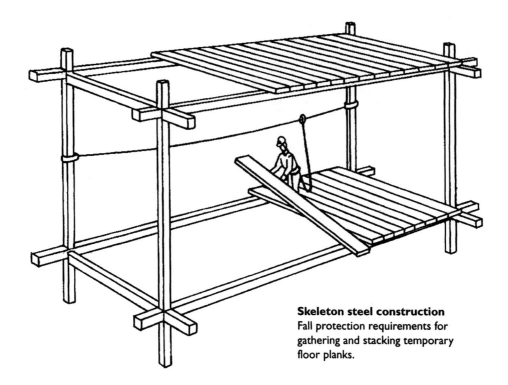

Skeleton steel construction
Fall protection requirements for gathering and stacking temporary floor planks.

(iii) When gathering and stacking temporary floor planks from the last panel, the employees assigned to such work shall be protected by safety belts with safety lines attached to a catenary line or other substantial anchorage.

Flooring—Other Construction

1926.750(c) Flooring—other construction.

(1) In the erection of a building having double wood floor construction, the rough flooring shall be completed as the building progresses, including the tier below the one on which floor joists are being installed.

(2) For single wood floor or other flooring systems, the floor immediately below the story where the floor joists are being installed shall be kept planked or decked over.

Steel Erection—Bolting, Riveting, Fitting-Up and Plumbing-Up

In the section "Bolting, riveting, fitting-up and plumbing-up" in Subpart R of the construction standards for steel erection, there are some provisions related to fall prevention and fall protection.

1926.752(e)

Wood planking shall be of proper thickness to carry the working load, but shall be not less than 2 inches thick full size undressed, exterior grade plywood, at least 3/4-inch thick, or equivalent material.

1926.752(f)

Metal decking of sufficient strength shall be laid tight and secured to prevent movement.

1926.752(g)

Planks shall overlap the bearing on each end by a minimum of 12 inches.

1926.752(h)

Wire mesh, exterior plywood, or equivalent, shall be used around columns where planks do not fit tightly.

1926.752(i)

Provisions shall be made to secure temporary flooring against displacement.

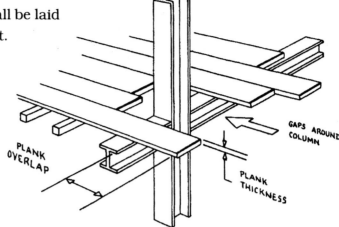

Open space around column requires wire mesh or plywood guard.

1926.752(j)

All unused openings in floors, temporary or permanent, shall be completely planked over or guarded in accordance with Subpart M of this part.

1926.752(k)

Employees shall be provided with safety belts in accordance with 1926.104 when they are working on float scaffolds.

STAIRWAYS AND LADDERS

29 CFR 1926 Subpart X (§1050 to 1060 and Appendix A)

Ladders and stairways on construction sites are covered by Subpart X of OSHA's Construction Standards. A synopsis of the general requirements follows.

♦ A stairway or ladder must be provided at all personnel points of access where there is a break in elevation of 19 inches (48 cm) or more, and no ramp, runway, sloped embankment, or personnel hoist is provided.

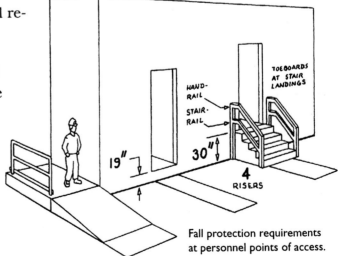

Fall protection requirements at personnel points of access.

- A double-cleated ladder or two or more separate ladders must be provided when ladders are the only means of access or exit from a working area for 25 or more employees, or when a ladder is to serve simultaneous two-way traffic.

- When a building or structure has only one point of access between levels, that point of access shall be kept clear to permit free passage of employees. When work must be performed or equipment must be used such that free passage at that point of access is restricted, a second point of access shall be provided and used.

- When a building or structure has two or more points of access between levels, at least one point of access shall be kept clear to permit free passage of employees.

Typical straight ladders

DOUBLE CLEAT

SINGLE CLEAT

EXTENSION LADDER

1 TO 4 LADDER PITCH

- Employers shall provide and install all stairway and ladder fall protection systems required by this subpart and shall comply with all other pertinent requirements of this subpart before employees begin the work that necessitates the installation and use of stairways, ladders, and their respective fall protection systems.

- When guardrail systems are used around holes which are used as points of access (such as ladderways), they shall be provided with a gate, or be so offset that a person cannot walk directly into the hole. [1926.502(b)(13)]

Safe use of portable ladders will be discussed at the end of Chapter 4.

Stair Openings on Construction Sites

1926.1052(c)(12) Stairways—Stairrails and handrails.

Unprotected sides and edges of stairway landings shall be provided with guardrail systems. Guardrail system criteria are contained in subpart M of this part.

Guardrail systems around holes which are used as points of access

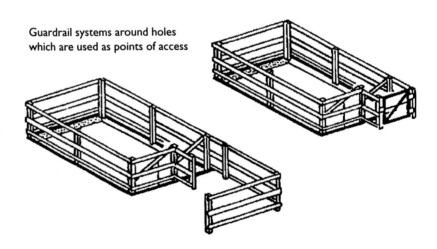

Training Requirements for Stairways and Ladders

The training requirements for stairways and ladders on construction sites are quoted below.

1926.1060(a)

The employer shall provide a training program for each employee using ladders and stairways, as necessary. The program shall enable each employee to recognize hazards related to ladders and stairways, and shall train each employee in the procedures to be followed to minimize these hazards.

(1) The employer shall ensure that each employee has been trained by a competent person in the following areas, as applicable:

  (i) The nature of fall hazards in the work area;

  (ii) The correct procedures for erecting, maintaining, and disassembling the fall protection systems to be used;

  (iii) The proper construction, use, placement, and care in handling of all stairways and ladders;

  (iv) The maximum intended load-carrying capacities of ladders and

  (v) The standards contained in this subpart.

Retraining

1926.1060(b)

Retaining shall be provided for each employee as necessary so that the employee maintains the understanding and knowledge acquired through compliance with this section.

FIXED STAIRS

The Construction and General Industry Standards agree on the subject of railings and guards, except that the Construction Standards require them for "stairways having four or more risers or rising more than 30 inches (76 cm), whichever is less." [1926.1052(c)(1)]

1910.23(d) Stairway railings and guards.

1910.23(d)(1) Every flight of stairs having four or more risers shall be equipped with standard stair railings or standard handrails as specified in paragraphs (d)(1)(i) through (v) of this section, the width of the stair to be measured clear of all obstructions except handrails:

(i) On stairways less than 44 inches wide having both sides enclosed, at least one handrail, preferably on the right side descending.

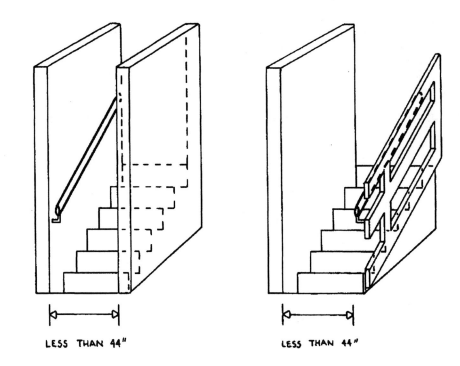

Railing requirements
for stairways
less than 44" wide,
closed and one side open

LESS THAN 44"   LESS THAN 44"

(ii) On stairways less than 44 inches wide having one side open, at least one stair railing on open side.

(iii) On stairways less than 44 inches wide having both sides open, one stair railing on each side.

(iv) On stairways more than 44 inches wide but less than 88 inches wide, one handrail on each enclosed side and one stair railing on each open side.

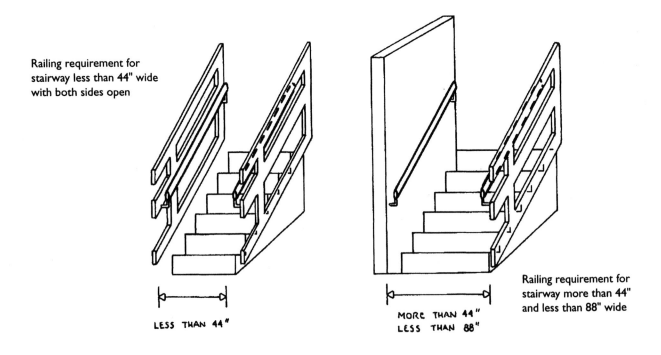

Railing requirement for
stairway less than 44" wide
with both sides open

Railing requirement for
stairway more than 44"
and less than 88" wide

LESS THAN 44"   MORE THAN 44"
                     LESS THAN 88"

(v) On stairways 88 or more inches wide, one handrail on each enclosed side, one stair railing on each open side, and one intermediate stair railing located approximately midway of the width.

Winding Stairs

1910.23(d)(2) and 1926.1052(c)(2)

Winding stairs and spiral stairs shall be equipped with a handrail offset to prevent walking on all portions of the treads having width less than 6 inches.

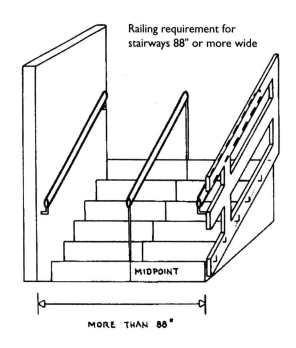

Railing requirement for stairways 88" or more wide

MIDPOINT

MORE THAN 88"

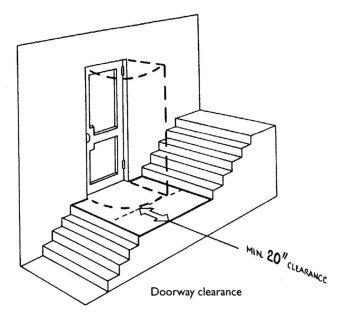

MIN. 20" CLEARANCE

Doorway clearance

Doors/Gates That Open Directly onto a Stairway

1910.23(a)(10) and 1926.1052(a)(4)

Where doors or gates open directly on a stairway, a platform shall be provided, and the swing of the door shall not reduce the effective width to less than 20 inches.

Stair Width and Angle of Rise

1910.24(d) Stair width.

Fixed stairways shall have a minimum width of 22 inches.

1910.24(e) Angle of stairway rise.

Fixed stairs shall be installed at angles to the horizontal of between 30 and 50. Any uniform combination of rise/tread dimensions may be used that will result in a stairway at an angle to the horizontal within the permissible range....

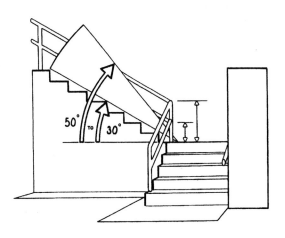

50° TO 30°

Rise requirement for fixed stairways

Handrails

1910.23(e)(5) Specifications for handrails.

(i) A handrail shall consist of a lengthwise member mounted directly on a wall or partition by means of brackets attached to the lower side of the handrail so as to offer no obstruction to a smooth surface along the top and both sides of the handrail. The handrail shall be of rounded or other section that will furnish an adequate handhold for anyone grasping it to avoid falling. The ends of the handrail should be turned in to the supporting wall or otherwise arranged so as not to constitute a projection hazard.

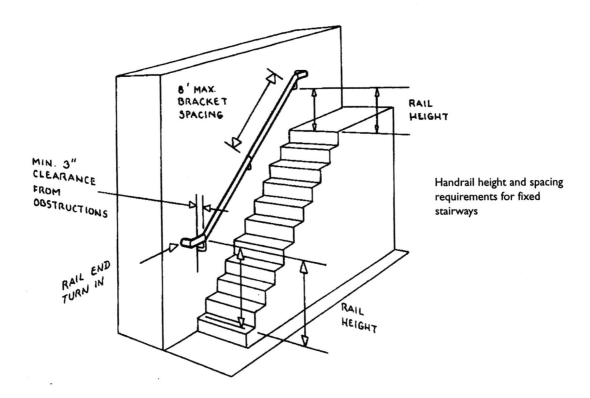

Handrail height and spacing requirements for fixed stairways

Height

(ii) The height of handrails shall be not more than 34 inches nor less than 30 inches from upper surface of handrail to surface of tread in line with face of riser or to surface of ramp.

When revised Construction Standards for stairs were issued, OSHA changed the height specification for stairrails:

1926.1052(c)(3)(i)

Stairrails installed after March 15, 1991, shall be not less than 36 inches (91.5 cm) from the upper surface of the stairrail system to the surface of the tread, in line with the face of the riser at the forward edge of the tread.

1926.1052(c)(6)

The height of handrails shall be not more than 37 inches (94 cm) nor less than 30 inches (76 cm) from the upper surface of the handrail to the surface of the tread, in line with the face of the riser at the forward edge of the tread.

1926.1052(c)(7)

When the top edge of a stair rail system also serves as a handrail, the height of the top edge shall be not more than 37 inches (94 cm) nor less than 36 inches (91.5 cm) from the upper surface of the stair rail system to the surface of the tread, in line with the face of the riser at the forward edge of the tread.

Size

1910.23(e)(5)(iii)

The size of handrails shall be:

♦ When of hardwood, at least 2 inches in diameter

♦ When of metal pipe, at least 1¹/₂ inches in diameter

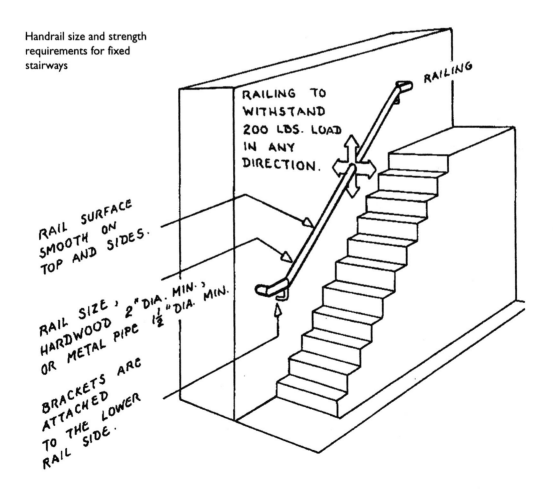

Handrail size and strength requirements for fixed stairways

The length of brackets shall be such as will give a clearance between handrail and wall or any projection thereon of at least 3 inches. The spacing of brackets shall not exceed 8 feet.

Strength Requirement

1910.23(e)(5) (iv)

The mounting of handrails shall be such that the completed structure is capable of withstanding a load of at least 200 pounds applied in any direction at any point on the rail.

1926.1052(c)(5)

Handrails and top rails of stair rail systems shall be capable of withstanding, without failure, a force of at least 200 pounds (890 n) applied within 2 inches (5 cm) of the top edge, in any downward or outward direction, at any point along the top edge.

Clearance of Rails from Wall or Object

1910.23(e)(6)

All handrails and railings shall be provided with a clearance of not less than 3 inches between the handrail or railing and any other object.

1926.1052(c)(11)

Handrails that will not be a permanent part of the structure being built shall have a minimum clearance of 3 inches (8 cm) between the handrail and walls, stair rail systems, and other objects.

OTHER FLOOR OPENINGS

Other floor openings that must be guarded include ladderways, hatchways, chutes, skylights, pits, trap doors, manholes, and temporary openings.

Ladderways

1910.23(a)(2)

Every ladderway floor opening or platform shall be guarded by a standard railing with standard toeboard on all exposed sides (except at entrance to opening), with the passage through the railing either provided with a swinging gate or so offset that a person cannot walk directly into the opening.

(See illustration for similar guarding of stairway openings on construction sites.)

Hatchways and Chutes

1910.23(a)(3)

Every hatchway and chute floor opening shall be guarded by one of the following:

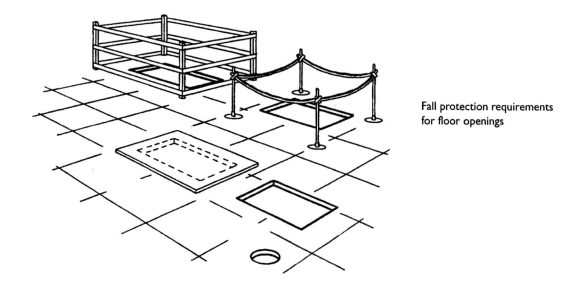

Fall protection requirements
for floor openings

(i) Hinged floor opening cover of standard strength and construction equipped with standard railings or permanently attached thereto so as to leave only one exposed side. When the opening is not in use, the cover shall be closed or the exposed side shall be guarded at both top and intermediate positions by removable standard railings.

(ii) A removable railing with toeboard on not more than two sides of the opening and fixed standard railings with toeboards on all other exposed sides. The removable railings shall be kept in place when the opening is not in use.

Where operating conditions necessitate the feeding of material into any hatchway or chute opening, protection shall be provided to prevent a person from falling through the opening.

Skylights

1910.23(a)(4)

Every skylight floor opening and hole shall be guarded by a standard skylight screen or a fixed standard railing on all exposed sides.

1910.23(e)(8)

Skylight screens shall be of such construction and mounting that they are capable of withstanding a load of at least 200 pounds applied perpendicularly at any one area on the screen. They shall also be of such construction and mounting that under ordinary loads or impacts, they will not deflect downward sufficiently to break the glass below them. The construction shall be of grillwork with openings not more than 4 inches long or of slatwork with openings not more than 2 inches wide with length unrestricted.

Pits and Trapdoors

1910.23(a)(5)

Every pit and trapdoor floor opening, infrequently used, shall be guarded by a floor opening cover of standard strength and construction. While the cover is not in place, the pit or trap opening shall be constantly attended by someone or shall be protected on all exposed sides by removable standard railings.

Manholes

1910.23(a)(6)

Every manhole floor opening shall be guarded by a standard manhole cover which need not be hinged in place.

While the cover is not in place, the manhole opening shall be constantly attended by someone or shall be protected by removable standard railings.

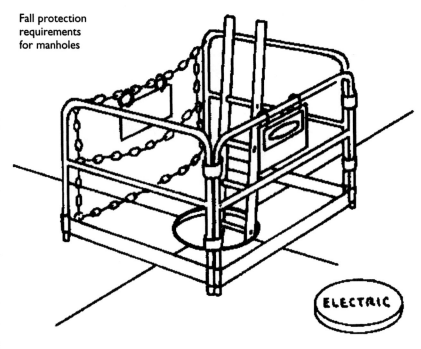

Fall protection requirements for manholes

Temporary Openings

1910.23(a)(7)

Every temporary floor opening shall have standard railings, or shall be constantly attended by someone.

FLOOR HOLES

Accessible Holes

1910.23(a)(8)

Every floor hole into which persons can accidentally walk shall be guarded by either:

(i)   A standard railing with standard toeboard on all exposed sides, or

(ii) A floor hole cover of standard strength and construction. While the cover is not in place, the floor hole shall be constantly attended by someone or shall be protected by a removable standard railing.

Inaccessible Holes

1910.23(a)(9)

Every floor hole into which persons cannot accidentally walk (on account of fixed machinery, equipment, or walls) shall be protected by a cover that leaves no openings more than 1 inch wide. The cover shall be securely held in place to prevent tools or materials from falling through.

Protection of Holes on Construction Sites

1926.502(b)(11)

When guardrail systems are used at holes, they shall be erected on all unprotected sides or edges of the hole.

Holes for Passage of Materials

1926.502(b)(12)

When guardrail systems are used around holes used for the passage of materials, the hole shall have not more than two sides provided with removable guardrail sections to allow the passage of materials.

When the hole is not in use, it shall be closed over with a cover, or a guardrail system shall be provided along all unprotected sides or edges.

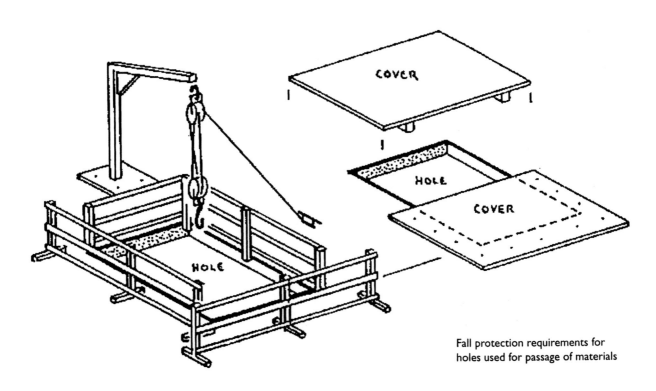

Fall protection requirements for holes used for passage of materials

Guardrail Systems for Hoisting Areas

1926.502(b)(10)

When guardrail systems are used at hoisting areas, a chain, gate or removable guardrail section shall be placed across the access opening between guardrail sections when hoisting operations are not taking place.

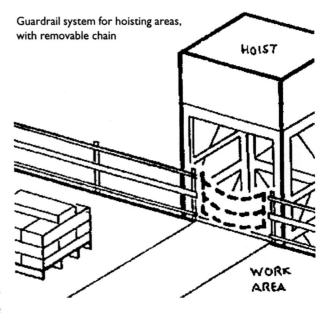

Guardrail system for hoisting areas, with removable chain

WALL OPENINGS AND HOLES

1910.23(b) Protection for wall openings and holes.

1910.23(b)(1) Every wall opening from which there is a drop of more than 4 feet shall be guarded by one of the following:

(i) Rail, roller, picket fence, half door, or equivalent barrier. Where there is exposure below to falling materials, a removable toe board or the equivalent shall also be provided. When the opening is not in use for handling materials, the guard shall be kept in position regardless of a door on the opening. In addition, a grab handle shall be provided on each side of the opening with its center approximately 4 feet above floor level and of standard strength and mounting.

(ii) Extension platform onto which materials can be hoisted for handling and which shall have side rails or equivalent guards of standard specifications.

Wall Opening Barriers

1910.23(e)(9)

Wall opening barriers (rails, rollers, picket fences, and half doors) shall be of such construction and mounting that, when in place

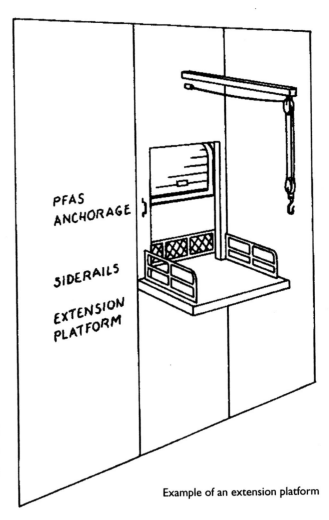

Example of an extension platform

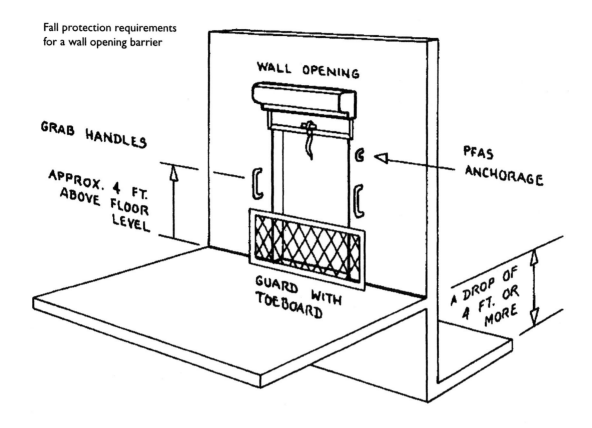

Fall protection requirements for a wall opening barrier

at the opening, the barrier is capable of withstanding a load of at least 200 pounds applied in any direction (except upward) at any point on the top rail or corresponding member.

Wall Opening Grab Handles

1910.23(e)(10)

Wall opening grab handles shall be not less than 12 inches in length and shall be so mounted as to give 3 inches clearance from the side framing of the wall opening.

The size, material, and anchoring of the grab handle shall be such that the completed structure is capable of withstanding a load of at least 200 pounds applied in any direction at any point of the handle.

Wall Opening Screens

1910.23(e)(11)

Wall opening screens shall be of such construction and mounting that they are capable of withstanding a load of at least 200 pounds applied horizontally at any point on the near side of the screen.

They may be of solid construction, of grillwork with openings not more than 8 inches long, or of slatwork with openings not more than 4 inches wide with length unrestricted.

Chute Wall Openings

1910.23(b)(2)

Every chute wall opening from which there is a drop of more than 4 feet shall be guarded by one or more of the barriers specified in paragraph (b)(1) of this section or as required by the conditions.

Window Wall Openings

1910.23(b)(3)

Every window wall opening at a stairway landing, floor, platform, or balcony, from which there is a drop of more than 4 feet, and where the bottom of the opening is less than 3 feet above the platform or landing, shall be guarded by standard slats, standard grill work (as specified in paragraph (e)(11) of this section), or standard railing.

Where the window opening is below the landing, or platform, a standard toe board shall be provided.

1910.23(b)(4)

Every temporary wall opening shall have adequate guards but these need not be of standard construction.

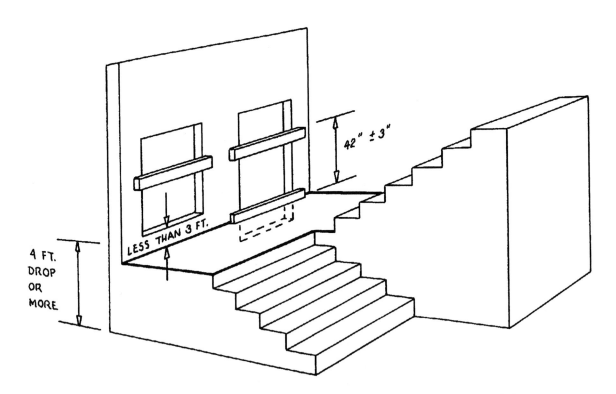

Guarding requirements for window wall openings at a stairway landing, floor, platform, or balcony

OUTLINE OF APPLICABLE REGULATIONS

The following table briefly summarizes the OSHA standards that apply to fall prevention and protection against falls and falling objects. To view any standard, go to the OSHA home page on the world wide web: **http://www.osha.gov/**. Navigate to the regulations page and then go to the standard number. Alternately, you can do a web site search on the name of the standard, but you are likely to get a lot of other "hits," too.

Construction Standards SUBJECT and NUMBER	General Industry Standards SUBJECT and NUMBER
Fall Protection, 29 CFR 1926 Subpart M (§500 to 503 and Appendices A - E)	**Walking-Working Surfaces, 29 CFR 1910 Subpart D(§21 to 32)**
• §1926.500 Application and definitions	• §1910.21 Definitions
• §1926.501 Duty to have fall protection	• §1910.22 General requirements
• §1926.502 Fall protection systems criteria and practices	• §1910.23 Guarding floor and wall openings and holes
• §1926.503 Training requirements	• §1910.24 Fixed industrial stairs
• Appendix A: Determining roof widths	• §1910.25 Portable wood ladders
• Appendix B: Guardrail systems	• §1910.26 Portable metal ladders
• Appendix C: Personal fall arrest systems	• §1910.27 Fixed ladders
• Appendix D: Positioning device systems	• §1910.28 Safety requirements for scaffolding
• Appendix E: Sample fall protection plans	• §1910.29 Manually propelled mobile ladder stands and scaffolds (towers)
Stairways and Ladders, 29 CFR 1926 Subpart X (§1050 to 1060 and Appendix A)	• §1910.30 Other working surfaces
• §1926.1050 Scope, application and definitions	**Powered Platforms, Manlifts and Vehicle-Mounted Work Platforms, 29 CFR 1910 Subpart F (§66, Appendices A-D, §67 to 70)**
• §1926.1051 General requirements	

Construction Standards SUBJECT and NUMBER	General Industry Standards SUBJECT and NUMBER
• §1926.1052 Stairways	• §1910.66 Powered platforms for exterior building maintenance
• §1926.1053 Ladders	• Appendix A: Guidelines (advisory)
• §1926.1060 Training requirements	• Appendix B: Exhibits (advisory)
• Appendix A: Ladders	• Appendix C: Personal fall arrest system (Section I—mandatory; Sections II and III—nonmandatory)
Personnel Hoists, 29 CFR 1926.552(c)	• Appendix D: Existing installations (mandatory)
Cranes and Derricks, 29 CFR 1926.550(g)	• §1910.67 Vehicle-mounted elevating and rotating work platforms
Steel Erection, 29 CFR 1926.750(b) and 1926.752(e)-(k)	• §1910.68 Manlifts
• Proposed Safety Standards for Steel Erection, published on 8/13/98 in the *Federal Register*, 63:43451-43513	**Electrical Transmission and Distribution**, 29 CFR 1910.269(e)(5) removal of covers, and 1910.269(g)(2) fall arrest equipment
General Requirements for Storage, 29 CFR 1926.250(b)	
Safety Belts, Lifelines and Lanyards, 29 CFR 1926.104	
Safety Nets, 29 CFR 1926.105	

ENDNOTES

1. Interpretation M-1, §1926.500 - Scope and Application, *Construction Resource Manual.*

2. J. Nigel Ellis, "Reviewing Fall Protection in General Industry," *Compliance Magazine,* September 1998, page 22.

Principles of Fall Protection

Safety Culture

"Fall hazards are in the eye of the beholder unless there is a safety culture," says J. Nigel Ellis, president of Dynamic Scientific Controls, in Wilmington, Delaware. Companies with safety cultures commit themselves to safe working conditions for all workers. That philosophy involves seeking out and controlling fall hazards. "Where there is no company-wide commitment to safety," he says, "workers are improperly prepared to take responsibility for their own protection."[1]

FALLS FROM ELEVATED WORK LOCATIONS

In his book on fall protection,[2] Nigel Ellis made the following observations about falls from elevated work locations [emphasis added]:

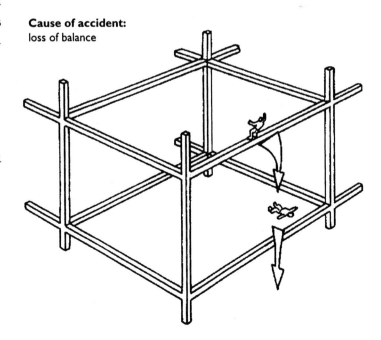

Cause of accident:
loss of balance

♦ "A momentary loss of balance resulting from a slip or trip can often lead to an elevated fall. *Grabbing on to something to catch oneself after balance is accidentally lost is rare.*"

♦ "[O]nce a person loses his or her balance and falls from elevation, whether it is 10 ft. or 200 ft., serious or fatal injury usually results. In fact, *the worst elevated fall hazards are from potential sudden collapse and from potential walking into holes* left after temporarily placed covers have been lifted."

♦ "Use of ladders was the number-one cause of injurious falls in 1992, according to an OSHA Training Institute study of OSHA investigations. ...The *fall risk is greatly increased if work is done from the ladder.*"

♦ "*Elevating personnel platforms or buckets and positioning portable stair towers on reasonably flat and stable ground further reduce risk* and allow work to be conducted if overreaching is not a reasonable foreseeability. However, if the possibility exists for climbing on the midrails of, for example, aerial lifts, and stretching outside the protection of the railing or barrier, then fall protection must be considered in addition to training workers in how to use access equipment properly or in the use of other equipment such as scaffolds."

Time vs. Distance

The chart below from the American Insurance Services Group[3] shows that a body in free fall covers distances quickly.

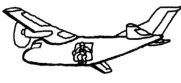

Time (Seconds)	Distance (Feet and Meters)
0.5	4 (1.2 m)
1.0	16 (4.9 m)
1.5	36 (11.0 m)
2.0	64 (19.5 m)

APPROXIMATE
FREE FALL SPEED

ONE SECOND	**10** MPH.
TWO SECONDS	**20** MPH.
THREE SECONDS	**60** MPH.

ELEMENTS OF A FALL HAZARD

According to Nigel Ellis, there are three main elements of a fall hazard:

1. As free fall distance increases, arresting forces or forces upon impact also increase.

2. Lack of adequate shock absorption at impact increases severity of injuries.

3. Position of victim when fall is arrested and until rescue.

Free-Fall Distance

When we refer to free-fall distance, we mean the distance of travel before fall arrest equipment is activated or until impact, whichever occurs first. OSHA measures this distance from foot level of the subject before the fall to foot level after the fall, but for purposes of planning for job safety, it is better to measure it from head level to the stopping point.

"A 6-ft. lanyard, for instance, attached at foot level or below could result in free falling 12 feet before the equipment is activated. Since free falling is a transfer from potential to kinetic energy, the longer the free-fall distance, the higher the forces generated on impact."[4]

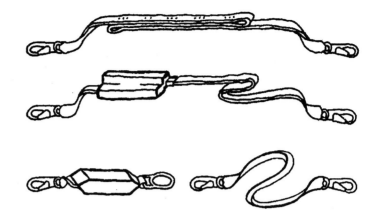

Typical lanyards with built-in shock-absorbing devices

Limiting the free-fall distance to less than 2 feet is the most effective way to prevent serious injuries. Decreasing the total fall distance should also be a safety planning objective, in order to decrease the chance of striking an object or part of a structure while falling.

"When free falling cannot practically be held below 2 ft., adequate shock absorption and proper body support become more critical, along with rapid rescue techniques."[5]

Shock Absorption

A relatively safe level for arresting forces is around 650 pounds.

Workers have been able to practice using fall protection equipment without suffering injuries when shock absorption features of fall arrest equipment reduce the forces acting on the body to this level or lower.

For this reason, lanyards with built-in shock absorbing devices are recommended. A lanyard is a short, flexible rope or synthetic web strap that connects a harness or safety belt to an anchor point or to a grab device on a lifeline.

Body Support

A properly designed full body harness will support the body in a relatively upright position after a fall, allowing the victim to breathe normally and to experience relatively little discomfort from being suspended while awaiting rescue.

There are five main functions of body support systems, each of which requires different design features:

Full-body harness support in a full arrest situation

1. **Fall arrest:** full body harness with a D-ring in the back. Must be used in combination with a fall arrest device.

2. **Climbing protection**: harness with D-ring in front or saddle belt with front O-rings, in combination with carrier rail or cable.

3. **Work positioning**: strap with adjustable lanyard or rebar chain and hook used in combination with one of the following:

Fall arrest harness   Climbing protection harness   Full restraint harness

   ○ saddle belt with O-rings in front
   ○ lineman's belt with a D-ring on both sides
   ○ boatswain's chair
   ○ tree trimmer's belt
   ○ full body harness with work-positioning belt

4. **Fall restraint**: full body harness with a D-ring on both sides, in combination with lifelines of a limited length.

5. **Rescue and retrieval**: full body harness with a D-ring in back or two shoulder rings (or wristlets, as a last resort), in combination with a retrieval line and suitable winch.

Typical rebar chain assembly

100 PERCENT FALL PROTECTION PROGRAM

"100% fall protection means that no exposure to an elevated fall hazard is permitted without backup protection. It means continuous protection. Exposure can be prevented by 1) establishing walls, floors and guardrails; 2) using work platforms and aerial lifts; 3) implementing an operational change; or 4) restricting workers' travel. Hazardous areas can be determined by warning lines 6 or more feet from an exposed edge.

"When the prevention of fall hazard exposure is not practical to the work method, personnel nets or personal fall protection equipment can be designed to mitigate the effects of elevated falls."[6]

Implementing an Effective Program

The steps to follow in implementing an effective fall protection program were outlined in a recent article in *Compliance Magazine:*[7]

- **Establish a fall hazard committee.** Groups represented by the committee in a plant environment typically are from health and safety, manufacturing, skilled trades, purchasing, unions, and engineering. The committee is responsible for identifying and evaluating fall hazards and proposing controls for fall hazards.

- **Designate program coordinators.** Responsibilities include, but are not limited to, implementing a comprehensive and continuous process to identify fall hazards. Individuals in this position ensure coordination of proposed controls with engineering and report on solutions and progress of the program.

- **Train the workforce.** In order to effectively implement the program, in-depth training must be provided to committee members, coordinators, engineers, at-risk workers, and trainers.

- **Implement fall hazard controls.** The implementation of controls should be carried out through the conventional line and staff organizations. The committee should monitor the process to ensure satisfactory completion and to communicate successes and problems to other areas of the organization.

- **Evaluate implemented controls.** The committee, in conjunction with engineering and management, should ensure that there is a viable system in place to monitor and evaluate the implemented controls to determine if there were any oversights in the design and implementation processes. There should be a good feedback mechanism for accomplishing the possible need for changes in a responsive way. The evaluation process also should consider technological advances as they may relate to upgrading existing controls.

Hazard Analysis and Pre-Inspection

"Any project will pose multiple fall hazards, including form work, brick work, open sided floors, stairwells, elevator shafts, window and wall openings, excavations, scaffolding, roofing work, etc. Pre-planning each exposure is a daunting task. ...Planning leads directly to equipment selection."[8]

A complete analysis should be done before designing or specifying the fall protection that is necessary for each job.

1. Identify the fall hazards that are associated with the work to be done, including access to and egress from the elevated location.

2. Plan work to eliminate exposure to falls whenever possible, and restrict access to areas where falls of 6 feet or more may occur.

3. Consider the feasibility of installing guardrails or other barriers to prevent falls.

4. Consider the feasibility of scaffolding or the use of manlifts, aerial lifts, or suspended platforms.

5. When fall prevention measures are not feasible due to the work location or sequence of tasks, select a suitable fall arrest system.

6. Evaluate requirements for vertical and horizontal mobility.

7. Identify anchor points for lifelines or lanyards.

8. Determine environmental conditions or other factors that may require additional precautions and/or maintenance.

Hazard of Falling through Elevated Work Surface

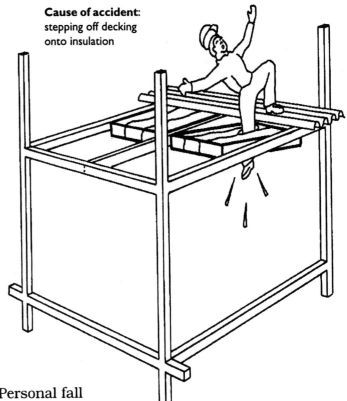

Cause of accident: stepping off decking onto insulation

The inspection prior to work that was briefly referenced above must include a physical survey to determine whether or not the walking or working surface has holes, air duct openings, skylights, or deteriorated areas through which a person could fall to a lower level.

OSHA does not require a person who is only performing an inspection to fully comply with fall protection requirements; however, it is prudent to make reasonable provisions for fall protection anyway.

The employer has a duty to cover or guard holes and protect employees from falling through weak or deteriorated surfaces.

◆ **Holes, air ducts, skylights, etc.:** Personal fall arrest systems, covers, or guardrail systems must be erected around holes that are more than 6 feet above lower levels. Covers on holes in elevated walking/working surfaces and roofs must be able to support at least twice the weight of employees, equipment, and materials that may be imposed on the cover at any one time. To prevent accidental displacement resulting from wind, equipment, or workers' activities, all covers must be secured in place. All covers must be color coded or bear the markings "HOLE" or "COVER."[9]

○ It should be noted that many new skylights are made of load-bearing materials such as plastic reinforced with wire mesh or Lexan and are designed to sustain a 200-lb. load. Even so, because of a NIOSH recommendation, many of the newer skylights have a warning label that says, "DO NOT SIT, STAND OR STEP."

○ "The problem with skylights is that they often look opaque. People mistake them for solid surfaces and think they'll bear their weight, but actually they may only support 8 pounds...."[10]

♦ **Deteriorated areas**: Placing large and sturdy sheets of plywood over deteriorated areas to spread the load over a larger area and securing them in place may be a possible solution when the condition of areas of a floor or roof are suspect.

"The most dangerous fall hazard is a sudden collapse. Renovating buildings with suspect floors or roofs calls for an engineer's plan for demolition, such as described in OSHA 1926.850(a), before contractors or employees are permitted to use them for access."[11]

HIERARCHY OF FALL PROTECTION SOLUTIONS

"Good fall protection control management calls for a priority system to tackle foreseeable fall hazards, as follows, in this order:

1. Eliminating fall hazards

2. Preventing fall hazards

3. Arresting falls

4. Administrative techniques."[12]

Examples of administrative techniques would include access restrictions, warning lines, safety monitors, etc.

Hierarchy of Work Platforms

"...From this primary hierarchy of fall protection arises another hierarchy—that of work platforms and how workers access them. In order of desirability, they are:

1. Eliminate the need for access/fall protection

2. Engineered platforms

3. Aerial platforms

4. Scaffolds (temporary platforms)

5. Work positioning using belts/seats

6. Ladders and administrative techniques."[13]

LIMITATIONS OF AND REQUIREMENTS FOR A FALL PROTECTION PLAN

Relying on a Fall Protection Plan is an option that is only available to employees engaged in leading edge work, precast concrete erection work, or residential construction work, who can demonstrate that it is infeasible or that it creates a greater hazard to use conventional fall protection equipment.

Requirements that apply to a Fall Protection Plan can be summarized as follows:

- ◆ The plan must be prepared by a qualified person and must be implemented under the supervision of a competent person.

- ◆ It must apply to a specific site and must be kept up to date. Changes must be approved by a qualified person.

- ◆ A copy of the plan, with all approved changes, must be kept at the job site.

- ◆ The plan must document the reasons for using it as a substitute for compliance with OSHA requirements.

Contents of a Fall Protection Plan

A Fall Protection Plan must identify each location where conventional fall protection methods cannot be used. Each such location must be classified as a Controlled Access Zone. It must include the names or other means of identifying each employee who is designated to work in the Controlled Access Zone, and it must prohibit all others from entering it.

A Fall Protection Plan must describe other measures (such as scaffolds, ladders, or aerial lifts) that will reduce or eliminate the fall hazard for workers who use conventional fall protection systems. A safety monitoring system may only be used as a last resort.

SYNOPSIS

Effective fall protection requires analysis and planning, because there are many different types of hazards and various control options. When it is impossible to meet regulatory requirements for fall protection, there must be formal planning and communication of control measures.

Although 100% fall protection is not a regulatory requirement, it is a desirable goal. Fail-safe provisions for fall protection are needed because of the high severity of injuries that are likely to result from falls from an elevated work location.

ENDNOTES

1. Janet Willen, "How to Prevent Falls in the Workplace," *eNSC*, August 1998.

2. J. Nigel Ellis, Ph.D., CSP, P.E., *Introduction to Fall Protection* (Des Plaines, IL: American Society of Safety Engineers, 1993), page 37.

3. American Insurance Services Group, "Fall Management Program," *Construction Management Report*, September 1995, page 1.

4. J. Nigel Ellis, "Reviewing Fall Protection in General Industry," *Compliance Magazine*, September 1998, page 22.

5. *Ibid.*

6. Nigel Ellis, *Introduction to Fall Protection*, page 58.

7. Bob Wujek and Joseph Feldstein, "Fall Protection: Beyond Harnesses and Lanyards," *Compliance Magazine*, January 1999, pages 20–21.

8. Charles E. Paulson, "Fall Protection: Constructive Change," *Professional Safety*, December 1995, page 39.

9. U.S. DOL-OSHA Publication No. 3146, "Fall Protection in Construction," page 14.

10. Paul Keane of NIOSH quoted by Sarah Wortham, "How to Pitch Rooftop Safety," *Safety & Health* (Itasca, IL: National Safety Council, April 1997), page 59.

11. Nigel Ellis, *Introduction to Fall Protection*, page 142.

12. *Ibid.*, page 86.

13. *Ibid.*, page 86.

Prevention of Falls and Falling Objects

Design of Barriers

The main focus of this chapter is the design of barriers to prevent people from falling to a lower level or to prevent objects from falling onto workers below.

COMPARISON OF GUARDRAIL SPECIFICATIONS

A guardrail system is an acceptable means of providing fall protection in both the Construction Standards (29 CFR Part 1926) and the General Industry Standards (29 CFR Part 1910).

The specifications for guardrails in both sets of standards are very similar. Following is a comparison of requirements and guidelines for guardrails.

Guardrail Specifications	
Construction	**General Industry**
◆ Top rail 42" ± 3" high	◆ Top rail 42" high
◆ Midrail ≥ 21" high	◆ Midrail about halfway between top rail and floor
◆ Ends of rails should not overhang posts (exception allowed where there is no hazard)	◆ Ends of rails should not overhang posts (exception allowed where there is no hazard)

Guardrail Specifications—Construction Standards

1926.502(b)(1)

Top edge height of top rails, or equivalent guardrail system members, shall be 42 inches (1.1 m) plus or minus 3 inches (8 cm) above the walking/working level. When conditions warrant, the height of the top edge may exceed the 45-inch height, provided the guardrail system meets all other criteria of this paragraph.

NOTE: When employees are using stilts, the top edge height of the top rail, or equivalent member, shall be increased an amount equal to the height of the stilts.

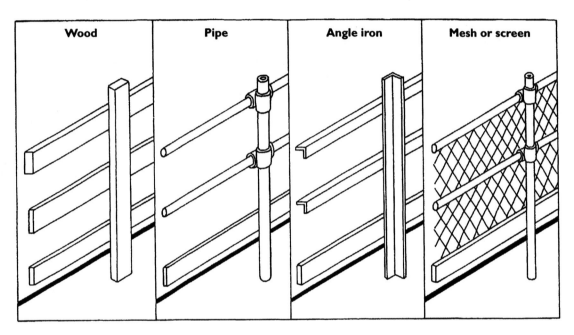

Typical guardrail construction materials

1926.502(b)(2)

Midrails, screens, mesh, intermediate vertical members, or equivalent intermediate structural members shall be installed between the top edge of the guardrail system and the walking/working surface when there is no wall or parapet wall at least 21 inches (53 cm) high.

(i) Midrails, when used, shall be installed at a height midway between the top edge of the guardrail system and the walking/working level.

(ii) Screens and mesh, when used, shall extend from the top rail to the walking/working level and along the entire opening between top rail supports.

(iii) Intermediate members (such as balusters), when used between posts, shall be not more than 19 inches (48 cm) apart.

(iv) Other structural members (such as additional midrails and architectural panels) shall be installed such that there are no openings in the guardrail system that are more than 19 inches (.5 m) wide.

1926.502(b)(7)

The ends of all top rails and midrails shall not overhang the terminal posts, except where such overhang does not constitute a projection hazard.

Guardrail Specifications—General Industry Standards

1910.23(e)(1)

A standard railing shall consist of top rail, intermediate rail, and posts, and shall have a vertical height of 42 inches nominal from upper surface of top rail to floor, platform, runway, or ramp level. The top rail shall be smooth-surfaced throughout the length of the railing. The intermediate rail shall be approximately halfway between the top rail and the floor, platform, runway, or ramp. The ends of the rails shall not overhang the terminal posts except where such overhang does not constitute a projection hazard.

Guardrail Strength

Construction

♦ ≥ 200 lbs. for top rail (without reducing height of cables, if used, to less than 39 inches high)

♦ ≥ 150 lbs. for midrails, screens, panels, etc

General Industry

♦ ≥ 200 lbs. for top rail

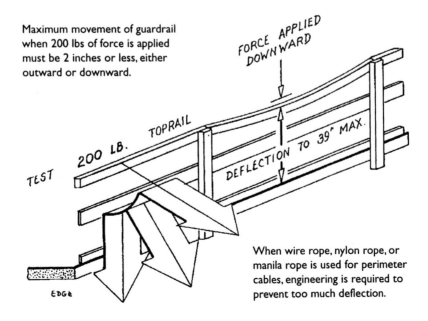

Maximum movement of guardrail when 200 lbs of force is applied must be 2 inches or less, either outward or downward.

When wire rope, nylon rope, or manila rope is used for perimeter cables, engineering is required to prevent too much deflection.

Guardrail Strength—Construction Standards

1926.502(b)(3)

Guardrail systems shall be capable of withstanding, without failure, a force of at least 200 pounds (890 N) applied within 2 inches (5.1 cm) of the top edge, in any outward or downward direction, at any point along the top edge.

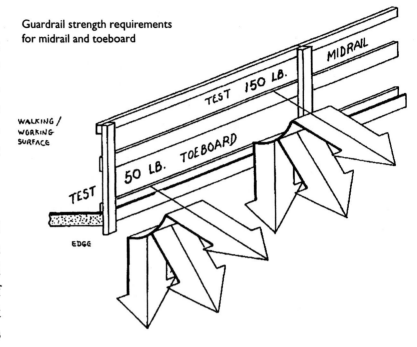

Guardrail strength requirements for midrail and toeboard

1926.502(b)(4)

When the 200 pound (890 N) test load specified in paragraph (b)(3) of this section is applied in a direction, the top edge of the guardrail shall not deflect to a height less than 39 inches (1.0 m) above the walking/working level. Guardrail system components selected and constructed in accordance with the Appendix B to subpart M of this part will be deemed to meet this requirement.

1926.502(b)(5)

Midrails, screens, mesh, intermediate vertical members, solid panels, and equivalent structural members shall be capable of withstanding, without failure, a force of at least 150 pounds (666 N) applied in any downward or outward direction at any point along the midrail or other member.

Guardrail Strength—General Industry Standards

1910.23(e)(3)(iv)

The anchoring of posts and framing of members for railings of all types shall be of such construction that the completed structure shall be capable of withstanding a load of at least 200 pounds applied in any direction at any point on the top rail.

Guardrail Materials—Construction Standards

1926.502(b)(6)

Guardrail systems shall be so surfaced as to prevent injury to an employee from punctures or lacerations, and to prevent snagging of clothing.

Guardrail Materials

Construction	**General Industry**
◆ Smooth surface on rails	◆ Smooth surface throughout length of railing
◆ Rails at least ¼" thick	
◆ No banding materials	
◆ Flag wire rope guardrails at 6' intervals	
◆ Frequently inspect manila, plastic or synthetic rope, if used	

1926.502(b)(8)

Steel banding and plastic banding shall not be used as top rails or midrails.

1926.502(b)(9)

Top rails and midrails shall be at least one-quarter inch (0.6 cm) nominal diameter or thickness to prevent cuts and lacerations. If wire rope is used for top rails, it shall be flagged at not more than 6-foot intervals with high-visibility material.

1926.502(b)(15)

Manila, plastic or synthetic rope being used for top rails or midrails shall be inspected as frequently as necessary to ensure that it continues to meet the strength requirements of paragraph (b)(3) of this section.

Wood Rails—Construction Standards

1926 Subpart M, Appendix B (non-mandatory)

(1) For wood railings: Wood components shall be minimum 1500 lb-ft/in(2) fiber (stress grade) construction grade lumber; the posts shall be at least 2-inch by 4-inch (5 cm x 10 cm) lumber spaced not more than 8 feet (2.4 m) apart on centers; the top rail shall be at least 2-inch by 4-inch (5 cm x 10 cm) lumber, the intermediate rail shall be at least 1-inch by 6-inch (2.5 cm x 15 cm) lumber. All lumber dimensions are nominal sizes as provided by the American Softwood Lumber Standards, dated January 1970.

Guardrail Materials—General Industry Standards

1910.23(e)(3)(i)

For wood railings, the posts shall be of at least 2-inch by 4-inch stock spaced not to exceed 6 feet; the top and intermediate rails shall be of at least 2-inch by 4-inch stock. If top rail is made of two right-angle pieces of 1-inch by 4-inch stock, posts may be spaced on 8-foot centers, with 2-inch by 4-inch intermediate rail.

Wood Rails

Construction	General Industry
◆ Grade of wood specified	◆ At least 2" x 4" top rails and 2" x 4" posts spaced ≤ 6' apart; or
◆ 2" x 4" posts spaced ≤ 8' apart	◆ Two right angle 1" x 4" posts spaced ≤ 8'
◆ Top rail = 2" x 4"; midrail ≥ 1" x 6"	◆ Midrail ≥ 2" x 4"

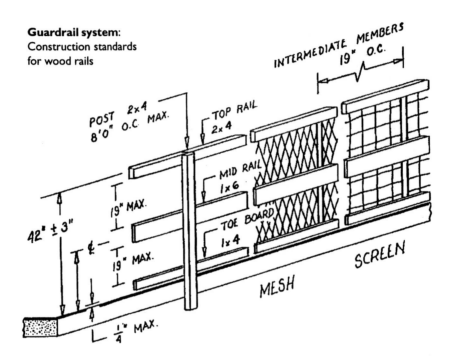

Guardrail system:
Construction standards
for wood rails

Pipe Rails

[Same requirements for Construction as for General Industry]

1926 Subpart M, Appendix B (non-mandatory)

(2) For pipe railings: posts, top rails, and intermediate railings shall be at least one and one-half inches nominal diameter (schedule 40 pipe) with posts spaced not more than 8 feet (2.4 m) apart on centers.

1910.23(e)(3)(ii)

For pipe railings, posts and top and intermediate railings shall be at least 1½ inches nominal diameter with posts spaced not more than 8 feet on centers.

Pipe Rails

Construction

◆ Posts, top rails, and midrails ≥ 1½" diameter pipe

◆ Posts ≤ 8' apart

General Industry

◆ Posts, top rails and midrails ≥ 1½" diameter pipe

◆ Posts ≤ 8' apart

Structural Steel Rails

Construction

◆ Posts, top rails, and midrails ≥ 2" x 2" x ⅜" angles

◆ Posts ≤ 8' apart

General Industry

◆ Posts, top rails, and midrails ≥ 2" x 2" x ⅜" angles or other metal shapes of equivalent bending strength

◆ Posts ≤ 8' apart

Structural Steel Rails

[Similar requirements for Construction as for General Industry]

1926 Subpart M, Appendix B (non-mandatory)

(3) For structural steel railings: posts, top rails, and intermediate rails shall be at least 2-inch by 2-inch (5 cm x 10 cm) by ⅜-inch (1.1 cm) angles, with posts spaced not more than 8 feet (2.4 m) apart on centers.

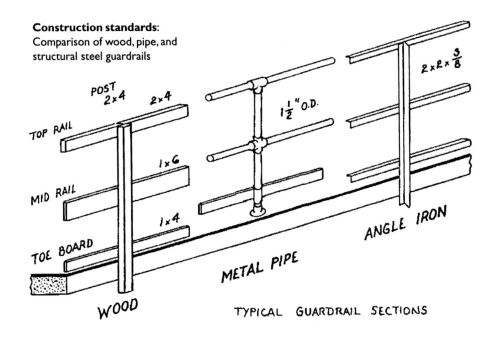

Construction standards:
Comparison of wood, pipe, and structural steel guardrails

TYPICAL GUARDRAIL SECTIONS

1910.23(e)(3)(iii)

For structural steel railings, posts and top and intermediate rails shall be of 2-inch by 2-inch by ⅜-inch angles or other metal shapes of equivalent bending strength with posts spaced not more than 8 feet on centers.

SAFETY RULES FOR GUARDRAILS

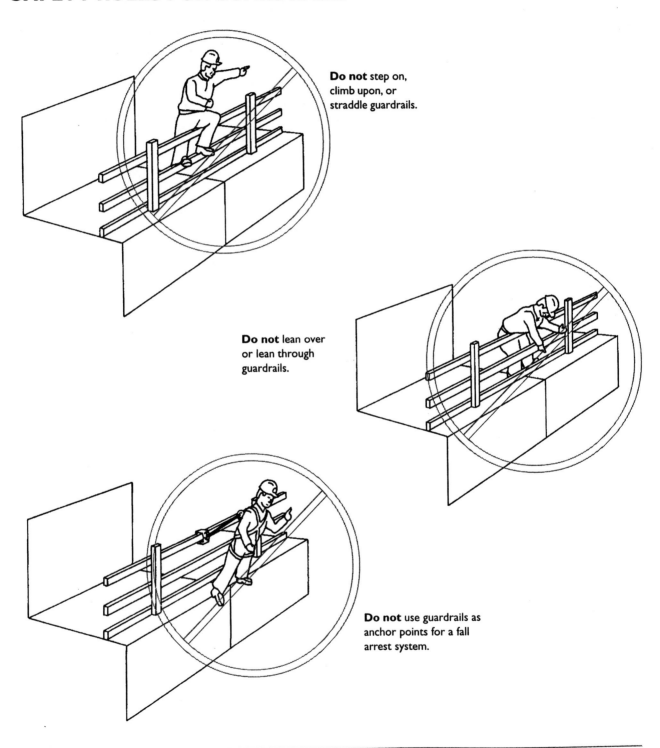

Do not step on, climb upon, or straddle guardrails.

Do not lean over or lean through guardrails.

Do not use guardrails as anchor points for a fall arrest system.

PROPOSED STEEL ERECTION STANDARDS

Perimeter Safety Cables on Multistory Structures

Proposed Appendix F to 1926 Subpart R—Installation of Perimeter Safety Cables:

Non-Mandatory Guidelines for Complying with Sec. 1926.756(f) To Protect the Unprotected Side or Edge of a Walking/Working Surface.

In multistory structures, the project structural engineer of record (SER) may facilitate the ease of erecting perimeter safety cables, where structural design allows, by placing column splices sufficiently high so as to accommodate perimeter safety cables located at 42–45 inches above the finished floor.

The SER may also consider allowing holes to be placed in the column web, when the column is oriented with the web perpendicular to the structural perimeter, at 42–45 inches above the finished floor and at the midpoint between the finished floor and the top cable. When holes in the column web are allowed for perimeter safety cables, the column splice must be placed sufficiently high so as not to interfere with any attachments to the column necessary for the column splice.

Column splices are recommended to be placed at every other or fourth levels as design allows. Column splices at third levels are detrimental to the erection process and should be avoided if possible.

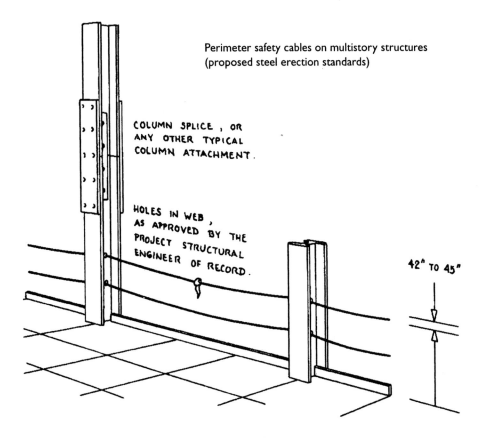

Perimeter safety cables on multistory structures
(proposed steel erection standards)

COLUMN SPLICE, OR ANY OTHER TYPICAL COLUMN ATTACHMENT.

HOLES IN WEB, AS APPROVED BY THE PROJECT STRUCTURAL ENGINEER OF RECORD.

42" TO 45"

Protections against falling objects:
a) hard hats
b) guardrails
c) canopies and barricades
d) moving objects away from elevated
   edges

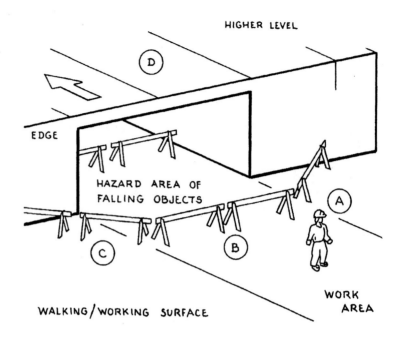

PROTECTION AGAINST FALLING OBJECTS

Protection against falling objects, according to OSHA's construction standards in Subpart M, include the following precautions:

- ◆ Wearing hard hats on construction sites

- ◆ Installing toeboards, screens, or guardrail systems that will prevent objects from falling from higher levels

- ◆ Erecting a canopy or barricading the area below and prohibiting entry into the danger zone

- ◆ Keeping objects far enough from the edge to prevent them from falling onto someone below

Where tools, equipment or materials are piled higher than the top edge of a toeboard, paneling or screening shall be installed from the surface or toeboard up to the top rail or midrail, for a distance sufficient to protect people below.

When guardrail systems are used, openings must be small enough to effectively prevent passage of objects.

Toeboards—Construction Standards

1926.502(j)

(1) Toeboards, when used as falling object protection, shall be erected along the edge of the overhead walking/working surface for a distance sufficient to protect employees below.

(2) Toeboards shall be capable of withstanding, without failure, a force of at least 50 pounds (222 N) applied in any downward or outward direction at any point along the toeboard.

Toeboards

Construction

◆ ≥ 3.5" high

◆ ≤ ¼" clearance

◆ Solid material or material with openings of 1" or less

General Industry

◆ 4" high*

◆ ≤ ¼" clearance

◆ Solid material or material with openings of 1" or less

* 4" high (nominal) as per text below.

---

(3) Toeboards shall be a minimum of 3½ inches (9 cm) in vertical height from their top edge to the level of the walking/working surface. They shall have not more than ¼-inch (0.6 cm) clearance above the walking/working surface. They shall be solid or have openings not over 1 inch (2.5 cm) in greatest dimension.

Toeboards—General Industry Standards

1910.23(e)(4), First paragraph

A standard toeboard shall be 4 inches nominal in vertical height from its top edge to the level of the floor, platform, runway, or ramp. It shall be securely fastened in place and with not more than ¼-inch clearance above floor level. It may be made of any substantial material either solid or with openings not over 1 inch in greatest dimension.

Guardrails—Protection against Falling Objects

Construction

◆ Paneling or screening

◆ Openings too small to allow materials to fall

General Industry

◆ Paneling

Guardrails for Protection against Falling Objects—Construction Standards

1926.502(j)(4)

Where tools, equipment, or materials are piled higher than the top edge of a toeboard, paneling or screening shall be erected from the walking/working surface or toeboard to the top of a guardrail system's top rail or midrail, for a distance sufficient to protect employees below.

1926.502(j)(5)

Guardrail systems, when used as falling object protection, shall have all openings small enough to prevent passage of potential falling objects.

Guardrails for Protection against Falling Objects—General Industry Standards

1910.23(e)(4), Second paragraph

Where material is piled to such height that a standard toeboard does not provide protection, paneling from floor to intermediate rail, or to top rail shall be provided.

GENERAL REQUIREMENTS FOR STORAGE

29 CFR 1926.250(b) and 1926.520(j)(6)–(8)

1926.250(b) Material storage.

General requirements for material stored in buildings under construction

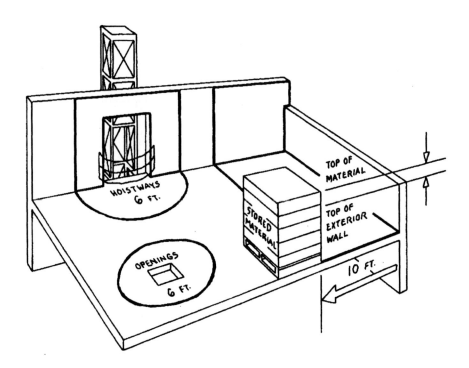

1926.250(b)(1)

Material stored inside buildings under construction shall not be placed within 6 feet of any hoistway or inside floor openings, nor within 10 feet of an exterior wall which does not extend above the top of the material stored.

Working on Stored Materials in Storage Areas

1926.250(b)(2)

Each employee required to work on stored material in silos, hoppers, tanks, and similar storage areas shall be equipped with personal fall arrest equipment meeting the requirements of Subpart M of this part.

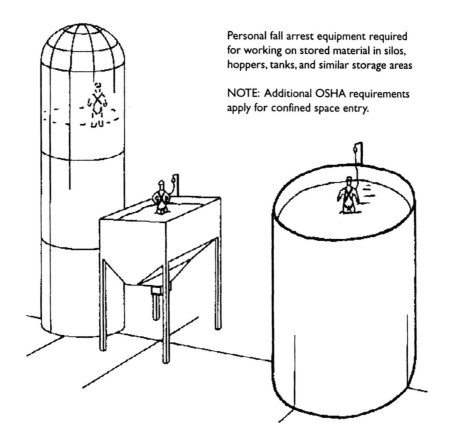

Personal fall arrest equipment required for working on stored material in silos, hoppers, tanks, and similar storage areas

NOTE: Additional OSHA requirements apply for confined space entry.

Storage on Scaffolds

1926.250(b)(5)

Materials shall not be stored on scaffolds or runways in excess of supplies needed for immediate operations.

Overhand Bricklaying

1926.502(j)(6)

During the performance of overhand bricklaying and related work:

(i) No materials or equipment except masonry and mortar shall be stored within 4 feet (1.2 m) of the working edge.

(ii) Excess mortar, broken or scattered masonry units, and all other materials and debris shall be kept clear from the work area by removal at regular intervals.

Roofing Work—Storage

1926.502(j)(7)

During the performance of roofing work:

(i) Materials and equipment shall not be stored within 6 feet (1.8 m) of a roof edge unless guardrails are erected at the edge.

(ii) Materials which are piled, grouped, or stacked near a roof edge shall be stable and self-supporting.

Canopies

1926.502(j)(8)

Canopies, when used as falling object protection, shall be strong enough to prevent collapse and to prevent penetration by any objects which may fall onto the canopy.

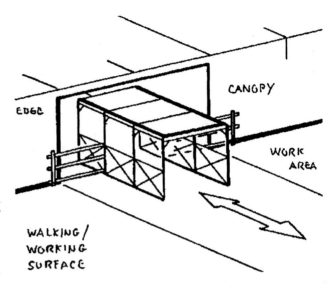

Debris Nets

"Debris nets are designed to catch falling debris, such as tools, foreign objects, falling concrete and other construction debris, and to protect workers and pedestrians below....

Typical net sizes range from ¼-in. to ¾-in. mesh. To catch large and heavy objects as well as small and light objects, smaller mesh nets can be used in conjunction with larger mesh and stronger personnel nets.

...Nets also can be used to catch both personnel and debris. In these cases, personnel nets must be used in conjunction with debris nets, and the nets must be cleared of debris on a regular basis to help ensure a falling worker's protection. Use of pivoting brackets can help to keep the net from interfering with crane loads, and also simplify attachment of the net section to supporting cables."[1]

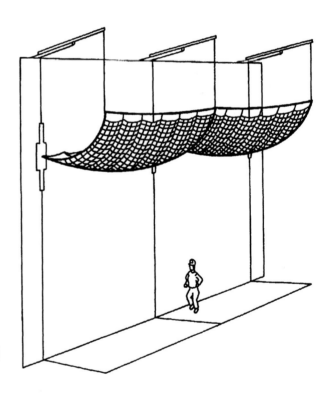

Interim Storage of Temporary Flooring Used in Steel Erection

Contractors have been cited under 29 CFR 1926.250(b)(1), when temporary flooring, in use during skeleton steel construction in tiered buildings, is bundled and placed over the edge of outer periphery while waiting to be picked up by a crane or derrick for movement to another tier.

Cause of accident:
falling objects from stored
or hoisted material

...The temporary flooring is, in fact, in-process equipment—not stored material, covered under the provisions of Subpart R—Steel Erection.... Temporary flooring not actually in use and placed in an area on the jobsite for an indefinite time would be considered as stored material...

The temporary flooring, when not in use as a floor, shall be properly bundled and braced to prevent movement until ready for use at the next tier.[2]

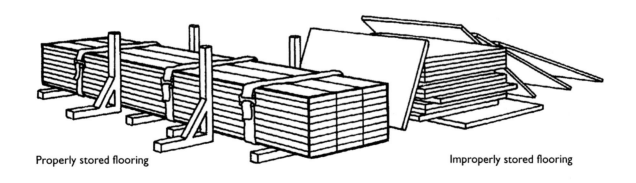

Properly stored flooring   Improperly stored flooring

PROTECTION AGAINST FALLING OBJECTS— GENERAL INDUSTRY

1910.22(d) Floor loading protection.

(1) In every building or other structure, or part thereof, used for mercantile, business, industrial, or storage purposes, the loads approved by the building official shall be marked on plates of approved design which shall be supplied and securely affixed by the owner of the building, or his duly authorized agent, in a conspicuous place in each space to which they relate. Such plates shall not be removed or defaced but, if lost, removed, or defaced, shall be replaced by the owner or his agent.

(2) It shall be unlawful to place, or cause, or permit to be placed, on any floor or roof of a building or other structure a load greater than that for which such floor or roof is approved by the building official.

Hazard of Objects Falling through Wall Hole

1910.23(b)(5)

Where there is a hazard of materials falling through a wall hole, and the lower edge of the near side of the hole is less than 4 inches above the floor, and the far side of the hole more than 5 feet above the next lower level, the hole shall be protected by a standard toeboard, or an enclosing screen either of solid construction, or as specified in paragraph (e)(11) of this section.

REMEMBER

Properly designed barriers will prevent many accidents and are required in permanent installations at a height of 4 feet.

Guardrail systems are generally considered to be the most effective means of preventing falls, and should be an option that receives preferential consideration for temporary exposures to potential falls of 6 feet or more.

Test Your Knowledge

How much slack is allowed in perimeter cables used as guardrails?

(HINT: Review guardrail strength requirements.)

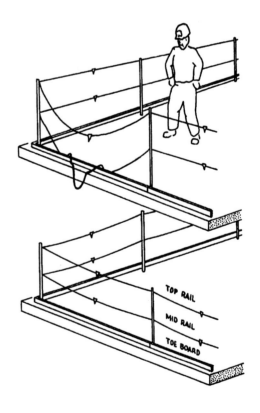

ENDNOTES

1. J. Nigel Ellis, Ph.D., CSP, P.E., *Introduction to Fall Protection* (Des Plaines, IL: American Society of Safety Engineers, 1993), pages 90–91.

2. OSHA Instruction, Directive No. STD 3-6.1, 1926.250(b)(1), Material Storage—As Related to Interim Storage of Temporary Flooring Used in Steel Erection, October 30, 1978.

Fall Protection

Accident Prevention

Analyze the following accidents and think about the recommendations you would make to prevent a recurrence. Record your comments. As you progress through this chapter, add to the list of recommendations any regulatory requirements or safety rules that apply that are not already listed.

ACCIDENTS

Fall from Scaffold — Lanyard Broke

(From an August 1992 NIOSH Alert)

On December 18, 1988, a 27-year-old male cement finisher died when he fell from a suspension scaffold and his safety lanyard snapped. The victim and a co-worker were dismantling suspended scaffolding at the 160-foot level inside a 172-foot high, circular concrete silo. Both men were wearing safety belts with nylon rope lanyards secured to independent lifelines.

The accident occurred when the victim lost his balance and fell off an unguarded end of the scaffold. The coworker stated that he saw the victim fall and jerk upward as the lanyard caught him. When the victim's weight dropped back on the lanyard, it snapped, allowing him to fall onto a concrete floor.

Examination of the lanyard after the event showed burn damage at several places, including the point of failure. The employer did not control inspection or distribution of this fall protection equipment. Instead, the equipment was kept in a common supply bin where the workers could readily obtain it when needed and return it when work was completed. The lanyard had been returned to the storage bin even though it had probably been damaged earlier during cutting and welding operations.[1]

Recommendations to Prevent Recurrence

_____
_____
_____
_____
_____
_____
_____
_____

Catwalk to Descent System

(From the Dallas Morning News, October 28, 1998)

Addison's Water Tower Theatre canceled its Sunday production of _Working_ a day after a cast member fell about 25 feet from a catwalk in front of an audience of about 160.

Actor Bill Jenkins, portraying a steel worker in the musical adapted from Studs Terkel's book of interviews with working people, said he suffered vertebrae damage in the fall Saturday night and will undergo reconstructive surgery....

In the final scene of the play, Mr. Jenkins walks out onto a catwalk and hooks himself to a harness and line that lowers him to the stage.... The play had run for a couple of weeks without mishap....

"I hook onto a carabiner that has a spring latch—it's a climbing rig—and I think I didn't make sure the catch was on right," he said Sunday from his room at Medical City Dallas Hospital. "I tried to relax as I fell, and I think that helped."[2]

Recommendations to Prevent Recurrence

_____
_____
_____
_____
_____
_____
_____
_____

Iron Workers

(From eNSC, January 1999)

On September 29, 1997, two iron workers hung 20 minutes in body harnesses above the turbulent water of New York's East River, waiting for rescue workers. They survived with only minor lacerations and pulled muscles.[3]

Recommendations to Prevent Recurrence

_____

_____

_____

_____

_____

_____

_____

_____

FALL ARREST SYSTEMS

If it is not feasible to prevent falls by means of guardrails or other barriers, then a personal fall arrest system should be used to prevent injury in case of a fall.

The anchor point, harness or other body support, and the connecting means must be compatible and designed for the specific application in order to provide effective protection.

Connecting means include lanyards and lifelines and associated hardware. Locking snap hooks are required.

Lifeline systems are points of attachment for fall protection lanyards. They may be mounted either vertically or horizontally and are generally intended to provide mobility to personnel working in elevated areas. Lifelines must not be used for any purpose other than fall protection.

Lifelines should be used when there is a danger of falling due to overreaching or work near an un-

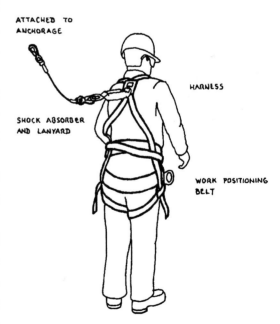

Components of a personal fall arrest system
NOTE: Do not mix and match parts from different manufacturers. Accidental disconnection could result!

Types of snaphooks

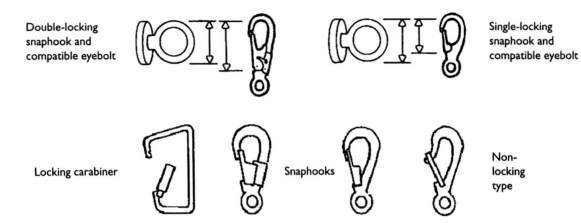

Double-locking snaphook and compatible eyebolt

Single-locking snaphook and compatible eyebolt

Locking carabiner   Snaphooks   Non-locking type

protected edge and on certain types of ladders and suspended scaffolds. Separate lifelines should be used for fall protection when work is done on suspended platforms.

Note that personnel who install lifelines must be protected from falls at all times by using retractable lanyards or by tying off to structural steel or other approved anchor points.

Strength Limited by Means of Attachment

A personal fall arrest system must be attached to an anchorage in a way that does not significantly reduce its strength.

For example, a good method of attachment might be a snaphook connected to an eyebolt that is the right size to accept it. A method that could reduce the strength of the system might be tying a knot in a rope lanyard or lifeline.

A serious problem could also result from tying off a rope lanyard or lifeline around an "H"-beam or an "I"-beam, because the cutting action of the beam edges can reduce the rope's strength by as much as 70 percent. *Use a crossarm strap or specially designed clamp on an I-beam or an H-beam!*

"The strength of an eye-bolt is rated along the axis of the bolt and its strength is greatly reduced if the force is applied at an angle to this axis (in the direction of shear)."[4]

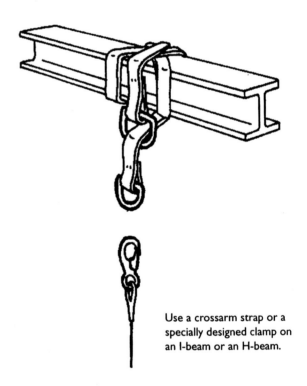

Use a crossarm strap or a specially designed clamp on an I-beam or an H-beam.

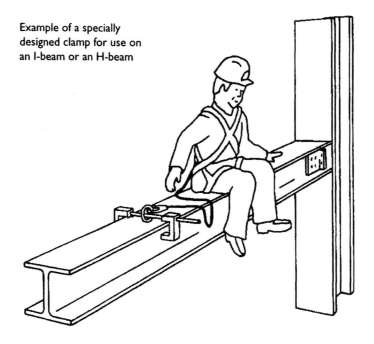

Example of a specially designed clamp for use on an I-beam or an H-beam

Manual vs. Automatic Equipment

A fall arrest system should operate automatically in the event of a fall.

"Requiring a worker to manually operate or manipulate a safety device during a panic situation introduces a significant potential for human error. Such error should be designed out. A fall arrest system is not mountaineering or fire rescue equipment, nor a restraint tool, nor for positioning. The latter require tremendous levels of skill that are only obtained through extensive amounts of initial and periodic training. Safety equipment that functions automatically can be more reliable for fall arrest and emergency escape."[5]

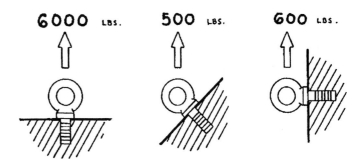

This illustration shows a reduction in strength for one particular anchor bolt. You must refer to manufacturer's data for a specific bolt.

Personal Lifelines (Backup) vs. Positioning Lines (Primary)

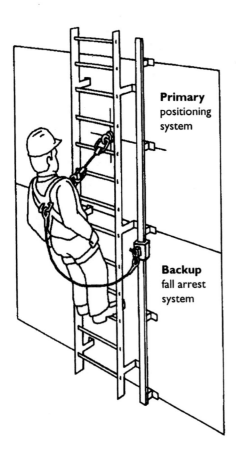

Primary positioning system

Backup fall arrest system

It is important to distinguish between a lifeline or lanyard that is used as a work tool to hold a worker in a certain position (for primary protection against falls) and a system that is only relied upon when a fall occurs (backup protection).

"For instance, if a worker locks a self-retracting lanyard/lifeline device and leans out against the line, that worker has forfeited his or her backup protection. If a situation such as form work calls for a work tool, then a second, separate fall arrest system is required.

"If a worker uses a primary positioning line and a backup lifeline, a second anchorage and body support are required. In principle, safety systems and work tools should be completely independent of one another. ... An exception might be when a portable tripod with adequate strength is used to anchor both lines because of the need to keep the lines directly overhead and centered in the opening. Yet when a saddle belt or boatswain's chair is used, a separate full body harness is required because most saddle belts are worn loosely for comfort and the wearer may fall out if a fall occurs."[6]

SAFETY BELTS, LIFELINES, AND LANYARDS

29 CFR 1926.104

Following are the first four rules in OSHA's Construction Standards on safety belts, lifelines and lanyards:

1926.104(a)

Lifelines, safety belts, and lanyards shall be used only for employee safeguarding. Any lifeline, safety belt, or lanyard actually subjected to in-service loading, as distinguished from static load testing, shall be immediately removed from service and shall not be used again for employee safeguarding.

Example of a work positioning belt, full body harness, shock absorbing device, and lanyard

Lifelines

1926.104(b)

Lifelines shall be secured above the point of operation to an anchorage or structural member capable of supporting a minimum dead weight of 5,400 pounds.

1926.104(c)

Lifelines used on rock-scaling operations, or in areas where the lifeline may be subjected to cutting or abrasion, shall be a minimum of ⅞-inch wire core manila rope. For all other lifeline applications, a minimum of ¾-inch manila or equivalent, with a minimum breaking strength of 5,400 pounds, shall be used.

Typical combination of safety belt with lanyard

1926.104(d)

Safety belt lanyard shall be a minimum of ½-inch nylon, or equivalent, with a maximum length to provide for a fall of no greater than 6 feet. The rope shall have a nominal breaking strength of 5,400 pounds.

Engineering of Anchor Points

Sufficiently strong anchor points must be carefully planned to provide continuous and complete protection while work is being done, including access to and egress from the elevated work area.

The primary considerations in the selection and design of anchor points should be these:

1. Support that is independent of the work surface, when possible, so that a collapse or fall of the work surface will not result in failure of fall arrest equipment. When this is not possible, use a structural member that is not likely to fail catastrophically.

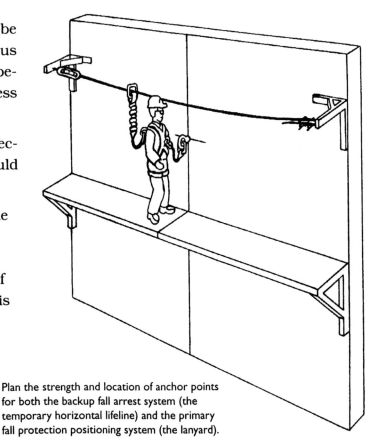

Plan the strength and location of anchor points for both the backup fall arrest system (the temporary horizontal lifeline) and the primary fall protection positioning system (the lanyard).

2. Anchor points that are clearly marked (i.e., painted with a bright color) and easy for workers to identify.

3. A shoulder-level anchor point for a harness-lanyard combination or an overhead anchor point for lifelines or fall arrest devices.

4. Adequate strength with an acceptable safety factor.

5. Horizontal lines for sideways movement that enable the device or attachment point to remain overhead so that a fall arrest occurs within a vertical plane. Moving away from a fixed anchor point to one side or the other can allow a dangerous "swing" (pendulum-like) fall to occur.

6. Minimum clearance above grade or any obstruction that will help prevent collisions during a fall.

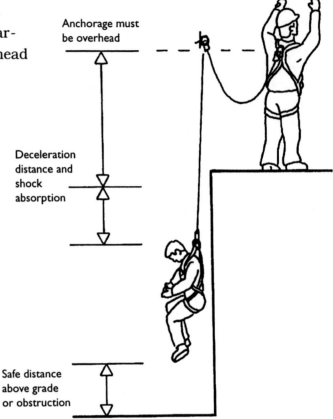

Considerations for the selection of anchor points

Anchorage must be overhead

Deceleration distance and shock absorption

Safe distance above grade or obstruction

In some situations a portable anchorage will provide a possible solution to potential swing-fall problems by keeping the anchor point overhead.

In the illustration of a portable anchorage on the next page, it is important to emphasize the need to ensure that the pipe or railing is sufficiently strong to be relied upon for fall protection.

Strength of anchor points can be determined by architects or engineers

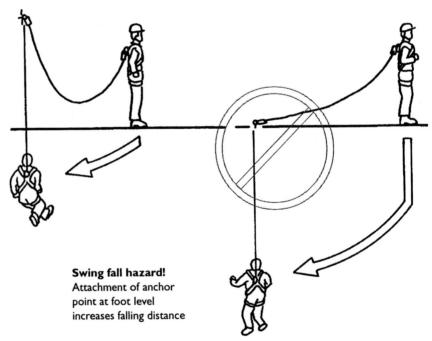

Swing fall hazard!
Attachment of anchor point at foot level increases falling distance

through modeling, calculations, or testing, and these strength determinations should be documented on engineering drawings. However, structures, beams, foundations, ladders, railings, etc. should be analyzed for corrosion and deterioration before they are approved and marked as anchor points.

Typical portable anchorage

Plan Ahead!

≥ **5400 lbs.** dead weight for anchorage of lifeline that will allow a fall of up to 6 feet

≥ **3000 lbs.** per attached worker, required strength for positioning system

General Guidelines for Anchorages

1. Plan ahead
2. Involve everyone
3. Rely on technical staff for guidance
4. Decide whether permanent anchorages should be created
5. Plan for rescue in case of a fall
6. Separate anchorages for each worker when possible
7. Choose anchorages directly above work area
8. Check for hazards below

Determining the strength of anchorage points: A full-sized pickup truck weighs less than 3000 lbs.

(From Occupational Health & Safety, March 1998)

"Plan anchorages in advance, and as completely as possible.

◆ Plan ahead and include everyone involved with the project. The safety director, architect, designer, general contractor, subcontractors and their crews, and appropriate personnel from the client company can all provide needed input in selecting safe and workable anchorages based on the type of work being done and on changes in the structure as different stages in the construction process are reached. A group effort will help all possibilities to be explored in determining the best anchorages.

◆ Contact technical staff at key fall protection equipment companies for additional guidance if needed.

◆ Determine whether permanent anchorages should be created for future work.

◆ As part of the planning process, discuss how a worker would be rescued in the event of a fall from each anchorage. Determine what rescue equipment should be on site.

◆ Plan to use separate anchorages for each worker wherever possible and make sure each anchorage is capable of supporting at least 5,000 pounds per attached worker, or 3,600 pounds when certified by an engineer or other properly qualified professional. Also note how the number of workers requiring tie-off changes with each stage of the project.

◆ Whenever possible, choose anchorages situated directly above the work area to avoid swing injuries. Also review areas below the anchorage and work area for possible structures or lower levels that could pose additional hazards during a fall.

◆ Choose anchorages that, in combination with fall protection equipment, allow for safe clearance should a fall occur."[7]

Guidelines for Minimum Sizes and Conditions of Anchor Points

Minimum recommended sizes and conditions of anchor points are outlined below:

◆ **Pipe**
  ○ 2-inch schedule 10 carbon steel or nickel. These metals must be identified with a magnet. Pipe that does not attract a magnet shall not be used, except for 2-inch schedule 10 stainless steel.
  ○ The span between pipe supports must not be greater than 20 feet for any size pipe.
  ○ 3-inch metal pipe or larger sizes may be used if it is in good condition. The pipe length must be continuous for at least two supports on either side of the attachment.
  ○ *Never* tie off to any plastic pipe or electrical conduit.
  ○ *Do not* tie off to insulated pipe of any size without prior approval of the Safety Department.

♦ **Structural steel**

○ 2½-inch x 2½-inch by ⅜-inch angle. Span must be 20 feet or less.

○ *Never* use guardrails.

Temporary Horizontal Lifelines

Horizontal lifelines placed in skeletal steel structures (e.g., pipe racks, etc.) shall be ⅜-inch cable or larger and shall be secured on each end by at least two cable clamps.

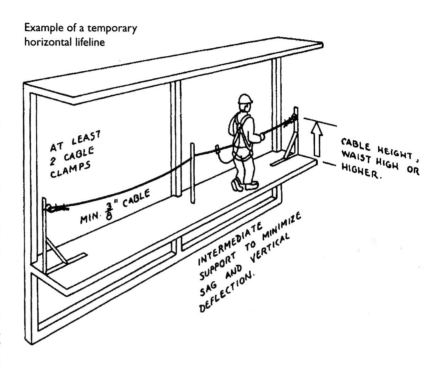

Example of a temporary horizontal lifeline

Intermediate supports must be adequate to minimize sag and vertical deflection under expected conditions of use and worst-case fall scenario.

"Based on testing, engineered horizontal lifelines are capable of absorbing the force of several workers falling, and up to three workers have been tested with both weights and personnel with little effect on maximum arrest force at cable termination (T_3). A 20% increase in force per worker (up to three workers) is believed satisfactory.

It should be noted that configurations of use of horizontal lifelines must be designed so that the fall of one worker does not reasonably cause another worker to fall from his or her work position. Horizontal lifelines must not be used by workers to support their balance or weight at any time. Horizontal lifelines are for emergency fall arrest use only. Also to be noted: Use a second suspension system for supporting the weight of the scaffold, tools, etc."[8]

As mentioned previously, horizontal lifelines should be positioned so that they provide points of attachment at waist level or higher.

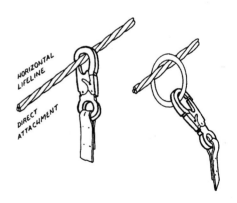

Methods of attaching the personal fall arrest system to the horizontal lifeline

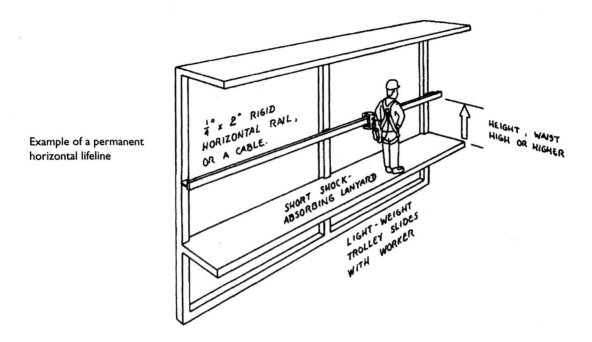

Example of a permanent horizontal lifeline

Permanent Horizontal Lifelines

"Permanent horizontal lifeline systems should be designed to last as long as the structure to which they are attached. They can consist of a ¼ in. x 2 in. rigid horizontal rail, or cable that allows a light-weight trolley to slide easily with the worker.

"Since these systems are attached to the structure at regular intervals, they can accommodate several workers simultaneously (one trolley per worker). Special sections can allow the trolley to go continuously around corners so workers do not have to disconnect. The fixed rail trolley can be easily attached and detached at protected access/egress points.

"For crane runways, elevated catwalks and piperacks, permanent systems installed at waist height can provide continuous horizontal mobility with protection. For waist-height installations, a short shock-absorbing lanyard is permanently attached to the trolley to limit arresting forces on the worker and system."[9]

Vertical Lifelines

Vertical lifelines are used as part of a personal fall arrest system when vertical mobility is required. They may consist of:

♦ Static lifelines made of synthetic fiber rope or wire rope (cable) which are equipped with approved sliding rope grabs; or

♦ Lanyards or lifelines with self-retracting reels that are connected directly to a body harness.

When vertical lifelines are used, each person must be provided with a separate lifeline.

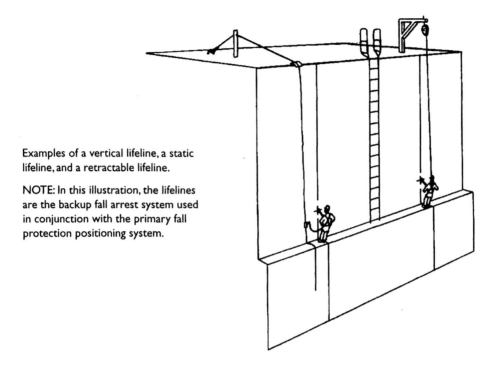

Examples of a vertical lifeline, a static lifeline, and a retractable lifeline.

NOTE: In this illustration, the lifelines are the backup fall arrest system used in conjunction with the primary fall protection positioning system.

Static Lifelines

Static rope lifelines with rope grabs are required for personnel working from two-point suspension scaffolds. They are recommended for other operations where tie-off points are limited and vertical mobility is required, such as erection of scaffolds and structural steel.

Sliding rope grabs, approved for the size of the rope, must be used to secure a safety lanyard to a vertical lifeline. Rope grabs shall be positioned on the lifeline above shoulder level or higher.

RETRACTABLE LIFELINES AND LANYARDS

Retractable lifeline devices shall be secured by means of shackles and wire rope chokers or synthetic slings. Synthetic or natural fiber rope shall not be used to secure these devices.

A retractable lifeline should be equipped with a rope (¼-inch synthetic fiber) tag line extending from the reel (when lifeline is fully retracted) to elevations below the point of attachment or to the ground, as applicable.

Miller Equipment lists the following limitations on the use of their retractable lifelines in their "Miller Series 52/55 Operation and Maintenance Manual."[10] [pages 4–10]

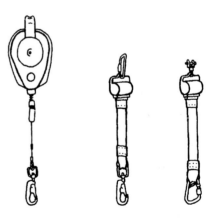

Typical retractable lifeline and lanyards

Limitations on Miller Retractable Lifelines

♦ "Only trained personnel should use this device."

♦ "The lifeline must be kept clean."

♦ "The equipment should be installed overhead and used in such a manner as to reduce the potential for a pendulum fall."

♦ "Allow 42" of clearance below the work surface in the event of a free fall."

♦ "The unit must be mounted to an overhead anchor by the anchorage handle using a locking carabiner, or by another Miller-approved mounting device such as Miller tripods, Quad Pods, davit systems, wall mounts, etc."[11]

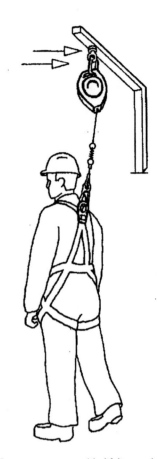

Securing a retractable lifeline and lanyard to an anchorage point

Testing and Safe Use of Retractable Lifelines

Safe Practices

♦ "With the device in the mounted position, test lifeline retraction and tension by pulling out several feet of lifeline and allow it to retract back into the unit. Always maintain a light tension on the lifeline as it retracts. The lifeline should pull out freely and retract all the way back into the unit."

♦ "If the lifeline does not pull out smoothly or sticks when retracting, pull all of the lifeline out of the housing and allow it to retract slowly under tension."

♦ "Do not pull lifeline out of the housing or let it retract while the unit is laying flat because proper lifeline retraction may not be achieved. Always inspect and operate the unit in a mounted position."

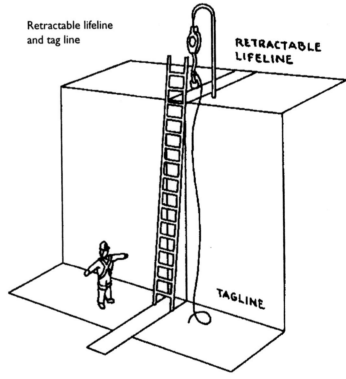

Retractable lifeline and tag line

RETRACTABLE LIFELINE

TAGLINE

- "The braking mechanism can be tested by grasping the end of the lifeline above the impact indicator and applying a sharp steady pull downward which will engage the brakes. There should be no slippage of the lifeline while the brakes are engaged. Once tension is released, the brakes will disengage and the unit will return to the retractable mode."

- "If the unit has a retrieval mode (Series 52), check it for proper function according to the manufacturer's directions prior to each use of the lifeline."[12]

Unsafe Use of Retractable Lifelines

Prohibitions

- "Do not use the unit if the cable doesn't retract."

- "Do not use the unit if the lifeline brakes do not engage."

- "Do not use the unit if the load impact indicator has been activated."

- "Do not attempt to service the unit; if it does not operate satisfactorily or requires repairs, return the unit to Miller or an authorized service center."

- "Do not lubricate this device."

- "Never use the device when the red colored length of cable shows. This is an indication that the unit is approaching maximum cable extension. Check the maximum cable length required before using to ensure the unit has sufficient capacity."

- "Do not allow lifeline in any application to bend or be subjected to fall arresting forces over structural members or edges."

- **"Failure to follow these instructions could cause serious injury or death."**[13]

DBI/SALA Tips on Retracting Lifelines

DBI/SALA also supplies self-retracting lifelines, and includes additional pointers in their "User Instruction Manual for Self-Retracting Lifelines":

- "When working with SRL, take note to allow lifeline to recoil back into device under control. A short tag line may be required to extend or retract lifeline during connection and disconnection operations."

- "Allowing lifeline to be fully extended for long periods of time may cause premature weakening of the retraction spring."[14]

OTHER CONNECTING DEVICES

The most common connecting device in a fall arrest system is a rope or webbing lanyard, preferably a shock-absorbing type. It could also be a rope grab or a retractable lifeline or lanyard.

Connector toggles are devices that lock into structural steel bolt holes to provide an attachment point for a safety lanyard. These devices should be used by structural iron connectors and bolt-up personnel during steel erection.

Concrete form tie-offs are devices that attach to patented concrete forms to provide an attachment point for lanyards. They should be used when placing concrete forms at elevations where a fall exposure exists.

Each time you use a snaphook to make a connection, LOOK AT YOUR CONNECTION and make sure it is locked in position on the anchor bolt, tie-off point, or D-ring.

Never rely only on the sound of the snaphook snapping into place. This has been a fatal mistake for some!

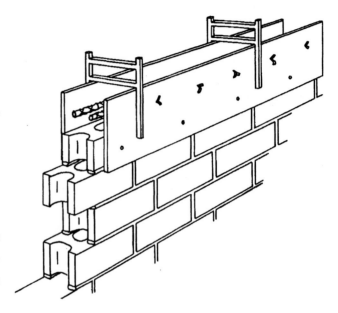

Concrete form tie-offs are devices that attach to patented concrete forms to provide an attachment point for lanyards. They should be used when placing concrete forms at elevations where a fall exposure exists.

EQUIPMENT MANUFACTURERS

Two of the best known manufacturers of fall protection equipment are Miller Equipment (now owned by a company called Dalloz Fall Protection) and DBI/SALA.

Compatibility of Components

In their instruction manuals, both companies warn against mixing and matching fall protection system components:

Miller Equipment

"To ensure that accidental disengagement cannot occur, a competent person must ensure system compatibility."[15]

DBI/SALA

"DBI/SALA full body harnesses are designed for use with DBI/SALA approved components (lanyards, energy absorbers, self retracting lifelines, etc.) Use of this harness with non-approved components may jeopardize compatibility between equipment which could affect the reliability and safety of the complete system. Contact DBI/ SALA if you have questions about compatibility of components."[16]

Questions about Your Fall Protection Equipment

If you have questions about your fall protection equipment that are not answered in the user instruction manual you received along with your equipment, here are the numbers to call:

Dalloz/Miller Equipment: **1-800-873-5242**

DBI/SALA: **1-800-328-6146**

Miller Equipment

Limitations of Equipment

Determine visually that your connection is secure.

(The following material has been excerpted from the Miller Equipment's "Instruction and Warning Information.")

♦ Maximum working load is 310 lbs., unless labeled otherwise.[page 3]

♦ Shock absorbers can elongate up to 3½ feet. This elongation distance must be considered when choosing a tie-off point. [page 10]

♦ Make sure snap hook is positioned so that its keeper is never load bearing. [page 11]

Primary Protection Requires Backup

(From Miller Equipment's "Instruction and Warning Information")

♦ Miller urges the use of the combination [of a fall arrest system in conjunction with personal positioning] system whenever possible, since a personal positioning system is not designed for fall arrest purposes. By using this combination system, the fall arrest components will be activated should the worker suffer a fall while working or changing positions. [page 7]

♦ Because the suspension system components [such as a boatswain's chair used in window washing and painting industries] are not designed to arrest a free fall, a back-up fall arrest system should be used in conjunction with the personal suspension system. This fall arrest system will only activate should the worker experience a free fall. [page 8]

Heat Limits

(From Miller Equipment's "Instruction and Warning Information")

- ◆ Lanyards made of nylon and corduroy should not be used above 200°F. [page 18]

- ◆ Lanyards made of polyester (Dacron®) should not be used above 180°F. [page 18]

Safe Use of PFAS

(From Miller Equipment's "Instruction and Warning Information")

- ◆ Always check for obstructions below the work area to make sure potential fall path is clear. [page 3]

- ◆ As a general rule, Miller recommends that a fall arrest system be used any time a working height of four feet or more is reached.[page 6]

- ◆ Visually check all buckles [of body harness] to assure proper and secure connections before each use. [page 10]

- ◆ Fall protection connecting devices should be attached to the back D-ring of a full body harness or body belt. [page 10]

- ◆ Side, front, and chest d-rings should be used for positioning only. [page 10]

- ◆ Shoulder D-rings should be used for retrieval only. [page 10]

- ◆ Always visually check that each snap hook freely engages D-ring or anchor point and that its keeper is completely closed. [page 10]

- ◆ Tie off in a manner that limits free fall to the shortest possible distance. (Six feet maximum) [page 10]

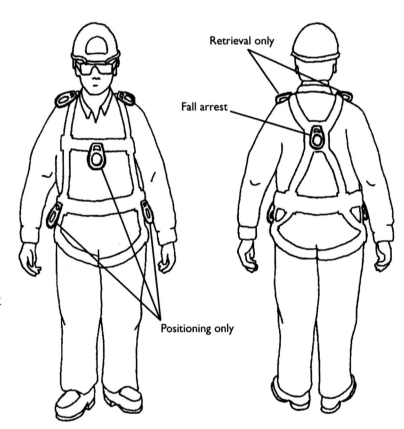

D-ring locations and recommended uses

◆ Do not wrap lanyards around sharp or rough edges. Use a cross arm strap to wrap around surface and connect to lanyard snap hook. For extremely sharp surfaces, use wear pad to protect strap from damage. [page 11]

◆ Always work directly under the anchor point to avoid a swing fall injury. [page 12]

When making connections to web loops of a body harness, locking carabiners may be used, but snaphooks are not recommended.

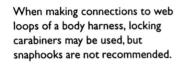
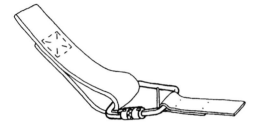
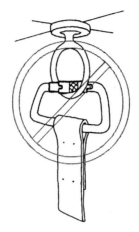

Use caution to ensure that backbone of carabiner (*not* its gate) bears the load. As a general rule, never allow the gate of a carabiner to be load-bearing.

Unsafe Use of PFAS
(From Miller Equipment's "Instruction and Warning Information")

Prohibitions

◆ Do not tie knots in lanyards. [page 11]

◆ Never use an anchor point which will not allow snap hook keeper to close. [page 12]

◆ Do not attach multiple lanyards together, or attach a lanyard back onto itself. [page 11]

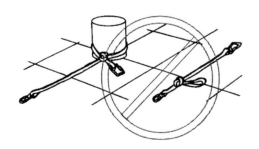

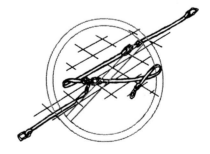

DBI/SALA Instructions

(The following information has been excerpted from DBI/SALA's "User Instruction Manual: Full Body Harnesses.")

Limitations

(From DBI/SALA's "User Instruction Manual: Full Body Harnesses")

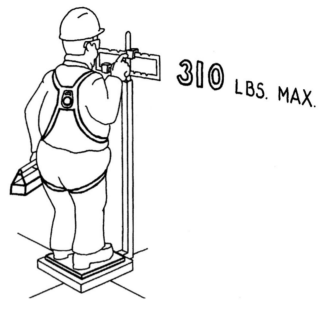

- ◆ DBI/SALA full body harnesses are designed for use by persons with a combined weight (person, clothing, tools, etc.) of no more than 310 lbs. [page 10]

- ◆ Pregnant women or minors must not use full body harnesses. [page 12]

Environmental Factors

(From DBI/SALA's "User Instruction Manual: Full Body Harnesses")

- ◆ Full body harnesses with Kevlar web should be used when working with tools, materials, or environments of high temperatures; or near flammable materials...[page 9]

- ◆ Avoid working in environments where the harness will come in contact with, or abrade against, abrasive surfaces. Kevlar webbing has exceptional cut and slash resistance but it does not have equivalent abrasion resistance to polyester webbing.[page 10]

- ◆ Harnesses made of Kevlar 29 webbing are specifically designed for high temperature environments, but they also have limitations. Kevlar 29 begins to char at 800–900°F.; it can withstand limited contact exposure to temperatures up to 1000°F. Polyester loses strength at temperatures between 300–400°F. The PVC coating has a melting point of approximately 350°F. [page 10]

- ◆ Harnesses with PVC coated hardware should be used when working in potentially explosive environments. [page 9]

- ◆ Even those harnesses incorporating PVC coated hardware are classified as non-sparking, precautions should be taken. Make certain the hardware is corrosion free before use to reduce the risk of incendiary sparking that can occur where corroded materials scrape against other materials (i.e. subsystem components). [page 10]

- ◆ Solutions containing acid or caustic chemicals, especially at elevated temperatures, may damage DBI/SALA full body harnesses. When working with such chemicals, frequent inspection of the entire full body harness must be completed. Consult DBI/SALA if doubt exists concerning the use of this equipment around chemical hazards. [page 9]

Safe Use of PFAS

(From DBI/SALA's "User Instruction Manual: Full Body Harnesses")

DBI/SALA Safety Tips

◆ DBI/SALA does not recommend connecting a lanyard to a self-retracting lifeline. Special applications do exist where it may be permissible. The 964DEP extension may be used inline between a self retracting lifeline and harness.

◆ Avoid working where your connecting subsystem may cross or tangle with that of another worker. Do not allow the connecting subsystem to pass under arms or between legs. [page 14]

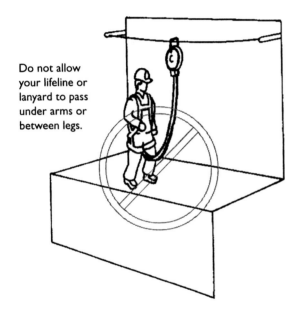

Do not allow your lifeline or lanyard to pass under arms or between legs.

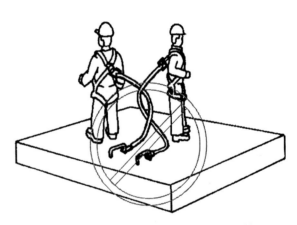

Avoid working where you can get tangled or crossed up with a co-worker.

◆ The user must have a rescue plan and the means at hand to implement it should a fall occur. [page 14]

◆ When connecting a lanyard to a rope grab, connect one end to the attachment point of the rope grab (i.e., handle, o-ring, etc.) and connect the other end to the body support.

  ○ Some rope grabs may be supplied with permanently attached lanyard or energy absorbing lanyard. For these cases, use of an additional lanyard connected between the rope grab and the body support is not recommended.

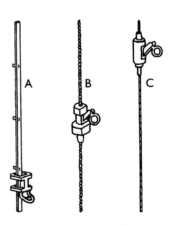

Examples of rope grabs
A. Fixed rail system with sliding sleeve grab
B. Rope lifeline with rope grab
C. Wire lifeline with wire grab

○ In all cases, ensure the length of the lanyard does not exceed the rope grab manufacturer's recommended maximum connection length. [Page 4 of DBI/SALA's "User Instruction Manual for Web and Rope Lanyards Used in Personal Restraint, Work Positioning, Suspension and Rescue Systems"][17]

Unsafe Use of PFAS

(From DBI/SALA's "User Instruction Manual: Full Body Harnesses")

DBI/SALA Prohibitions

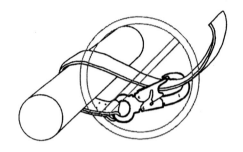

◆ Do not hook lanyard back onto itself (choker style). [page 23]

◆ Do not use hooks or connectors that will not completely close over the attachment object (for these situations, use a "tie-off" adaptor or other anchorage connector to allow a compatible connection). [page 23]

◆ Snap hooks and carabiners shall not be connected to each other. [page 23]

◆ Do not attach two snap hooks into one D-ring. [page 23]

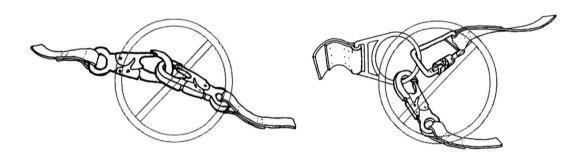

Pitfalls to Avoid When Using Fall Protection Equipment

Common problems to be anticipated and overcome include the following:

1. **Transition points**
   Do not allow unprotected exposure while traveling to or returning from the work station or during the progress of the work.

2. **Multiple users**
   Make sure that the anchor points are strong enough to safely hold the number of workers who are attached, or provide additional tie-off points.

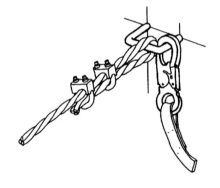

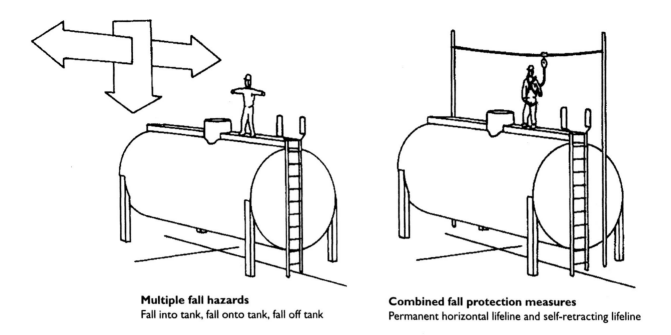

Multiple fall hazards
Fall into tank, fall onto tank, fall off tank

Combined fall protection measures
Permanent horizontal lifeline and self-retracting lifeline

3. Multiple fall hazards

In some situations, a fall arrest system may need to be used in combination with fall prevention measures such as perimeter guardrails or a catch platform, or covers over skylight openings or holes in roofs. In other situations, both horizontal and vertical fall protection may be needed.

Examples include tank car loading and unloading, tank truck cleaning, water cooler tower construction, water treatment facilities, and work on dome-shaped roofs and roofs with steep slopes.

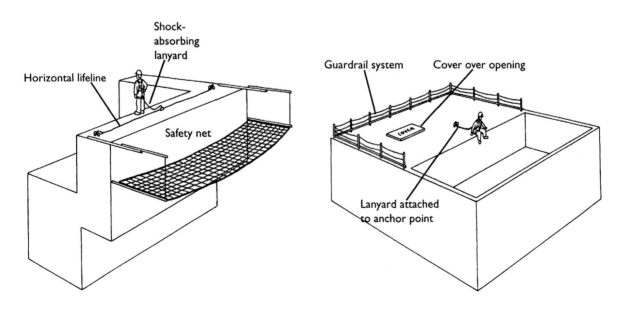

Examples of multiple fall protection exposures and suitable fall protection measures

4. Mixing and matching components

A personal fall arrest system should be designed, tested, and used as a system. Components from different manufacturers should not be randomly mixed.

5. Rollout

Rollout caused by a twisting action can be a major problem with nonlocking snaphooks. Locking snaphooks, which are required by OSHA rules, will not open unless two separate forces are applied.

Rollout of a nonlocking snaphook caused by twisting

6. Unsafe anchor points

Do not tie off onto something just because the snap hook will fit around or through it. Such unsafe anchor points may be metal stud cutouts, wire rope, perimeter protection, rebar that is tied but not welded, 2 x 4s, and pipe or conduit hangers.

Do not tie off to unsafe anchor points!

7. Failure to consider stretch of lifeline

"A 100-ft. nylon rope will stretch elastically several feet in a fall, so that a fall within 15 ft. of grade could produce an injurious impact with the ground. Polyester has one-third of the rope stretch of nylon, and has better UV resistance."[18]

8. Loss of strength

Manufacturers will estimate approximate annual loss of strength in their lifelines, but only a pull-test of end samples of the rope can confirm how much strength has been lost.

9. Conditions that may damage components

Provisions must be made to protect synthetic materials from hot surfaces or contact with acids or corrosive materials.

○ Protection from heat may be provided by a section of slit air hose or a leather cover. Where welding is being done, Kevlar® or Nomex® sleeves should be used to protect synthetic materials against hot slag.

○ Lanyards and lifelines must also be protected against being cut by sharp or abrasive surfaces, such as plate glass window panes, angle iron, fabricated steel parts, and parapets. The lifeline must either be protected or changed to steel cable.

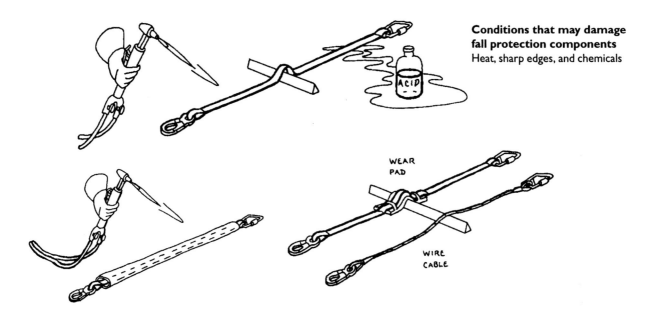

Conditions that may damage fall protection components
Heat, sharp edges, and chemicals

Many synthetic materials and leather are subject to damage by chemicals. Use lanyard made from wire rope, steel, or chemical-resistant material.

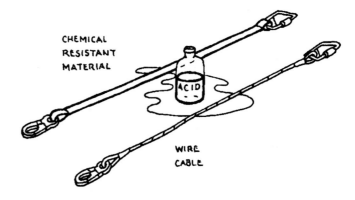

INSPECTION

Fall restraint devices should be inspected by a designated competent person when purchased and at six-month intervals. A record should be kept of these inspections. Bar coding of all fall arrest components facilitates tracking of inspections and service life. As mentioned above, end samples of lifelines should be tested on a regular basis for strength.

DBI/SALA has sample inspection forms in their instruction manuals.

Pre-Use Inspection

Fall restraint devices must be visually inspected by the user prior to use for defects such as the following:

◆ Cuts or abrasion

◆ Excessive wear

◆ Loose splices

◆ Defective or distorted hardware.

DBI/SALA recommends inspecting labels, too, and replacing them if they are illegible or missing.

Straps of Body Harness

Miller Equipment recommends grasping the webbing of each section of the body harness with hands about 6 to 8 inches apart. When the webbing is bent in an inverted "U" the surface tension makes damaged fibers or cuts easier to see.

(From Miller User Instruction Manual)

◆ Follow this procedure the entire length of the webbing, inspecting both sides of each strap. Watch for frayed edges, broken fibers, pulled stitches, cuts, burns, and chemical damage. [page 13]

◆ Broken webbing strands generally appear as tufts on the webbing surface. Any broken, cut or burned stitches will be readily seen. [page 14]

Hardware on Harness

(From Miller Equipment's "Instruction and Warning Information")

◆ Check D-rings and D-ring metal wear pad (if any) for distortion, cracks, breaks, and rough or sharp edges. The D-ring bar should be at a 90° angle with the long axis of the belt and should pivot freely. [page 14]

◆ Attachments of buckles and D-rings should be given special attention. Note any unusual wear, frayed or cut fibers, or distortion of the buckles or dees. [page 14]

◆ The tongue or billet of the belts receives heavy wear from repeated buckling and un-buckling. Inspect for loose, distorted or broken grommets. Belts should not have additional, punched holes. [page 14]

Lanyards

(From Miller Equipment's "Instruction and Warning Information")

When inspecting lanyards, begin at one end and work to the opposite end. Slowly rotate the lanyard so that the entire circumference is checked. Spliced ends require particular attention. [page 15]

◆ **Snaps:** Inspect closely for hook and eye distortions, cracks, corrosion, or pitted surfaces. The keeper (latch) should seat into the nose without binding and should not be distorted or obstructed. The keeper spring should exert sufficient force to firmly close the keeper. Keeper locks must prevent the keeper from opening when the keeper closes. [page 16]

Typical lanyards

SYNTHETIC

◆ **Thimbles:** The thimble must be firmly seated in the eye of the splice, and the splice should have no loose or cut strands. The edges of the thimble must be free of sharp edges, distortion, or cracks. [page 16]

◆ **Steel Lanyard:** While rotating the steel lanyard, watch for cuts, frayed areas, or un-usual wearing patterns on the wire. Broken strands will separate from the body of the lanyard. [page 16]

◆ **Web Lanyard:** While bending webbing over a pipe or mandrel, observe each side of the webbed lanyard. This will reveal any cuts or breaks. Swelling, discoloration, cracks, and πcharring are obvious signs of chemical or heat damage. Observe closely for any breaks in the stitching. [page 16]

◆ **Rope Lanyard:** Rotation of the rope lanyard while inspecting from end-to-end will bring to light any fuzzy, worn, broken or cut fibers. Weakened areas from extreme loads will appear as a noticeable change in original diameter. The rope diameter should be uniform throughout, following a short break-in period. [page 17]

◆ **Miller Sofstops:** The outer portion of the pack should be examined for burn holes and tears. Stitching on areas where the pack is sewn to d-rings, belts, or lanyards should be examined for loose strands, rips and deterioration. [page 17]

Additional Notes on Snaphooks

Snaphooks in particular should be closely examined. A malfunctioning snaphook could accidentally open and become disconnected from a lifeline, which could result in a fall.

- ◆ Check regularly to be sure that snaphook closes fully and locks reliably each time pressure is released. Check the spring on the mechanism that opens the snaphook.

- ◆ Keep snaphooks free of accumulated dirt or particles. Wash or clean hooks regularly.

- ◆ Check for any sign of wear, abrasion, damage, or tampering.

Typical locking snaphooks in locked and open positions

HOW TO PUT ON A BODY HARNESS

The following steps for putting on a full body harness have been outlined by Miller Equipment on pages 20–21 of "Instruction and Warning Information":[19]

1. Hold harness by back D-ring. Shake harness to allow all straps to fall into place.

2. If waist and/or leg straps are buckled, release straps and unbuckle at this time.

3. Slide straps over shoulders so D-ring is located in middle of back between shoulder blades.

4. Connect waist strap. Waist strap should be tight, but not binding.

5. Pull buckle portion of leg strap between legs and connect to opposite end of leg strap. Repeat with second leg strap.

6. After all straps have been buckled, tighten all friction buckles so that harness fits snug but allows full range of movement.

7. If harness contains a chest strap, pull strap around shoulder strap and fasten in midchest area. Tighten to keep shoulder straps taut.

8. To remove harness, reverse procedures.

9. Miller recommends reconnecting the waist strap after removing harness. This gives workers a starting point when next attempting to put harness on.

10. Miller recommends hanging the harness by back d-ring to help it keep its shape when not in use.

CLEANING AND STORAGE

DBI/SALA's recommendations[20] for cleaning and storage of body harnesses, published in their "User Instruction Manual: Full Body Harnesses," are listed below. Their recommendations for cleaning lanyards are almost exactly the same as Miller's.[21]

1. Clean full body harness with water and a mild soap solution. Do not use bleach or bleach solutions. ...Wipe off hardware with clean, dry cloth, and hang to air dry. Do not force dry with heat. An excessive buildup of dirt, paint, etc. may prevent the full body harness from working properly, and in severe cases degrade the webbing to a point where it weakens and should be removed from service. [page 24]

2. Additional maintenance and servicing procedures (i.e., replacement parts) must be completed by a factory authorized service center. Authorization must be in writing. Do not attempt to disassemble the unit. [page 25]

3. Store full body harnesses in a cool, dry, clean environment out of direct sunlight. Avoid areas where chemical vapors may exist. Thoroughly inspect the full body harness after any period of extended storage. [page 25]

Miller Equipment recommends wiping off all surface dirt with a sponge dampened in plain water. After squeezing the sponge dry, they say to dip the sponge in a mild solution of water and commercial soap or detergent. Then you are supposed to work up a thick lather, with a "vigorous back and forth motion." Then the harness or lanyard should be wiped dry with a clean cloth and hung freely to dry. [page 19]

Allow the harness or lanyard to dry in a protected area inside a building. Never use industrial solvents on synthetic materials.

Washing with soapy water is also recommended for fall arrester devices. Metal parts may be cleaned with approved solvents to remove caked materials or paint overspray. Do not oil moving parts unless the manufacturer's instructions specify this.

Store components made of synthetic materials out of direct sunlight in a cool, dry place.

Fall Protection Requirements vs. Confined Space Retrieval

Like a fall protection system, a confined space retrieval system uses a body harness and lifeline.

When it is worn by an authorized entrant for protection against a vertical fall hazard, it is considered a fall protection system; however, its main purpose is to rescue someone working inside the space without requiring the rescuer to enter the space, which could have a hazardous atmosphere or other dangers.

"The retrieval mechanism should have a minimum mechanical advantage of 4:1, such as a manually operated winch, because of the great difficulty of lifting dead weight vertically through a small opening. ...Architects and engineers should be strongly encouraged to design or redesign manway openings with no less than a 24-in. diameter clearance to facilitate prompt emergency retrieval. ...An opening of 18 in. or less promises a much more delayed rescue time, which could prove to be the fatal factor."[22]

Both Miller Equipment and DBI/SALA offer self-retracting lifelines that can double as retrieval devices when they are mounted on compatible tripods, davits, or ladder masts.

Rescue Considerations

1. Never put a person in a situation where prompt rescue would be impractical or extremely difficult in the event of a fall.

2. Rescue systems for above-ground rescue that do not have a built-in speed control require the presence of a trained rescue team.

3. Rescue equipment should be readily available. Options may include the following:

   ◆ Basket stretcher with lifting bridle

   ◆ Aerial lift

   ◆ Systems that include features for self-rescue or controlled descent

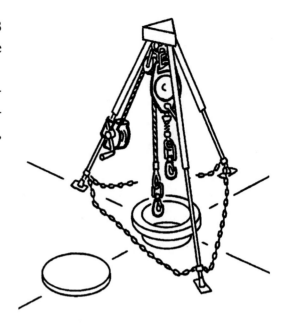

Confined space entry
Tripod with a lifeline for the retrieval system and a self-extracting lifeline for the fall protection system

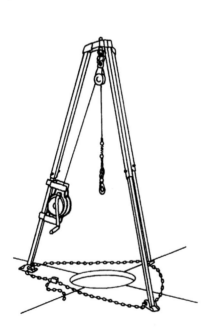

Tripod with lifeline and retrieval mechanism

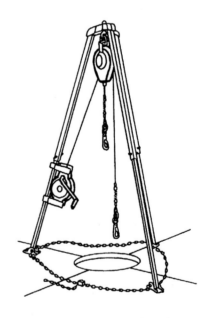

Tripod with lifeline, retrieval mechanism, and self-extracting lifeline

Self-Rescue

Some equipment can be used for fall protection and emergency escape, such as a self-retracting cable lifeline with a controlled descent feature.

Other controlled descent devices are designed only for escape purposes in case of an emergency such as a fire or medical situation while working in an elevated position, such as on an oil rig, overhead crane cab, or elevated platform on a tower or vessel.

SAFETY NETS

29 CFR 1926.105

1926.105(a)

Safety nets shall be provided when workplaces are more than 25 feet above the ground or water surface, or other surfaces where the use of ladders, scaffolds, catch platforms, temporary floors, safety lines, or safety belts is impractical.

1926.105(b)

Where safety net protection is required by this part, operations shall not be undertaken until the net is in place and has been tested.

1926.105(c)

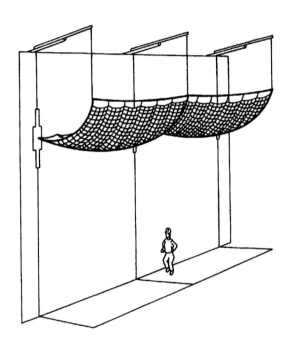

(1) Nets shall extend 8 feet beyond the edge of the work surface where employees are exposed and shall be installed as close under the work surface as practical but in no case more than 25 feet below such work surface. Nets shall be hung with sufficient clearance to prevent user's contact with the surfaces or structures below. Such clearances shall be determined by impact load testing.

(2) It is intended that only one level of nets be required for bridge construction.

Specifications

1926.105(d)

The mesh size of nets shall not exceed 6 inches by 6 inches. All new nets shall meet accepted performance standards of 17,500 foot-pounds minimum impact resistance as determined and certified by the manufacturers, and shall bear a label of proof test. Edge ropes shall provide a minimum breaking strength of 5,000 pounds.

Details of safety net specifications

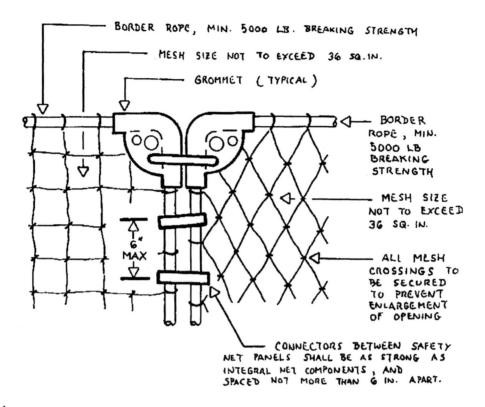

1926.105(e)

Forged steel safety hooks or shackles shall be used to fasten the net to its supports.

1926.105(f)

Connections between net panels shall develop the full strength of the net.

ENGINEERING AND EDUCATION

A fall arrest system is only as good as its weakest link. An engineering analysis of the strength of anchor points and the configuration of the system must be done for personal fall arrest systems to ensure safety.

In addition to engineering, the effectiveness of the system also depends on the training of workers who use fall arrest equipment and the development of safe work habits.

ENDNOTES

1. NIOSH Alert, "Preventing Worker Injuries and Deaths Caused by Falls from Suspension Scaffolds," August 1992, page 3.

2. "Actor injured in fall," *Dallas Morning News*, October 28, 1998, page 25A.

3. Renee Houston Zemanski, "Don't Fall for It! Wear Your Body Harness," *eNSC*, January 1999.

4. J. Nigel Ellis, *Introduction to Fall Protection* (Des Plaines, IL: American Society of Safety Engineers. 1993), page 209.

5. *Ibid.*, page 48.

6. *Ibid.*, page 48.

7. Steve Spotts, "Higher Ground," *Occupational Health & Safety*, March, 1998, pages 55-56.

8. Nigel Ellis, *Introduction to Fall Protection*, page 196.

9. *Ibid.*, page 107.

10. Miller Equipment, "Miller Series 52/55 Operation and Maintenance Manual," (Franklin, PA: Dalloz Fall Protection, 1999), pages 4–10.

11. *Ibid.*, pages 4, 5, 8.

12. *Ibid.*, pages 11–12.

13. *Ibid.*, pages 4–5.

14. DBI/SALA, "User Instruction Manual for Self-Retracting Lifelines" (Red Wing, MN: D.B. Industries, 1994), Section 3.5, Paragraph 3.

15. Miller Equipment, "Instruction and Warning Information," (Franklin, PA: Dalloz Fall Protection, 1999), page 2.

16. DBI/SALA, "User Instruction Manual: Full Body Harnesses," (Red Wing, MN: D.B. Industries, 1998), page 11.

17. DBI/SALA, "User Instruction Manual for Web and Rope Lanyards Used in Personal Restraint, Work Positioning, Suspension and Rescue Systems" (Red Wing, MN: D.B. Industries, 1998), page 4.

18. Nigel Ellis, *Introduction to Fall Protection*, page 149.

19. Miller Equipment, "Instruction and Warning Information," (Franklin, PA: Dalloz Fall Protection, 1999), pages 20–21.

20. DBI/SALA, "User Instruction Manual: Full Body Harnesses," (Red Wing, MN: D.B. Industries, 1998), pages 24–25.

21. Miller Equipment, "Instruction and Warning Information," (Franklin, PA: Dalloz Fall Protection, 1999), page 19.

22. Nigel Ellis, *Introduction to Fall Protection*, page 48.

Scaffolds

"The persistence of scaffolding hazards and the difficulty of dealing with them is illustrated by how long it took OSHA to revise the standard: The agency issued a notice of proposed rulemaking to revise the standard in November 1986 and did not release the final rule until November 1996—10 years later. Underscoring the importance of the issue: *About two-thirds of the construction work force frequently uses scaffolds,* OSHA estimates."[1]

SCAFFOLDS—GENERAL REQUIREMENTS

"The general requirements for scaffolding (which were revised in 1996) are contained in 29 CFR 1926.451—Subpart L. Highlights include the following:

♦ A 10-foot trigger height for fall protection.

♦ Extensive training for all those working on scaffolds, including a trained 'competent person' to oversee scaffold erection, dismantling and use.

♦ Guardrail requirements that mandate the minimum height of the top rail for scaffolds at 36 inches until January 2000; after that, the height of the top rail for manufactured scaffolds must be at least 38 inches.

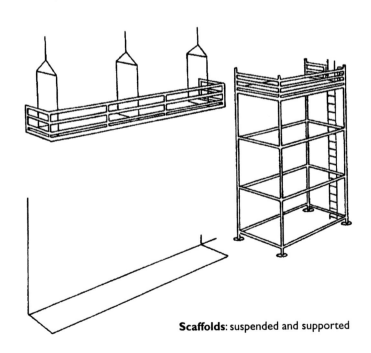

Scaffolds: suspended and supported

- Required inspections before each work shift and after any event that could affect the structural integrity of the scaffold.

- Required protection for work involving over-hand bricklaying from supported scaffolds, including a guardrail or personal fall arrest system to be in place on all sides, except the side where work is being done.

- A review of the 23 different scaffold types and the technical criteria employers should use when designing, installing, and loading these specified types of scaffolds, as well as related guardrail and fall-protection systems."2

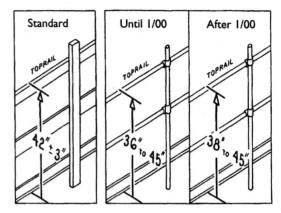

Standard guardrail system
Scaffold guardrail system height (until Jan. 1, 2000)
Scaffold guardrail system height (after Jan. 1, 2000)

Fall protection requirements on supported scaffolds for work involving overhead bricklaying

Preventing Falls Caused by Collapse/Upsetting of Scaffold

A scaffold and its components must be able to support without failure at least four times the maximum intended load in addition to its own weight.

1926.451(f)(7)

Scaffolds shall be erected, moved, dismantled, or altered only under the supervision and direction of a competent person qualified in scaffold erection, moving, dismantling or alteration. Such activities shall be performed only by experienced and trained employees selected for such work by the competent person.

1926.451(f)(9)

Where swinging loads are being hoisted onto or near scaffolds such that the loads might contact the scaffold, tag lines or equivalent measures to control the loads shall be used.

Bad Weather Rules

1926.451(f)(8)

Employees shall be prohibited from working on scaffolds covered with snow, ice, or other slippery material except as necessary for removal of such materials.

1926.451(f)(12)

Work on or from scaffolds is prohibited during storms or high winds unless a competent person has determined that it is safe for employees to be on the scaffold and those employees are protected by a personal fall arrest system or wind screens. Wind screens shall not be used unless the scaffold is secured against the anticipated wind forces imposed.

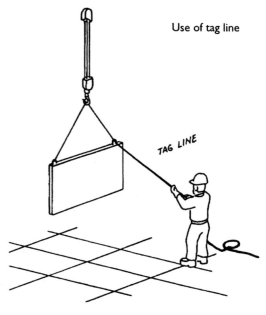

Use of tag line

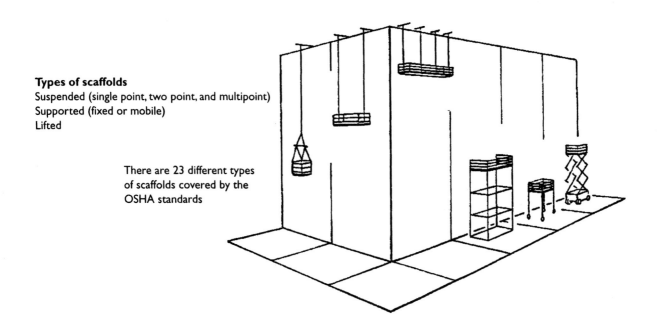

Types of scaffolds
Suspended (single point, two point, and multipoint)
Supported (fixed or mobile)
Lifted

There are 23 different types of scaffolds covered by the OSHA standards

OSHA Inspection Procedures

Following are excerpts from OSHA's "Inspection Procedures for Enforcing Subpart L, Scaffolds Used in Construction."[3]

- ◆ [T]he employer is required to have a competent person who has the training and experience necessary to make determinations as to fall protection and the integrity of scaffolds and that the scaffold is maintained and used in a safe manner. NOTE: OSHA recognizes that an employer may have more than one competent person on the worksite to deal with different aspects of scaffolding.

- ◆ Paragraph (b)(1) allows exceptions to the full planking of platforms, but requires that the platform be planked or decked "as fully as possible." Employers may leave an opening between uprights and planking but the opening may not exceed 9½ inches.

- ◆ Full planking/decking rules do not apply to platforms used only as walkways and platforms used only by employees while performing scaffold erection or dismantling. However, in these cases, OSHA requires enough planking to provide safe working conditions; i.e., they must be at least 18 inches wide or have guardrails and/or personal fall arrest systems.

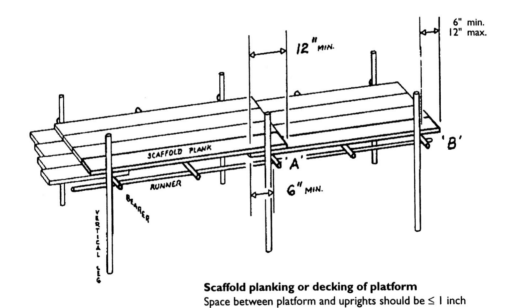

Scaffold planking or decking of platform
Space between platform and uprights should be ≤ 1 inch

Note that each end of a platform must extend over the centerline of its support by at least 6 inches, unless cleated or restrained by hooks or equivalent means.

The end of the platform may not extend more than 12 inches if the platform is up to 10 feet long, and it may not extend more than 18 inches if the platform is longer than 10 feet, unless the end is designed and installed to support the weight of employees and/or materials without tipping, or unless it has guardrails which block access by employees to the cantilevered end.

SUPPORTED SCAFFOLDS

◆ Fall protection for supported scaffolds usually consists of guardrails. However, there may be some unique situations in which a properly anchored personal fall arrest system may be necessary on a supported scaffold, such as when overreaching guardrails may occur.

◆ Poles, legs, posts, frames and uprights must be plumb and braced to prevent swaying and displacement.

◆ Both base plates and mud sills or other adequate firm foundations are required.

Footings for supported scaffolds

A concrete slab would be considered a firm foundation—mud sills would not be necessary.

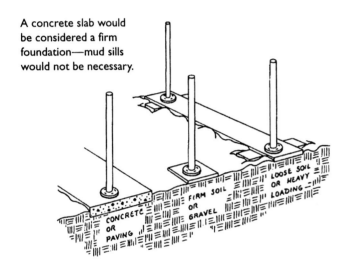

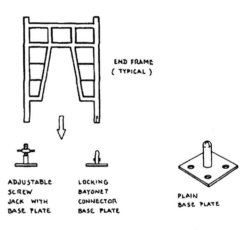

Typical welded frame scaffold, showing adjustable screw jack with base plate, and locking bayonet connector base plate

1926.451(e)(1)

When scaffold platforms are more than 2 feet (0.6 m) above or below a point of access, portable ladders, hook-on ladders, attachable ladders, stair towers (scaffold stairways/towers), stairway-type ladders (such as ladder stands), ramps, walkways, integral prefabricated scaffold access, or direct access from another scaffold, structure, personnel hoist, or similar surface shall be used. Crossbraces shall not be used as a means of access.

Scaffold poles, legs, posts, frames, and uprights must be plumb and braced to prevent swaying and displacement. (The example illustrated is a bricklayers square scaffold made of wood.)

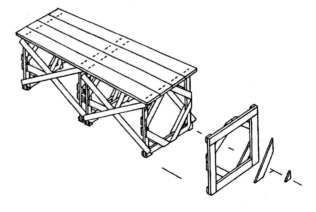

Acccess to scaffold platform

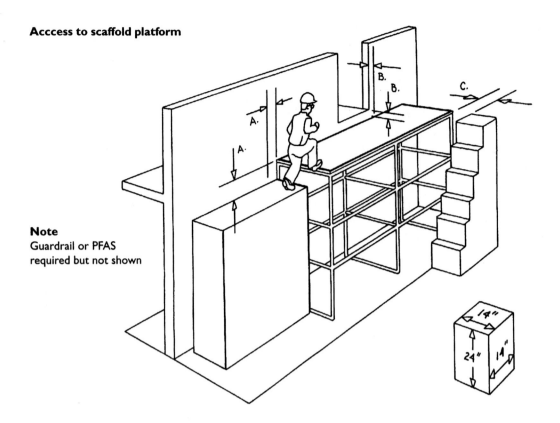

Note
Guardrail or PFAS
required but not shown

◆ Direct access to a supported scaffold must be less than 24 inches away vertically and less than 14 inches away horizontally.

◆ At all points where the scaffold platform changes direction, any platform that rests on a bearer at an angle other than a right angle shall be laid first, and platforms which rest at right angles over the same bearer shall be laid second, on top of the first platform.

◆ Guys, ties, and braces must be installed at each end of the scaffold and at horizontal intervals of 30 feet or less.

◆ Vertical and horizontal tie-ins are required per manufacturer's recommendations on all supported scaffolds with a height to

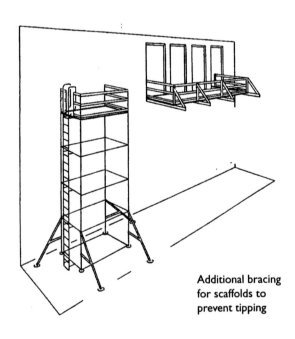

Additional bracing
for scaffolds to
prevent tipping

Typical tube and coupler scaffold

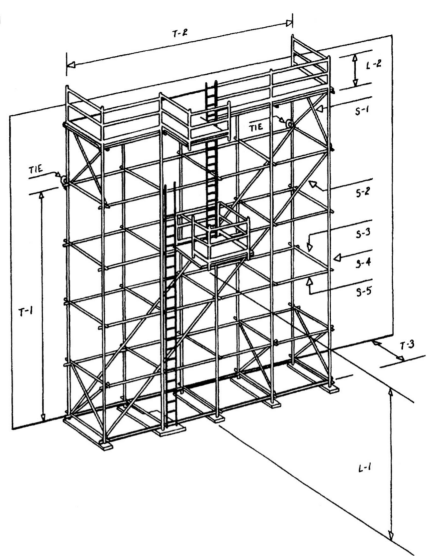

Scaffold
S-1   Cross bracing
S-2   Diagonal bracing
S-3   Bearer
S-4   Post
S-5   Runner

Ladders for access
L-1   Landing rest area located at ≤ 20-foot intervals
L-2   Ladder must extend about 42 inches above platform

Ties
T1   Ties at intervals of ≤ 26 feet or 4 times T3
T2   Ties at ends and intervals of ≤ 30 feet
T3   Minimum width of base

base ratio of more than four times the minimum base width. They are to be installed to keep a scaffold from falling into and away from the structure.

♦ General guidelines indicate tie-ins should be installed at the closest horizontal member to the 4:1 height and at vertical intervals of 20 feet or less for scaffolds that are 3 feet or less wide, and at vertical intervals of 26 feet or less for scaffolds that are more than 3 feet wide.

♦ Additional bracing (ties, guys, braces, or outriggers) must be used to prevent tipping whenever an eccentric (unbalanced) load is applied to the scaffold.

Erection and Dismantling of Supported Scaffolds

Fall exposure during erection and dismantling of scaffolds must be addressed.

1926.451(e)(9)

(i)   The employer shall provide safe means of access for each employee erecting or dismantling a scaffold where the provision of safe access is feasible and does not create a greater hazard. The employer shall have a competent person determine whether it is feasible or would pose a greater hazard to provide, and have employees use, a safe means of access. This determination shall be based on site conditions and the type of scaffold being erected or dismantled.

(ii) Hook-on or attachable ladders shall be installed as soon as scaffold erection has progressed to a point that permits safe installation and use.

(iii) When erecting or dismantling tubular welded frame scaffolds, (end) frames, with horizontal members that are parallel, level, and not more than 22 inches apart vertically, may be used as climbing devices for access, provided they are erected in a manner that creates a usable ladder and provides good hand hold and foot space.

(iv) Cross braces on tubular welded frame scaffolds shall not be used as a means of access or egress.

A personal fall arrest system may be needed to control a fall during the installation or dismantling process. This can often be done by using overhead or portable anchor points. Another option is to use scaffold members as part of an engineered fall arrest system that achieves the objective of complete and continuous protection.

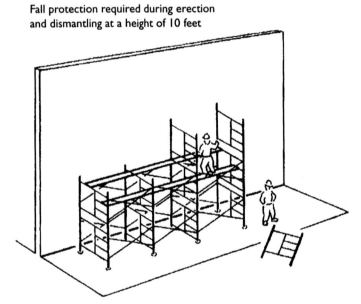

Fall protection required during erection and dismantling at a height of 10 feet

"Outrigger brackets equipped with cable railings snapped together one at a time could provide side protection. Tying in the scaffold approximately 5 ft. to 6 ft. above grade will overcome the critics' objection about scaffold tipover."[4]

Mixing and Matching Parts

1926.451(b)(10)

Scaffold components manufactured by different manufacturers shall not be intermixed unless the components fit together without force and the scaffold's structural integrity is maintained by the user. Scaffold components manufactured by different manufacturers shall not be modified in order to intermix them unless a competent person determines the resulting scaffold is structurally sound.

Use of Supported Scaffolds

♦ All employees who use scaffolds must be trained by a competent person to recognize the hazards of falls and falling objects and to learn control measures and applicable OSHA standards.

♦ Workers are not allowed to climb cross bracing to access or descend a scaffold. Properly designed fixed ladder access is preferred.

♦ The OSHA standard does not specifically prohibit climbing over or through a guardrail. Gates, removable rails, or chains across the point of access are preferred.

Proper use of supported scaffolds

♦ Workers must know the rated capacity of the scaffolds they use, as well as the approximate weight of materials and workers on the scaffold, so that appropriate steps are taken to ensure the scaffold is not overloaded.

♦ Only materials needed for the day's work are allowed to be stored temporarily on a scaffold.

Hazards of Falling Objects

1926.451(h) Falling object protection.

(1) In addition to wearing hardhats each employee on a scaffold shall be provided with additional protection from falling hand tools, debris, and other small objects through the installation of toeboards, screens, or guardrail systems, or through the erection of debris nets, catch platforms, or canopy structures that contain or deflect the

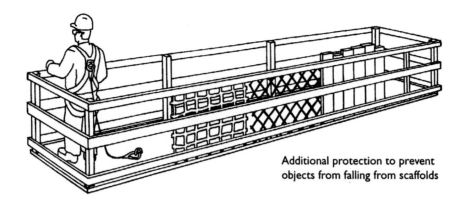

Additional protection to prevent
objects from falling from scaffolds

falling objects. When the falling objects are too large, heavy or massive to be contained or deflected by any of the above-listed measures, the employer shall place such potential falling objects away from the edge of the surface from which they could fall and shall secure those materials as necessary to prevent their falling.

1926.451(h)

(2) Where there is a danger of tools, materials, or equipment falling from a scaffold and striking employees below, the following provisions apply:

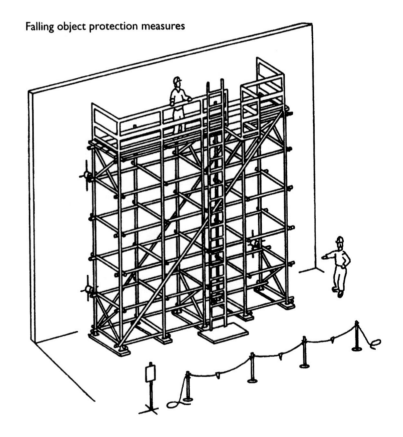

Falling object protection measures

    (i) The area below the scaffold to which objects can fall shall be barricaded, and employees shall not be permitted to enter the hazard area; or

    (ii) A toeboard shall be erected along the edge of platforms more than 10 feet (3.1 m) above lower levels for a distance sufficient to protect employees below, except on float (ship) scaffolds where an

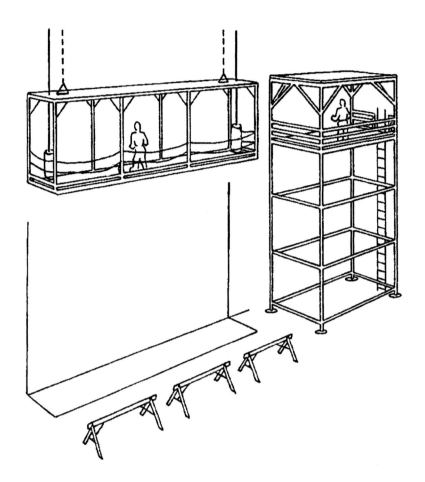

Protective measures to prevent falling objects from striking personnel on scaffolds. Illustration shows canopies for suspended and supported scaffolds.

edging of ¾ x 1½ inch (2 x 4 cm) wood or equivalent may be used in lieu of toeboards;

(iii) Where tools, materials, or equipment are piled to a height higher than the top edge of the toeboard, paneling or screening extending from the toeboard or platform to the top of the guardrail shall be erected for a distance sufficient to protect employees below; or

(iv) A guardrail system shall be installed with openings small enough to prevent passage of potential falling objects; or

(v) A canopy structure, debris net, or catch platform strong enough to withstand the impact forces of the potential falling objects shall be erected over the employees below.

MOBILE LADDER STANDS AND ROLLING SCAFFOLDS

1910.29(a)(2)(ii)

(a) The design working load of ladder stands shall be calculated on the basis of one or more 200-pound persons together with 50 pounds of equipment each.

(b) The design load of all scaffolds shall be calculated on the basis of:

 ◆ *Light*—Designed and constructed to carry a working load of 25 pounds per square foot.

 ◆ *Medium*—Designed and constructed to carry a working load of 50 pounds per square foot.

 ◆ *Heavy*—Designed and constructed to carry a working load of 75 pounds per square foot.

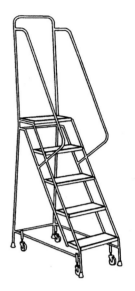

Typical mobile ladder stand

Maximum Height

1910.29 (a)(3)(i)

The maximum work level height shall not exceed four (4) times the minimum or least base dimensions of any mobile ladder stand or scaffold. Where the basic mobile unit does not meet this requirement, suitable outrigger frames shall be employed to achieve this least base dimension, or provisions shall be made to guy or brace the unit against tipping.

Typical rolling scaffold

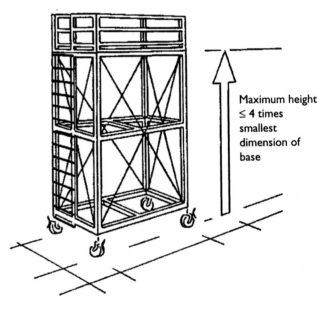

Maximum height ≤ 4 times smallest dimension of base

1910.29(a)(3)(ii)

The minimum platform width for any work level shall not be less than 20 inches for mobile scaffolds (towers). Ladder stands shall have a minimum step width of 16 inches.

Steps

1910.29(a)(3)(iv)

The steps of ladder stands shall be fabricated from slip resistant treads.

Planking

1910.29(a)(3)(v)

The work level platform of scaffolds (towers) shall be of wood, aluminum, or plywood planking, steel or expanded metal, for the full width of the scaffold, except for necessary openings. Work platforms shall be secured in place. All planking shall be 2-inch (nominal) scaffold grade minimum 1,500 f. (stress grade) construction grade lumber or equivalent.

Guardrails and Toeboards

1910.29(a)(3)(vi)

All scaffold work levels 10 feet or higher above the ground or floor shall have a standard (4-inch nominal) toeboard.

1910.29(a)(3)(vii)

All work levels 10 feet or higher above the ground or floor shall have a guardrail of 2- by 4-inch nominal or the equivalent installed no less than 36 inches or more than 42 inches high, with a mid-rail, when required, of 1- by 4-inch nominal lumber or equivalent.

Access and Egress

1910.29(a)(3)(viii)

A climbing ladder or stairway shall be provided for proper access and egress, and shall be affixed or built into the scaffold and so located that its use will not have a tendency to tip the scaffold. A landing platform shall be provided at intervals not to exceed 30 feet.

Guardrail, toeboard, and access requirements for mobile scaffolds

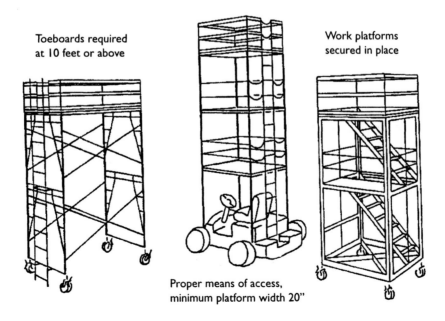

Toeboards required at 10 feet or above

Work platforms secured in place

Proper means of access, minimum platform width 20"

Casters and Leveling

1910.29(a)(4)(ii)

All scaffold casters shall be provided with a positive wheel and/or swivel lock to prevent movement. Ladder stands shall have at least two (2) of the four (4) casters and shall be of the swivel type.

1910.29(a)(4)(iii)

Where leveling of the elevated work platform is required, screw jacks or other suitable means for adjusting the height shall be provided in the base section of each mobile unit.

Safety Rules for Mobile Ladder Stands and Platforms

The following safety rules are quoted from American National Standard ANSI A14.7-1991, "Safety Requirements for Mobile Ladder Stands and Mobile Ladder Stand Platforms."[5]

Occupied units shall not be moved

- ◆ Occupied units shall not be moved.

- ◆ Units shall not be loaded beyond rated loads.

- ◆ Materials and equipment shall not be stored on the steps or platform of a unit.

- ◆ Additional height shall not be gained by the addition of any type extension or an object being placed on the unit.

- ◆ Foreign materials, such as mud and grease, shall be removed from a person's shoes prior to ascending a unit.

- ◆ Handrails should be used while ascending or descending the unit.

- ◆ The user shall face the ladder when ascending or descending a unit except when the slope of the ladder is 50 degrees or less above the horizontal.

- ◆ Overreaching, while on a unit, could cause instability and result in a fall. Always keep the unit in close proximity to the work. Descend and relocate the unit to prevent overreaching.

♦ Mobile ladder stands and ladder stand platforms are intended to be used only on a level surface. They are not to be used on uneven or sloping surfaces.

♦ Access to or egress from any step or platform from any other elevated surface shall be prohibited unless the unit has been positively secured against movement.

SUSPENDED SCAFFOLD ACCIDENTS

Analyze the following accidents and think about the recommendations you would make to prevent a recurrence. Record your comments. As you progress through this chapter, add to the list of recommendations any applicable regulatory requirements or safety rules that are not already listed.

Fall from Suspended Scaffold

"Gary Evans, 22, fell to his death from a scaffolding Wednesday while painting a new water tower for the Bolivar Water Supply Corp. in Bolivar, northwest of Denton. The 100-foot fall occurred about 4:50 p.m. ...Two co-workers said Mr. Evans ... was not wearing safety restraints. ...The men were moving the scaffolding to paint another part of the tower when a cable snapped."[6]

Recommendations to Prevent Recurrence

_____

_____

_____

_____

_____

_____

_____

_____

_____

Scaffold Hoist Defect

"On March 15, 1989, a 33-year-old male caulking mechanic died when the scaffold on which he was working failed and caused him to fall 60 feet to the ground. The victim and a coworker were caulking the exterior skin plate joints and windows of a new seven-story building. Most of the work on the lower levels of the building had previously been completed using a personnel hoist. The upper floors of the building could not be reached with this device, so the crew brought a suspension scaffold to the site on the day of the incident.

"Upon arrival, the crew found that workers from a window-washing firm had already rigged a two-point suspension scaffold on the building. An arrangement was made for one crew (containing one worker from each company) to work from the caulker's manlift while a second crew worked from the window washer's two-point suspension scaffold. The victim and one worker from the window-washing firm then ascended the building using the two-point suspension scaffold and began work at the sixth floor. Although the victim and his coworker had brought safety belts and lifelines to the site, this equipment had been left in the company truck, and none of the four workers were using any type of fall protection equipment.

"When work was completed at the sixth floor, the men began their descent. Suddenly, the victim's end of the scaffold dropped to a vertical position. The victim fell from the scaffold to the ground 60 feet below. The second man on the scaffold (the window washer) managed to cling to the scaffold and a nearby window ledge until he could be rescued.

"Inspection of the scaffold hoist revealed a defect in a centrifugal safety brake. This defect and the victim's possible failure to release the parking brake before beginning his descent caused one end of the scaffold to drop."[7]

Recommendations to Prevent Recurrence

_____

_____

_____

_____

_____

_____

_____

_____

_____

_____

SUSPENDED SCAFFOLDS

- ◆ For some types of scaffolds (such as single-point or two-point adjustable suspension scaffolds), both a guardrail system and personal fall protection are required.

- ◆ On some types of scaffolds, only personal fall arrest systems are required (catenary, float and needle beam scaffolds, boatswain's chairs, roof bracket scaffolds, and ladder jack scaffolds.

- ◆ When employees are installing suspension scaffold support systems, fall protection must be provided.

- ◆ Direct connections and counterweights used to balance adjustable suspension scaffolds must be capable of resisting at least four times the tipping moment of the scaffold,

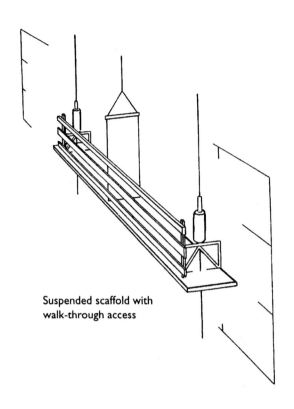

Suspended scaffold with walk-through access

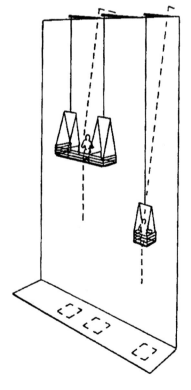

Both guardrails and a personal fall arrest system are required in these situations.

Single-point and two-point adjustable suspension scaffolds

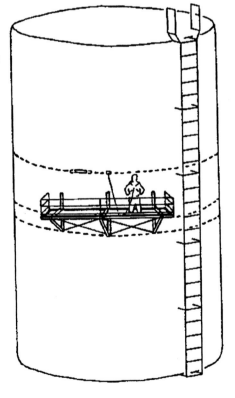

Tank builders' scaffold

Only a personal fall arrest system is required for boatswain's chairs and certain other scaffolds:
• catenary
• float
• needle beam
• roof bracket
• ladder jack

including stall loads. If the stall load has not been determined by a qualified person, check to see whether the scaffold is counterbalanced by at least 4 times the rated load of the hoist.

◆ Flowable materials are not allowed to be used as counterweights. Examples include sand bags or water buckets.

◆ Solid materials such as large blocks of concrete specifically designed for use as counterweights, or large ingots of metal (such as lead) are examples of acceptable counterweights.

◆ Suspension ropes and connecting hardware must support at least six times the maximum intended load.

◆ A worker may not use boxes, barrels, or any other object on top of platforms to increase the height of the working level.

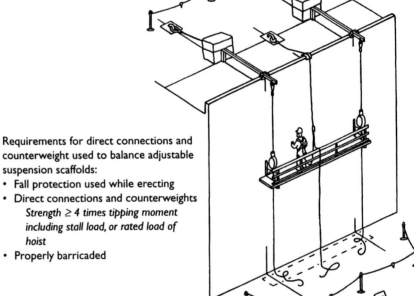

Requirements for direct connections and counterweight used to balance adjustable suspension scaffolds:
• Fall protection used while erecting
• Direct connections and counterweights
  Strength ≥ 4 times tipping moment including stall load, or rated load of hoist
• Properly barricaded

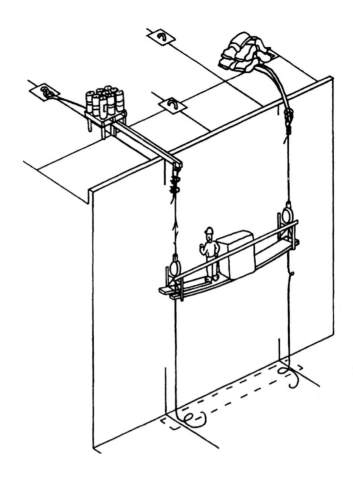

List below all the hazards you see in this drawing of a very bad scaffold setup.

Hazards

1. _____

2. _____

3. _____

4. _____

5 _____

Anchoring Fall Arrest Systems

◆ Attach personal fall arrest systems by lanyard to a vertical lifeline, horizontal lifeline, or scaffold structural member.

◆ Vertical lifelines are not allowed when overhead components are part of single-point or two-point adjustable suspension scaffolds.

◆ Vertical lifelines must be fastened to fixed safe anchorages that are independent of the scaffold.

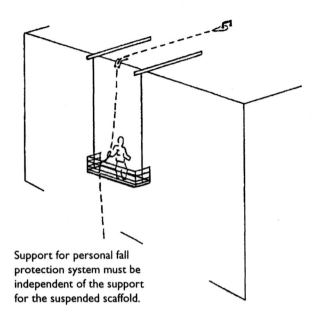

Support for personal fall protection system must be independent of the support for the suspended scaffold.

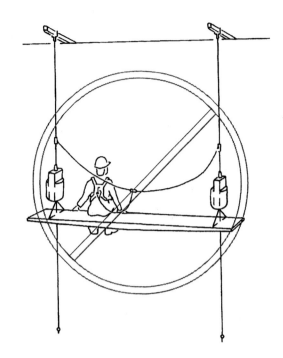

Do not attach vertical lifelines, support lines, and suspension ropes to each other OR to the same anchor points OR to the same point on the scaffold or PFAS.

♦ Horizontal lifelines must be secured to two or more structural members of the scaffold or looped around both suspension and independent lines.

♦ If lanyards are connected to horizontal lifelines or structural members on single-point or two-point adjustable suspension scaffolds, the scaffold must have additional independent support lines and automatic locking devices to stop the fall of the scaffold.

♦ Vertical lifelines, independent support lines, and suspension ropes must not be attached to each other, nor to the same anchor points, nor to the same point on the scaffold or personal fall arrest system.

Hoist Ropes

♦ There must be no less than 4 wraps of wire rope left on the drum of winding drum hoists at the lowest point of scaffold travel.

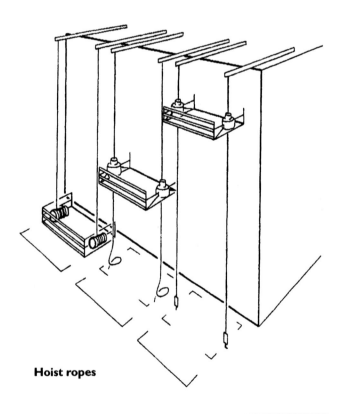

Hoist ropes

◆ Ropes must be of one continuous length, without repairs. Wire suspension ropes may only be joined together by using eye splice thimbles connected with shackles or coverplates and bolts.

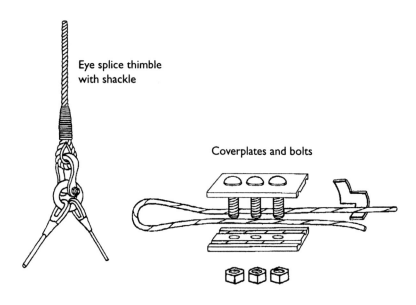

Eye splice thimble with shackle

Coverplates and bolts

◆ A competent person must inspect the hoist ropes prior to each shift and after every incident that could affect the integrity of the ropes. A rope must be replaced if it has any physical damage, kinks, 6 broken wires in one lay, or 3 broken wires in one strand in one lay, loss of one-third of its diameter, heat damage, or evidence of engagement of rope by the secondary brake during an overspeed condition.

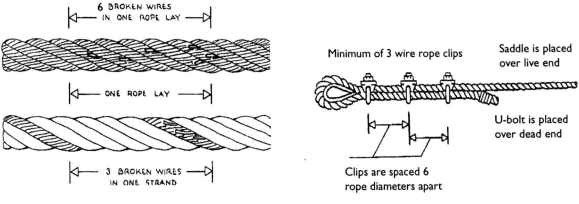

6 BROKEN WIRES IN ONE ROPE LAY

ONE ROPE LAY

3 BROKEN WIRES IN ONE STRAND

Look for these problems when inspecting hoist ropes

Minimum of 3 wire rope clips

Saddle is placed over live end

U-bolt is placed over dead end

Clips are spaced 6 rope diameters apart

◆ When wire rope clips are used, there must be a minimum of 3 clips and they must be spaced a minimum of 6 rope diameters apart. The U-bolt must be over the dead end. They must be inspected and retightened as necessary at the start of each work shift.

◆ No U-bolts are allowed at the point of suspension.

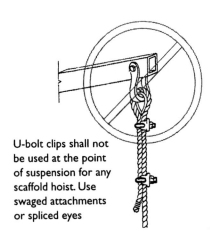

U-bolt clips shall not be used at the point of suspension for any scaffold hoist. Use swaged attachments or spliced eyes

Securing to Prevent Swaying

◆ Two-point and multi-point suspension scaffolds must be tied or secured to prevent swaying. Window cleaner's anchors are not allowed to be used for this purpose.

◆ No work is allowed on scaffolds during storms or high winds, unless workers are protected by a fall arrest system or wind screens.

Access

◆ When scaffold platforms are more than two feet above or below a point of access, use a portable ladder, hook-on ladder, attachable ladders, stairway-type ladders, ramps, prefabricated access, or direct access from another scaffold or other safe means of access. Position portable, hook-on, and attachable ladders so that the scaffold will not tip.

◆ Cross braces shall not be used for access.

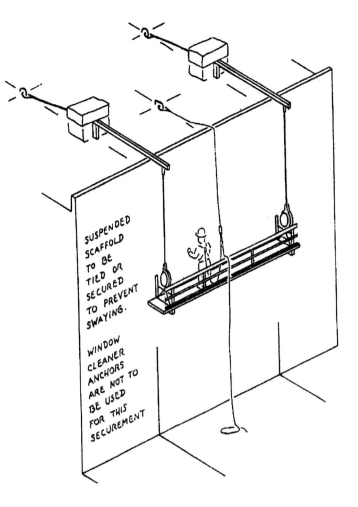

Rated load capacity for a one-person scaffold
250 pounds at center of span

Rated load capacity for a two-person scaffold
250 pounds 18" to left and right of center of span

Rated Load Capacity

Rated load capacity for different types of scaffolds are listed below:

- **Light duty**—25 lbs./square foot applied uniformly over span

- **Medium duty**—50 lbs./square foot applied uniformly over span

- **Heavy duty**—75 lbs./square foot applied uniformly over span

- **One person**—250 lbs. placed at the center of the span

- **Two-person**—250 lbs. placed 18" to the left and 250 lbs. placed 18" to the right of the center of the span

- **Three-person**—250 lbs. at the center plus 250 lbs. placed 18" to either side of the center

POWERED PLATFORMS FOR BUILDING MAINTENANCE

29 CFR 1910.66

OSHA's General Industry Standards contain special requirements for buildings that have permanently installed systems for suspended scaffolds for exterior or interior building maintenance. Such systems must be designed by a qualified engineer or architect in accordance with the provisions of 1910.66. There are some additional requirements that differ from OSHA's Construction Standards that apply to suspended scaffolds used on a temporary basis.

Emergency Planning

1910.66(e)(9)

Emergency planning. A written emergency action plan shall be developed and implemented for each kind of working platform operation. This plan shall explain the emergency procedures which are to be followed in the event of a power failure, equipment failure or other emergencies which may be encountered. The plan shall also explain that employees inform themselves about the building

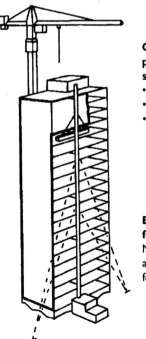

General Industry standards for permanently installed suspended scaffolds
- exterior or interior maintenance
- roof powered or ground rigged systems
- must be designed by a qualified engineer

Example of a powered platform for building construction
NOTE: A window-washing system is an example of a powered platform for building maintenance.

emergency escape routes, procedures and alarm systems before operating a platform. Upon initial assignment and whenever the plan is changed, the employer shall review with each employee those parts of the plan which the employee must know to protect himself or herself in the event of an emergency.

Secondary Suspension System

1910.66(f)(5)(ii)(L)

The platform shall be provided with a secondary wire rope suspension system if the platform contains overhead structures which restrict the emergency egress of employees. A horizontal lifeline or a direct connection anchorage shall be provided, as part of a fall arrest system which meets the requirements of Appendix C, for each employee on such a platform.

Vertical Lifeline

1910.66(f)(5)(ii)(M)

A vertical lifeline shall be provided as part of a fall arrest system which meets the requirements of Appendix C, for each employee on a working platform suspended by two or more wire ropes, if the failure of one wire rope or suspension attachment will cause the platform to upset. If a secondary wire rope suspension is used, vertical lifelines are not required for the fall arrest system, provided that each employee is attached to a horizontal lifeline anchored to the platform.

Single Point Suspended Scaffolds

1910.66(f)(5)(iii)(B)

Each single point suspended working platform shall be provided with a secondary wire rope suspension system, which will prevent the working platform from falling should there be a failure of the primary means of support, or if the platform contains overhead structures which restrict the egress of the employees. A horizontal life line or a direct connection anchorage shall be provided, as part of a fall arrest system which meets the requirements of appendix C, for each employee on the platform.

Emergency Power Backup Device

1910.66(f)(5)(ii)(N)

An emergency electric operating device shall be provided on roof powered platforms near the hoisting machine for use in the event of failure of the normal operating device located on the working platform, or failure of the cable connected to the platform. The emergency electric operating device shall be mounted in a secured compartment, and the compartment shall be labeled with instructions for use. A means for opening the compartment shall be mounted in a break-glass receptacle located near the emergency electric operating device or in an equivalent secure and accessible location.

Power to Ground-Rigged Working Platforms

1910.66(f)(5)(iv) Ground-rigged working platforms.

1910.66(f)(5)(iv)(B)

After each day's use, the power supply within the building shall be disconnected from a ground-rigged working platform, and the platform shall be either disengaged from its suspension points or secured and stored at grade.

Example of a ground-rigged working platform (stucco work in progress)

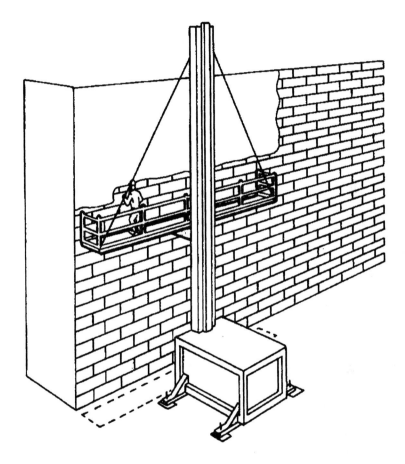

Suspension Ropes—Tags

1910.66(f)(7)(vi)

A corrosion-resistant tag shall be securely attached to one of the wire rope fastenings when a suspension wire rope is to be used at a specific location and will remain in that location. This tag shall bear the following wire rope data:

(A) The diameter (inches and/or mm);

(B) Construction classification;

(C) Whether non-preformed or preformed;

(D) The grade of material;

(E) The manufacturer's rated strength;

(F) The manufacturer's name;

(G) The month and year the ropes were installed; and

(H) The name of the person or company which installed the ropes.

1910.66(f)(7)(vii)

A new tag shall be installed at each rope renewal.

1910.66(f)(7)(viii)

The original tag shall be stamped with the date of the resocketing, or the original tag shall be retained and a supplemental tag shall be provided when ropes are resocketed. The supplemental tag shall show the date of resocketing and the name of the person or company that resocketed the rope.

Length and Fastening of Suspension Ropes

1910.66(f)(7)(ix)

Winding drum type hoists shall contain at least three wraps of the suspension wire rope on the drum when the suspended unit has reached the lowest possible point of its vertical travel.

1910.66(f)(7)(x)

Traction drum and sheave type hoists shall be provided with a wire rope of sufficient length to reach the lowest possible point of vertical travel of the suspended unit, and an additional length of the wire rope of at least four feet (1.2 m).

1910.66(f)(7)(xi)

The lengthening or repairing of suspension wire ropes is prohibited.

1910.66(f)(7)(xii)

Babbitted fastenings for suspension wire rope are prohibited.

Other Requirements for Powered Platforms

There are detailed instructions for inspection and maintenance of permanently installed powered platforms for building maintenance in Sections 1910.66(g) and (h). Training requirements are listed in Section 1910.66(i) and are supplemented by the following provision in Section I of Appendix C to 1910.66 (mandatory):

(d) Employee training considerations. Thorough employee training in the selection and use of personal fall arrest systems is imperative. As stated in the standard, before the equipment is used, employees must be trained in the safe use of the system. This should include the following: Application limits; proper anchoring and tie-off techniques; estimation of free fall distance, including determination of deceleration distance, and total fall distance to prevent striking a lower level; methods of use; and inspection and storage of the system. Careless or improper use of the equipment can result in serious injury or death. Employers and employees should become familiar with the material in this appendix, as well as manufacturer's recommendations, before a system is used. Of uppermost importance is the reduction in strength caused by certain tie-offs (such as using knots, tying around sharp edges, etc.) and maximum permitted free fall distance. Also, to be stressed are the importance of inspections prior to use, the limitations of the equipment, and unique conditions at the worksite which may be important in determining the type of system to use.

1910.66(i)(2)(i)

Working platforms shall not be loaded in excess of the rated load, as stated on the platform load rating plate.

1910.66(i)(2)(ii)

Employees shall be prohibited from working on snow, ice, or other slippery material covering platforms, except for the removal of such materials.

1910.66(i)(2)(iii)

Adequate precautions shall be taken to protect the platform, wire ropes and life lines from damage due to acids or other corrosive substances, in accordance with the recommendations of the corrosive substance producer, supplier, platform manufacturer or other equivalent information sources. Platform members which have been exposed to acids or other corrosive substances shall be washed down with a neutralizing solution, at a frequency recommended by the corrosive substance producer or supplier.

1910.66(i)(2)(iv)

Platform members, wire ropes and life lines shall be protected when using a heat producing process. Wire ropes and life lines which have been contacted by the heat producing process shall be considered to be permanently damaged and shall not be used.

1910.66(i)(2)(v)

The platform shall not be operated in winds in excess of 25 miles per hour (40.2 km/hr) except to move it from an operating to a storage position. Wind speed shall be determined based on the best available information, which includes on-site anemometer readings and local weather forecasts which predict wind velocities for the area.

1910.66(i)(2)(vi)

On exterior installations, an anemometer shall be mounted on the platform to provide information of on-site wind velocities prior to and during the use of the platform. The anemometer may be a portable (hand held) unit which is temporarily mounted during platform use.

1910.66(i)(2)(vii)

Tools, materials and debris not related to the work in progress shall not be allowed to accumulate on platforms. Stabilizer ties shall be located so as to allow unencumbered passage along the full length of the platform and shall be of such length so as not to become entangled in rollers, hoists or other machinery.

1910.66(j)

Personal fall protection. Employees on working platforms shall be protected by a personal fall arrest system meeting the requirements of Appendix C, Section I, of this standard, and as otherwise provided by this standard.

RECOGNIZE SCAFFOLD FALL POTENTIAL

There are many reasons that a worker might fall from a scaffold. Proper training of workers, along with engineering design, adequate supervision, and consistent enforcement of safe work practices, are the keys to preventing seriously disabling and fatal falls.

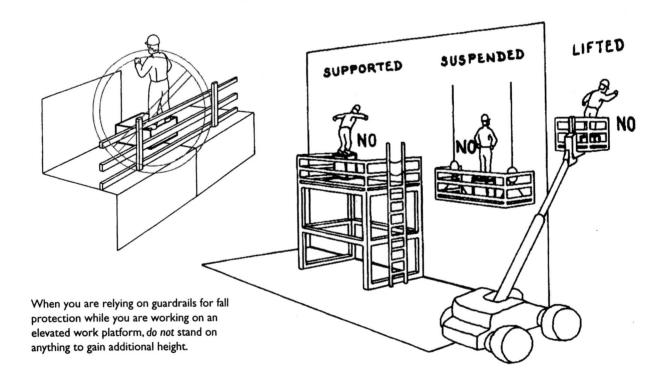

When you are relying on guardrails for fall protection while you are working on an elevated work platform, *do not* stand on anything to gain additional height.

ENDNOTES

1. Robert J. Derocher, "Safe Scaffolding," *Safety & Health*, March 1999, page 57.

2. *Ibid.*

3. OSHA Directive CPL 2-1.23, January 7, 1997, "Inspection Procedures for Enforcing Subpart L, Scaffolds Used in Construction," (U.S. DOL OSHA: **http://www.osha.slc.gov/ OshDoc/Directive.data/CPL 2-1 23.html**), 17 pages.

4. J. Nigel Ellis, *Introduction to Fall Protection* (Des Plaines, IL: American Society of Safety Engineers. 1993), page 68.

5. American National Standards Institute, "Safety Requirements for Mobile Ladder Stands and Mobile Ladder Stand Platforms," ANSI A14.7-1991 (Des Plaines, IL: American Society of Safety Engineers, 1991), pages 11–12.

6. "Man falls 100 feet to his death from scaffolding," *Dallas Morning News*, Thursday, July 11, 1996, page 26A.

7. National Institute of Occupational Safety and Health, "NIOSH Alert: Preventing Worker Injuries and Deaths Caused by Falls from Suspension Scaffolds," NIOSH Publication No. 92-108 (Cincinnati, OH: U.S. DHHS NIOSH, 1992), pages 3–4.

Ladders

PORTABLE LADDER ACCIDENTS

Analyze the following accidents and think about the recommendations you would make to prevent a recurrence. Record your comments. As you progress through this chapter, add to the list of recommendations any regulatory requirements or safety rules that apply that are not already listed.

Max the X-Ray Technician

"Max used the center (fly) section of an extension ladder to reach the top of a horizontal pressure tank in a factory. The tank was 12 ft. in diameter and 40 ft. long. X-ray tasks had been performed the same way for 25 years. In fact, factory managers frequently used the ladder's fly section independently because it was lightweight and portable, and its narrow base allowed access to the center of the tank.

"The working surface was concrete, covered with flux and other welding by-products; consequently, the working surface was slippery. This ladder did not have slip-resistant feet. As a result, Max could not secure the ladder to his satisfaction, so he blocked it with dunnage. He climbed 10 ft. and began to move horizontally to the round surface of the tank. There, he would leave the ladder and work directly on the tank's rounded surface. At this transition point, the bottom of the ladder kicked out, and Max fell."[1]

Recommendations to Prevent Recurrence

_____

_____

_____

_____

_____

_____

_____

Alan the Telecommunications Installer

"A 38-year-old telecommunications installer, Jantz was routinely tossing CAT-3 cable across ceiling rafters at a Dallas-area construction site. He positioned himself on the second rung down of a 12-foot tall fiberglass ladder, with his legs braced against the ladder's top for leverage. He threw a grouping of six cables, which then had to be dropped one at a time for future systems installation at individual workstations. As occasionally happens, he made a bad toss and tried to retrieve the cables for another throw.

"'When I tried to pull back, it was hung. I tried to whip it loose so I could retoss it to where I wanted it to go,' Jantz recalls. 'That didn't work, so I decided to give it a hard pull.'

"To his surprise, the cables were no longer snagged. As he gave the lines a backwards jerk, the cables flew toward him, and he began free falling backward in a split-second descent to concrete flooring below. The ladder never failed or moved...."[2]

Recommendations to Prevent Recurrence

_____

_____

_____

_____

_____

_____

_____

_____

_____

CAUSES OF LADDER ACCIDENTS

"In one-half of the ladder accidents investigated by BLS [Bureau of Labor Statistics], the worker carried materials in his/her hands as s/he climbed—a practice that contributes to slips (_Federal Register_ 13361). To avoid this situation, materials should be raised to the workstation on a tether.

"In other accidents, either the ladder or the worker slipped. To prevent this, a ladder should always have four-point contact with the working surface, and pressure on each leg should be proportional. In addition, the climber should always maintain three points of contact with the ladder (i.e., two feet and one hand). If the working surface is slippery or unstable, the worker must tie or strap the ladder to the rear surface at both the top and the bottom."[3]

Proper positioning of ladders
4-point contact with pressure on
each leg proportional

LADDERS

Basic Types

There are a lot of different types of ladders, but the basic types of ladders include portable and fixed ladders.

Portable ladders include stepladders, straight ladders, and extension ladders. These ladders may be made of wood, aluminum, or fiberglass. Most are purchased from manufacturers, but some are made on construction sites for access and are referred to as "job-made" ladders.

Fixed ladders are those that are an integral and permanent part of a structure.

Inspection

"'Lack of inspection is the weakest part of ladder use,' [Mark] Fullen [construction safety and health specialist at the West Virginia Safety and Health Extension] says. 'Often a ladder shows no sign of weakness. Yet wood will rot, metal will bend, and fiberglass can break. And not all these defects will be obvious to a casual observer.' A slight bend in a metal ladder could be a sign that it may collapse."[4]

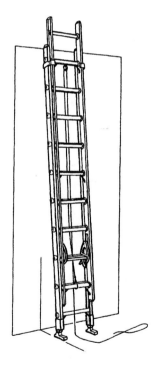

Typical extension ladder

1926.1053(b)(15)

Ladders shall be inspected by a competent person for visible defects on a periodic basis and after any occurrence that could affect their safe use.

1926.1053(b)(16)

Portable ladders with structural defects, such as, but not limited to, broken or missing rungs, cleats, or steps, broken or split rails, corroded components, or other faulty or defective components, shall either be immediately marked in a manner that readily identifies them as defective, or be tagged with "Do Not Use" or similar language, and shall be withdrawn from service until repaired.

1926.1053(b)(17)

Fixed ladders with structural defects, such as, but not limited to, broken or missing rungs, cleats, or steps, broken or split rails, or corroded components, shall be withdrawn from service until repaired. The requirement to withdraw a defective ladder from service is satisfied if the ladder is either:

(i)   Immediately tagged with "Do Not Use" or similar language;

(ii) Marked in a manner that readily identifies it as defective;

(iii) Or blocked (such as with a plywood attachment that spans several rungs).

1926.1053(b)(18)

Ladder repairs shall restore the ladder to a condition meeting its original design criteria, before the ladder is returned to use.

REQUIREMENTS THAT APPLY TO ALL LADDERS

- ◆ No oil or grease
- ◆ Never overloaded
- ◆ Used only as designed

1926.1053(b)(2)

Ladders shall be maintained free of oil, grease, and other slipping hazards.

1926.1053(b)(3)

Ladders shall not be loaded beyond the maximum intended load for which they were built, nor beyond their manufacturer's rated capacity.

1926.1053(b)(4)

Ladders shall be used only for the purpose for which they were designed.

(An example of an *improper* use of a ladder would be to place it horizontally and use it instead of a scaffold.)

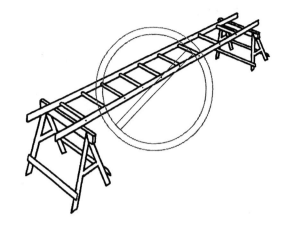

Skid-Resistant Material for Ladder Rungs

1926.1053(a)(6)(i)

The rungs and steps of fixed metal ladders manufactured after March 15, 1991, shall be corrugated, knurled, dimpled, coated with skid-resistant material, or otherwise treated to minimize slipping.

1926.1053(a)(6)(ii)

The rungs and steps of portable metal ladders shall be corrugated, knurled, dimpled, coated with skid-resistant material, or otherwise treated to minimize slipping.

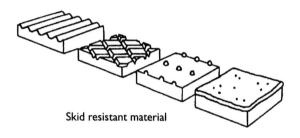

Skid resistant material

Other Ladder Construction Requirements

♦ Smooth, no splinters

♦ No painting of wood

♦ Nonconductive siderails around electrical equipment

1926.1053(a)(11)

Ladder components shall be surfaced so as to prevent injury to an employee from punctures or lacerations, and to prevent snagging of clothing.

1926.1053(a)(12)

Wood ladders shall not be coated with any opaque covering, except for identification or warning labels which may be placed on one face only of a side rail.

1926.1053(b)(12)

Ladders shall have nonconductive side rails if they are used where the employee or the ladder could contact exposed energized electrical equipment, except as provided in 1926.951(c)(1) of this part.

Offset Fixed Ladders with Platforms or Landings

1926.1053(a)(10)

Except when portable ladders are used to gain access to fixed ladders (such as those on utility towers, billboards, and other structures where the bottom of the fixed ladder is elevated to limit access), when two or more separate ladders are used to reach an elevated work area, the ladders shall be offset with a platform or landing between the ladders.

Basic Rules for Use of Ladders

1926.1053(b)(20)

When ascending or descending a ladder, the user shall face the ladder.

1926.1053(b)(21)

Each employee shall use at least one hand to grasp the ladder when progressing up and/or down the ladder.

1926.1053(b)(22)

An employee shall not carry any object or load that could cause the employee to lose balance and fall.

PORTABLE LADDERS

Most of the time, portable ladders are used without any type of personal fall arrest system. People are less likely to fall off portable ladders when they are used only for access to or egress from an elevated work location.

When work is done from a portable ladder, people are more likely to fall off. There are many instances when it would be safer to do work from a scaffold or a manlift. This should be considered when the job is planned.

"A worker cannot be effective standing on a ladder for hours at a time. If the work requires side-to-side

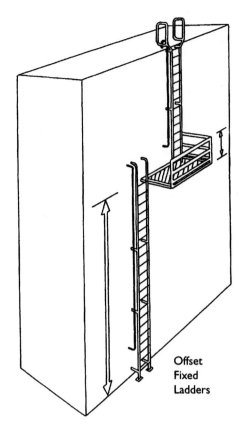

Offset Fixed Ladders

Maintain 3-point contact when climbing up or down

movement, a scaffold is preferable to a ladder due to risk of tipping. Moreover, if the work requires using tools with both hands, a ladder should not be used. The rule is that a worker should maintain three-point contact with a ladder at all times. That means both feet and one hand."[5]

An acceptable means of fall protection when working on a portable extension ladder is a vertical lifeline attached directly over the ladder. There are a couple of options:

1. The worker could connect the D-ring on the back of his/her body harness to a lanyard with a rope grab on a vertical wire rope lifeline, or

2. The worker could connect the D-ring on the back of his/her body harness to a retractable vertical lifeline that is anchored directly over the ladder.

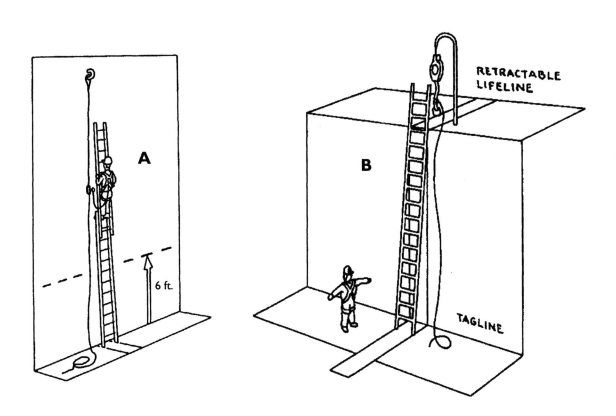

Fall protection when working from a portable ladder
A Vertical wire rope lifeline
B Retractable vertical lifeline

Stepladders

Stepladders are usually marked with roman numerals that indicate their ladder duty classification and maximum load:

	Load Rating	Duty Rating
IA	300 pounds	extra heavy duty
I	250 pounds	heavy duty
II	225 pounds	medium duty
III	200 pounds	light duty

Requirements related to inspection or use of stepladders include the following:

Typical stepladder

1926.1053(a)(8)

A metal spreader or locking device shall be provided on each stepladder to hold the front and back sections in an open position when the ladder is being used.

1926.1053(b)(13)

The top or top step of a stepladder shall not be used as a step.

1926.1053(b)(14)

Cross-bracing on the rear section of stepladders shall not be used for climbing unless the ladders are designed and provided with steps for climbing on both front and rear sections.

Placement of Straight Ladders

♦ Place foot of ladder at distance from wall or structure equal to about one-fourth (¼) of working length of ladder.

♦ For job-made ladders, place ladder at one-eighth (⅛) working length.

♦ Place ladder on stable and level surface or secure to prevent displacement.

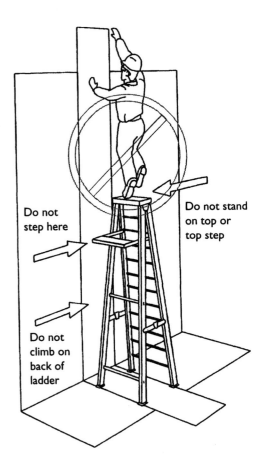

Do not step here

Do not stand on top or top step

Do not climb on back of ladder

Proper use of an A-frame stepladder

- Ladder must have safety feet or be secured on slippery surfaces such as flat metal or concrete.

- Secure ladder to prevent displacement when ladder could be moved by work activities or when placed in passageways, doorways, or driveways.

- Keep area around top and bottom of ladder clear.

- Top rails must be supported equally unless equipped with special attachment.

1926.1053(b)(5)(i)

Non-self-supporting ladders shall be used at an angle such that the horizontal distance from the top support to the foot of the ladder is approximately one-quarter of the working length of the ladder (the distance along the ladder between the foot and the top support).

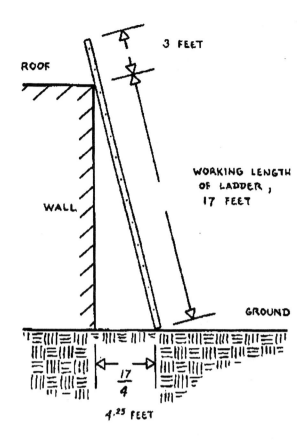

Proper placement of a straight ladder

1926.1053(b)(5)(ii)

Wood job-made ladders with spliced side rails shall be used at an angle such that the horizontal distance is one-eighth the working length of the ladder.

1926.1053 (b)(6)

Ladders shall be used only on stable and level surfaces unless secured to prevent accidental displacement.

1926.1053 (b)(7)

Ladders shall not be used on slippery surfaces unless secured or provided with slip-resistant feet to prevent accidental displacement. Slip-resistant feet shall not be used as a substitute for care in placing, lashing, or holding a ladder that is used upon slippery surfaces including, but not limited to, flat metal or concrete surfaces that are constructed so they cannot be prevented from becoming slippery.

Secure ladder footing to prevent accidental displacement

1926.1053 (b)(8)

Ladders placed in any location where they can be displaced by workplace activities or traffic, such as in passageways, doorways, or driveways, shall be secured to prevent accidental displacement, or a barricade shall be used to keep the activities or traffic away from the ladder.

1926.1053 (b)(9)

The area around the top and bottom of ladders shall be kept clear.

1926.1053 (b)(10)

The top of a non-self-supporting ladder shall be placed with the two rails supported equally unless it is equipped with a single support attachment.

Temporary Construction Ladders and Portable Straight Ladders

♦ Side rails must extend at least 3 feet above upper landing surface.

♦ Retractable lifeline should be placed at top of temporary construction ladders used for repeated access.

♦ Temporary construction ladders and portable straight ladders shall extend at least 36 inches above their uppermost landing and must be secured against displacement.

1926.1053(b)(1)

When portable ladders are used for access to an upper landing surface, the ladder side rails shall extend at least 3 feet (.9 m) above the upper landing surface to which the ladder is used to gain access; or, when such an extension is not possible because of the ladder's length, then the ladder shall be secured at its top to a rigid support that will not deflect, and a grasping device, such as a grabrail, shall be provided to assist employees in mounting and dismounting the ladder. In no case shall the extension be such that ladder deflection under a load would, by itself, cause the ladder to slip off its support.

Temporary construction ladder and portable straight ladder

A retractable lifeline should be placed at the top of each temporary construction ladder that is used for repeated access or egress to elevations. Personnel using these ladders should be required to secure the retractable lifeline to their safety harness while ascending or descending the ladder.

The reels of retractable lifelines should be secured above the highest point of access to temporary construction ladders that are subject to repeated use.

A tagline that extends from the level of the reel to the ground or floor should be attached to the end of the lifeline for convenience in hooking up to it when standing at the base of the ladder.

Safe practices for use of a portable ladder

A. Climbing up a ladder

B. Working on a ladder

C. Climbing down a ladder

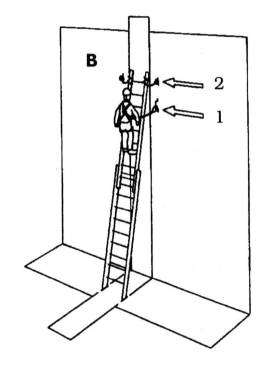

Safe Practices for Use of Portable Ladders

Portable ladders (straight ladders, extension ladders, A-frame ladders, etc.) do not require the retracting lifeline when they are used for access to an elevation to perform a single task.

When using these types of ladders without a retractable lifeline, the following safe work practices must be followed:

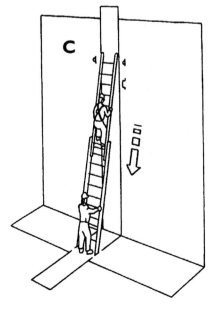

- ◆ When climbing a straight or extension ladder, another person must hold the ladder at its base until the ladder has been secured at the top.

◆ Likewise, when a ladder must be moved, one person must hold the ladder at its base while the other person unties the ladder and climbs down.

◆ When work will be done from a ladder (that is, it is not used just for access or egress to an elevation), the worker must first secure his or her safety lanyard after climbing to the work position, and shall then secure the ladder by tying it off.

◆ The safety lanyard shall be removed as the last action before descending the ladder.

◆ No objects, tools, or materials shall be carried by hand while climbing or descending ladders.

Knots

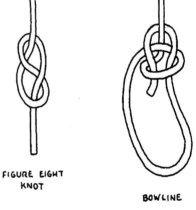

FIGURE EIGHT KNOT   BOWLINE

FIGURE EIGHT KNOT   BOWLINE

"The tracing, or follow through, of (the) figure eight knot for attachment around anchorage points has been recommended in at least one publication as a substitute for the bowline [which has been criticized because of its small bending radii, which can dramatically lower the tensile strength of the line].*

"The termination strength retention using the figure eight might be attributable to its construction, which bends more smoothly around two lines under stress, as opposed to the construction of a knot like the bowline, which bends sharply around and closely to one line....

"The ease of tying, untying, and correctly tying the tracing figure eight are other reasons for favoring it over the bowline, double bowline (double bight) and other variations. However, the properly-tied bowline is reported to be much stronger than many hitch knots and others that have one diameter rope bands and are subject to major stress."[6]

Neither a square knot nor a "granny" knot should be used for securing a ladder. A square knot joining two lines of different diameters may slip and fail.

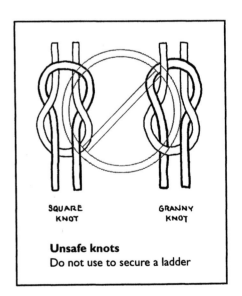

SQUARE KNOT   GRANNY KNOT

Unsafe knots
Do not use to secure a ladder

*NOTE: Explanation added.

Unsafe Practices

"Ladders are commonly misused in two ways:

◆ 'Walking' a ladder, or rocking it from side to side to move it.

◆ Using a folded-up stepladder as a straight ladder. A step-ladder, which is designed as a four-legged device, cannot safely be used as a two-legged straight ladder. According to Lhotka of ASSE, "The feet of the stepladder used this way do not sit squarely on the floor or ground, and they will slip out from under the user."[7]

"'Properly used ladders just don't fall out from under people, but people certainly do fall off ladders.' ...'You can't make a ladder that's safe if the people who use it don't use it safely.' A ladder has feet that grip the floor. But if a worker at the top leans way over the side to reach for something, even nonslip feet won't keep the ladder from tipping."[8]

1926.1053(a)(7)

Ladders shall not be tied or fastened together to provide longer sections unless they are specifically designed for such use.

1926.1053(b)(11)

Ladders shall not be moved, shifted, or extended while occupied.

Misuses of a ladder

A. Walking or rocking a ladder to move it

B. Using a folded-up stepladder as a straight ladder

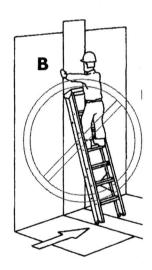

Do not overreach from a ladder. Instead, move the ladder.

It is considered unsafe to climb or work on straight ladders in the rain, or when there is lightning or high wind.

FIXED LADDER ACCIDENT

Painting Contractor

"Employees were sand blasting and painting a water tower. A worker was spray painting the inside of the riser of the tower. He was standing on a fixed ladder 40 feet above the riser floor without wearing any fall protection gear. Apparently he slipped and fell through an opening in the floor of the riser onto a standpipe."[9]

Recommendations to Prevent Recurrence

_____

_____

_____

_____

_____

_____

SUMMARY OF REQUIREMENTS FOR FIXED LADDERS

♦ Pitch must be no greater than 90 degrees.

♦ Side rails must extend 42 inches above top.

♦ If workers walk through top ladder extension, rails must be flared to a width of from 24 to 30 inches.

♦ If workers step to the side at the top of the ladder, the ladder extension must have steps or rungs (for grip).

♦ Ladders made of rungs or steps on a wall must have grab bars up to 42 inches above the access level or landing platform.

NOTE: OSHA's General Industry Standards for fixed ladders differ from the Construction Standards, which are newer, with respect to the height at which ladder cages or other fall protection systems are required.

❑ The General Industry Standards require cages or other protection for ladders over 20 feet high.

❑ The Construction Standards require cages or other protection for ladders that are 24 feet high or higher.

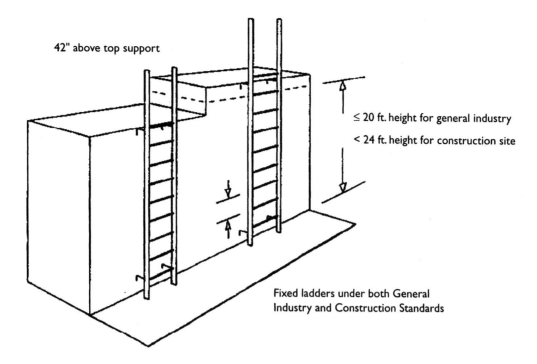

42" above top support

≤ 20 ft. height for general industry

< 24 ft. height for construction site

Fixed ladders under both General
Industry and Construction Standards

1926.1053(a)(27)

Individual-rung/step ladders, except those used where their access openings are covered with manhole covers or hatches, shall extend at least 42 inches (1.1 m) above an access level or landing platform either by the continuation of the rung spacings as horizontal grab bars or by providing vertical grab bars that shall have the same lateral spacing as the vertical legs of the rungs.

1926.1053(b)(5)(iii)

Fixed ladders shall be used at a pitch no greater than 90 degrees from the horizontal, as measured to the back side of the ladder.

1926.1053(a)(24)

The side rails of through or side-step fixed ladders shall extend 42 inches (1.1 m) above the top of the access level or landing platform served by the ladder. For a parapet ladder, the access level shall be the roof if the parapet is cut to permit passage through the parapet; if the parapet is continuous, the access level shall be the top of the parapet.

1926.1053(a)(25)

For through-fixed-ladder extensions, the steps or rungs shall be omitted from the extension and the extension of the side rails shall be flared to provide not less than 24 inches

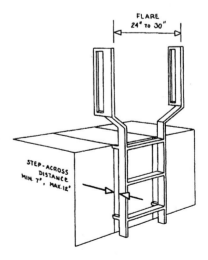

FLARE
24" to 30"

STEP-ACROSS
DISTANCE
MIN. 7", MAX. 12"

Example of through-fixed-ladder extension

(61 cm) nor more than 30 inches (76 cm) clearance between side rails. Where ladder safety devices are provided, the maximum clearance between side rails of the extensions shall not exceed 36 inches (91 cm).

1926.1053(a)(26)

For side-step fixed ladders, side rails and steps or rungs shall be continuous in the extension.

Clearance behind Ladder

1926.1053(a)(13)

The minimum perpendicular clearance between fixed ladder rungs, cleats, and steps, and any obstruction behind the ladder shall be 7 inches (18 cm), except in the case of an elevator pit ladder for which a minimum perpendicular clearance of 4½ inches (11 cm) is required.

Step-Across Distance

1926.1053(a)(16)

Through fixed ladders at their point of access/egress shall have a step-across distance of not less than 7 inches (18 cm) nor more than 12 inches (30 cm) as measured from the centerline of the steps or rungs to the nearest edge of the landing area. If the normal step-across distance exceeds 12 inches (30 cm), a landing platform shall be provided to reduce the distance to the specified limit.

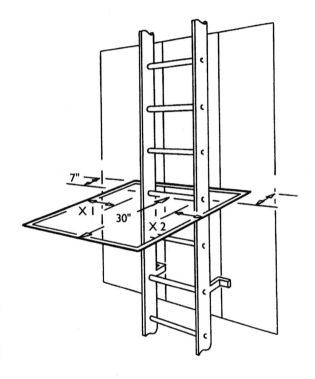

Clearances around a fixed ladder

Clearance on Climbing Side

1926.1053(a)(14)

The minimum perpendicular clearance between the centerline of fixed ladder rungs, cleats, and steps, and any obstruction on the climbing side of the ladder shall be 30 inches (76 cm), except as provided in paragraph (a)(15) of this section.

1926.1053(a)(15)

When unavoidable obstructions are encountered, the minimum perpendicular clearance between the centerline of fixed ladder rungs, cleats, and steps, and the obstruction on the climbing side of the ladder may be reduced to 24 inches (61 cm), provided that a deflection device is installed to guide employees around the obstruction.

1926.1053(a)(17)

Fixed ladders without cages or wells shall have a clear width to the nearest permanent object of at least 15 inches (30 cm) on each side of the centerline of the ladder.

Fall Protection Options

The General Industry Standards require ladder safety devices for fixed ladders over 20 feet high on towers, water tanks, and chimneys. Cages are required for other fixed ladders over 20 feet high, but ladder sections are limited to a maximum of 30 feet. Offset sections with landing platforms are required for ladders with more than one section.

1926.1053(a)(18)

Fixed ladders shall be provided with cages, wells, ladder safety devices, or self-retracting lifelines where the length of climb is less than 24 feet (7.3 m) but the top of the ladder is at a distance greater than 24 feet (7.3 m) above lower levels.

1926.1053(a)(19)

Where the total length of a climb equals or exceeds 24 feet (7.3 m), fixed ladders shall be equipped with one of the following:

(i) Ladder safety devices; or

(ii) Self-retracting lifelines, and rest platforms at intervals not to exceed 150 feet (45.7 m); or

(iii) A cage or well, and multiple ladder sections, each ladder section not to exceed 50 feet (15.2 m) in length. Ladder sections shall be offset from adjacent sections, and landing platforms shall be provided at maximum intervals of 50 feet (15.2 m).

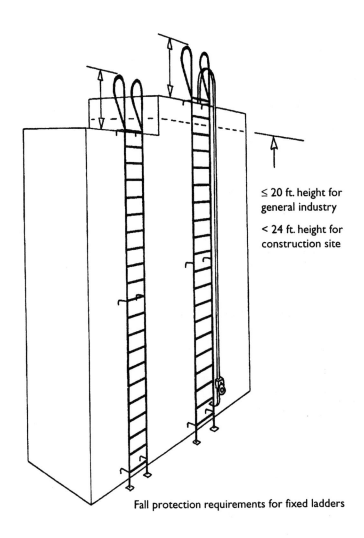

≤ 20 ft. height for general industry

< 24 ft. height for construction site

Fall protection requirements for fixed ladders

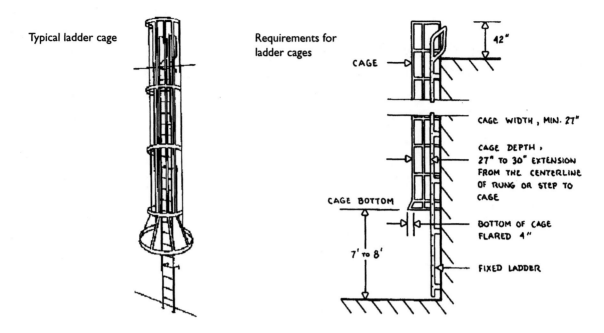

Typical ladder cage

Requirements for ladder cages

CAGE

42"

CAGE WIDTH, MIN. 27"

CAGE DEPTH, 27" TO 30" EXTENSION FROM THE CENTERLINE OF RUNG OR STEP TO CAGE

CAGE BOTTOM

BOTTOM OF CAGE FLARED 4"

7' TO 8'

FIXED LADDER

Ladder Cages

Fixed ladders that have permanently attached cages may be ascended or descended without additional fall protection.

1926.1053(a)(20)(iii)

Cages shall extend not less than 27 inches (66 cm), or more than 30 inches (76 cm) from the centerline of the step or rung (excluding the flare at the bottom of the cage), and shall not be less than 27 inches (68 cm) in width.

1926.1053(a)(20)(vii)

The bottom of the cage shall be at a level not less than 7 feet (2.1 m) nor more than 8 feet (2.4 m) above the point of access to the bottom of the ladder. The bottom of the cage shall be flared not less than 4 inches (10 cm) all around within the distance between the bottom horizontal band and the next higher band.

1926.1053(a)(20)(viii)

The top of the cage shall be a minimum of 42 inches (1.1 m) above the top of the platform, or the point of access at the top of the ladder, with provision for access to the platform or other point of access.

Ladder Safety Devices

1926.1053(a)(22)

Ladder safety devices, and related support systems, for fixed ladders shall conform to all of the following:

(i) They shall be capable of withstanding without failure a drop test consisting of an 18-inch (41 cm) drop of a 500-pound (226 kg) weight;

(ii) They shall permit the employee using the device to ascend or descend without continually having to hold, push, or pull any part of the device, leaving both hands free for climbing;

(iii) They shall be activated within 2 feet (.61 m) after a fall occurs, and limit the descending velocity of an employee to 7 feet/sec. (2.1 m/sec.) or less;

(iv) The connection between the carrier or lifeline and the point of attachment to the body belt or harness shall not exceed 9 inches (23 cm) in length.

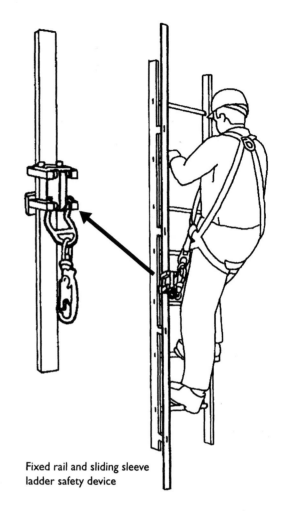

Fixed rail and sliding sleeve ladder safety device

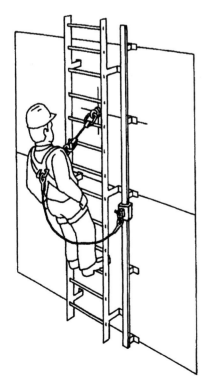

For work on ladder when 3-point contact cannot be maintained, worker should use BOTH positioning system and fall arrest system.

Fixed rail and trolley ladder safety device

1926.1053(a)(23)(ii)

Mountings for flexible carriers shall be attached at each end of the carrier. When the system is exposed to wind, cable guides for flexible carriers shall be installed at a minimum spacing of 25 feet (7.6 m) and maximum spacing of 40 feet (12.2 m) along the entire length of the carrier, to prevent wind damage to the system.

FALLS FROM LADDERS AT HOME

Remember that if you plan to work from the ladder or if you cannot maintain three-point contact, both a personal fall arrest system (lifeline for backup protection) and a positioning system (fall restraint system) should be used.

The following is an excerpt from an article about falls from ladders at home. The article appeared in the *Forum*, a publication of Consumer Benefits of America:[10]

"The Academy of Emergency Medicine reports a study showing that half of those injured in falls from ladders were hurt at home. They were working on projects such as painting or cleaning gutters and doing minor roof repairs. Broken bones were the most common injury, followed by sprains, bruises and cuts.

"Almost half of those injured said they fell because the ladder wasn't positioned correctly. It was on uneven or slippery ground, it wasn't securely resting against the house, or it was too upright. Reaching too far accounted for a third of falls, followed by slipping down the rungs.

"The Academy recommends:

- ◆ Make sure the ladder is on level ground.

- ◆ Place it an appropriate distance from the house.

- ◆ Have someone hold the ladder while you are climbing up or down.

- ◆ Don't reach too far to the left or right."

WHAT TO DO IF YOU FALL

Even if all OSHA regulations are followed, a fall from a ladder might still occur. Eagle Insurance Group has published the following "Tips When Falling" on their web page (http://www.eig.com).

- ◆ **Roll with the fall**. Bruise the meat; don't break the bones. Try to twist and roll backward, rather than falling forward. Roll onto the soft tissues of your buttocks, thigh, and large back muscles. Doing this protects the back of your head and your spine.

- ◆ **Turn quickly to look** at the spot where your body will hit the ground. This will help turn your body to your side, rather than falling on your back. It avoids impact to the spine, concussion to the head, and whiplash to the neck.

- **Relax** as much as possible when you begin to fall. You'll be more likely to roll with the fall than to strike an elbow or knee.

- **Shout and exhale** to reduce internal compression due to holding your breath. Cry out as those practicing martial arts do.

- **Slap the ground**. Don't "stiff-arm" the wall, floor, or ground when you fall. Slap the surface with your extended palm and inner forearm just before impact. This helps spread the impact and reduce the force of the fall. It avoids wrist, elbow, and shoulder dislocations.

- **Toss the load**. Protect yourself, instead of objects being carried, by letting go or tossing them clear when you start to fall. The potential cost in damage to materials or in cleanup time is usually much less than the cost of an injury.[11]

ENDNOTES

1. Barrett Miller, "Safe Ladder Management," *Professional Safety*, November 1997, pages 30–31.

2. David May, "Rise and Fall," *Occupational Safety & Health*, February 1999, page 40.

3. Barrett Miller, "Safe Ladder Management," *Professional Safety*, November 1997, page 30.

4. Tom Kabaker, "Step Up to Ladder Safety," *Safety & Health*, January 1999, page 62.

5. *Ibid.*, page 60.

6. J. Nigel Ellis, *Introduction to Fall Protection* (Des Plaines, IL: American Society of Safety Engineers. 1993), pages 96–97.

7. Tom Kabaker, "Step Up to Ladder Safety," *Safety & Health*, January 1999, page 61.

8. *Ibid.*, page 62.

9. OSHA, *Fatal Facts*, No. 23.

10. Consumer Benefits of America, "Home Repairs and Ladder Falls," *Forum*, Vol. 11, No. 2, June/July 1998, page 3.

11. David May, "Rise and Fall," *Occupational Health & Safety*, February 1999, page 42.

Elevating Personnel

ACCIDENTS

Analyze the following accidents and think about the recommendations you would make to prevent a recurrence. Record your comments. As you progress through this chapter, add to the list of recommendations any regulatory requirements or safety rules that apply that are not already listed.

Maintenance Repairman

"An employee needed to replace some burned-out bulbs approximately 15 feet above the ground. He flagged down a passing lift truck. While he was being raised his little finger became caught between the roller and mast and was amputated. He knew he was doing the wrong thing in not using a lift cage but said he was in a hurry. The lift truck operator said it wasn't unusual to lift the mechanic this way, he did it all the time."[1]

Recommendations to Prevent Recurrence

_____

_____

_____

_____

_____

_____

_____

_____

Mason Contractor

"A laborer and his foreman were riding a material hoist carrying two skids of bricks up to the work floor. The skid jack handle fell and jammed into the interior cross bracing bar of the hoist at the fifth floor level. At the sixth floor level, the foreman jumped off the hoist. He struck the protection platform bar and was subsequently knocked into the hoist shaft. He fell 60 feet to his death."[2]

Discussion

◆ What safety rules were violated?

◆ How are material hoists and personnel hoists different with regard to design features for safety?

Recommendations to Prevent Recurrence

_____

_____

_____

_____

_____

_____

_____

_____

_____

_____

MANLIFTS AND VEHICLE-MOUNTED WORK PLATFORMS

29 CFR 1910.67 and 1910.68

Fall protection design requirements for various types of aerial lifts are specified in ANSI standards:

◆ ANSI/SIA A92.2-1990 Vehicle-Mounted Elevating and Rotating Aerial Devices

◆ ANSI/SIA A92.3-1990 Manually Propelled Elevating Aerial Platforms

◆ ANSI/SIA A92.5-1990 Boom Supported Elevating Work Platforms

◆ ANSI/SIA A92.6-1990 Self-Propelled Elevating Work Platforms

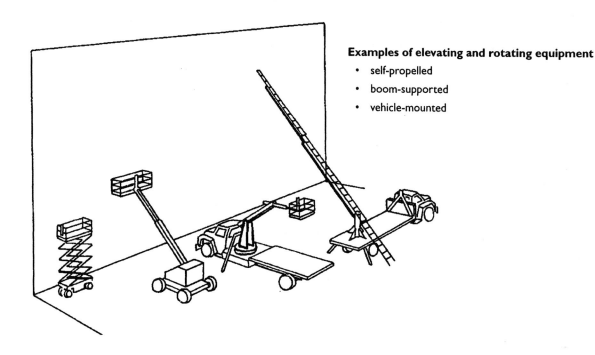

Examples of elevating and rotating equipment
- self-propelled
- boom-supported
- vehicle-mounted

ELEVATING AND ROTATING EQUIPMENT

Elevating and rotating equipment may be self-propelled, it may be supported on a boom that is mounted on a truck or mobile unit, or it may consist of a ladder that is mounted onto a base that rotates or swivels on a truck. Equipment in this category includes manlifts or scissor lifts and aerial lifts such as bucket trucks or cherry pickers.

"AWP's [aerial work platforms] are available in various shapes and sizes and have widely different characteristics. For example, some AWP's are designed only for inside work on slabs; some can be driven over uneven ground; and others have outriggers that enable leveling. Regardless of the type, however, *there is no substitute for job and product knowledge.*"[3]

Whenever personnel use manlifts or aerial lifts for work positioning, fall protection is always needed, because workers tend to reach outside the guardrails or aerial basket

Some lifts are designed only for inside work on slabs. Some can be driven over uneven ground.

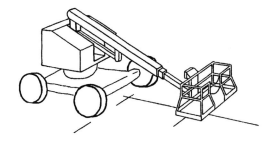

Types of Lifts

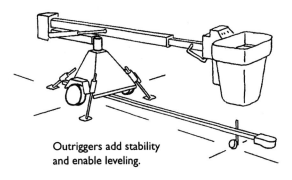

Outriggers add stability and enable leveling.

"A full body harness and a shock absorbing lanyard that can be anchored to the boom or another suitable location, preferably overhead, should serve as fall protection.

"NOTE: Aerial lift fall protection must be engineered, tested, and documented on an engineering drawing."[4]

Safety Rules for Aerial Lifts

PFAS must be worn if worker may reach outside guardrails or basket

1. Personnel who are elevated by aerial lifts must wear a body harness with a lanyard that is no longer than 4 feet and is properly connected to an approved anchor point. The anchor point must be capable of withstanding twice the maximum arrest force of the fall arrest device (to avoid potential tip-over).

2. When leaving an aerial basket or platform to perform work at a height of 10 feet or more above the ground, there must be an approved means of providing fall protection during the transition from the basket or platform to the work area.

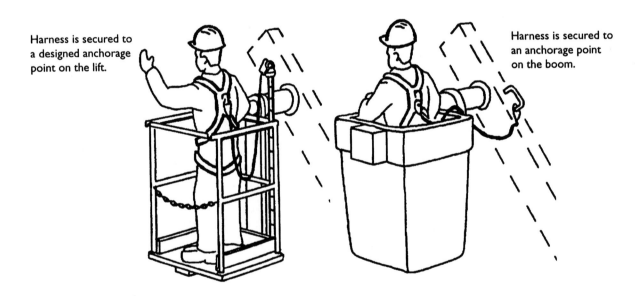

Harness is secured to a designed anchorage point on the lift.

Harness is secured to an anchorage point on the boom.

Harness must be worn to comply with OSHA's Construction Standard.

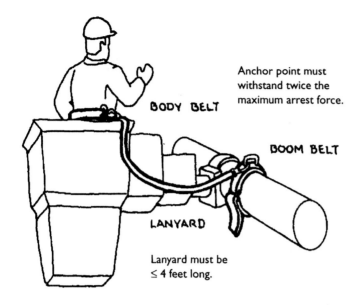

Anchor point must withstand twice the maximum arrest force.

BODY BELT

BOOM BELT

LANYARD

Lanyard must be ≤ 4 feet long.

Typical body belt with D-ring

Safety Rules for Stock Pickers

George Swartz in *Forklift Safety* gives the following description of the stock picker: "Order picking trucks allow the operator to ride up with the forks where he regulates travel, speed, elevation, and direction with onboard controls. These trucks are mainly used for assembling less than pallet load quantities. The order picker is a narrow-aisle straddle truck that contains the operator's platform. This model can usually lift at heights up to 15 to 20 feet with a load capacity of up to 2,500 pounds. Some heavy duty units can lift as high as 30 feet."[5]

1. Follow manufacturer's recommendations for fall protection. Retractable lines are preferable to lanyards.

2. Never stand or place your whole weight on a rack. Do not move across to the other side of a rack for any reason.

3. Do not step across an opening of more than 12 inches.

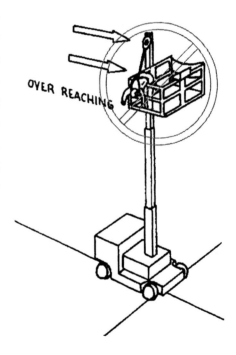

OVER REACHING

Stock pickers, do not overreach!

Scissor Lifts

Forklift Safety presents this description of the scissor lift: "Another type of unit similar to an order picker is a scissor lift. These models are mostly used for maintenance work or for taking inventory. It is important to block off areas where these units will operate to keep from

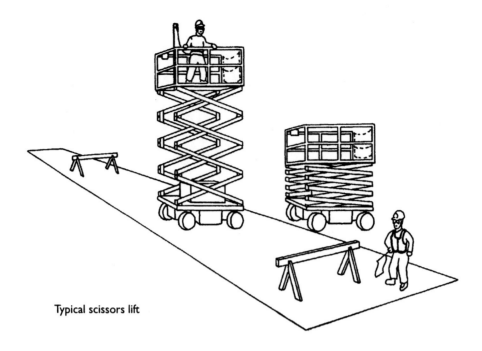

Typical scissors lift

being struck. They can be top heavy and must not make turns while elevated. While traveling the unit can be hazardous."[6]

Lift Cages/Working Platforms Elevated by Forklifts

In *Forklift Safety*, Swartz presents the following guidelines for using forklifts as elevated working platforms: "There are times when someone has to be lifted to an upper level to perform maintenance. ...To safeguard anyone who must be lifted by the machine [forklift], some basic principles must be followed:

◆ Only use an approved lifting cage. Many are sold commercially and offer protection as required. Be sure the power equipment manufacturer approves of this process. Check their operating guidelines or personally contact them.

◆ Proper hand railing on two sides and the front.

◆ Mid rail and toeboard.

◆ Moveable gate that locks into place.

◆ Nonskid walking surface.

◆ Slots to allow maximum width for the forks.

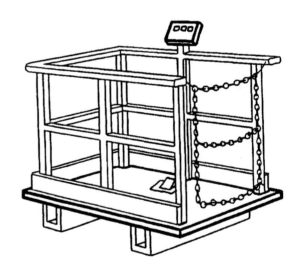

Lift cage or working platform elevated by forklift

◆ A high back that includes small enough metal grid mesh that prevents a finger from being injured if placed in the operating mechanism.

◆ An effective means of securing the platform to the mast of the lift truck.

◆ A means shall be provided to allow personnel on the platform to shut off the power to the truck.

...Workers should not be carried to the work site while on the platform. The platform should be inspected before being used. A critical safety requirement is to properly anchor the platform to the mast. A word of caution, some manufacturers only allow for a chain hook to be passed over a link to lock the platform to the mast. This hook can easily become undone which could allow the platform to slide off the forks. A high tensile bolt and nut or an approved clevis should be used for maximum safety when fastening the chain. A chain manufacturer can assist in this situation."[7]

Additional Recommendations for Personnel Platforms on Forklifts

Swartz provides these recommendations for working with personnel on elevated platforms: "Once elevated the communication between the worker and the operator should be such that both have an understanding of what is being said. Hand-held talk devices are a plus here. At no time should the operator desert the lift truck. At no time should the operator drive to another location with the work platform elevated. An added safety rule should allow for the worker to anchor a support line to the mast and platform while wearing a safety harness. Check with the safety harness manufacturer and lift truck manufacturer to ensure that this procedure is safe.

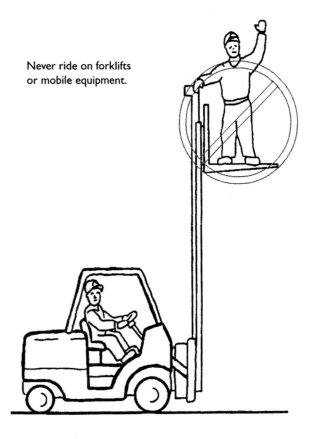

Never ride on forklifts or mobile equipment.

"Where the operator has to look up at the platform, or at a load, small wire mesh placed over the overhead guard adds to operator safety. Most overhead guards have large openings in them and could allow small pieces of product or tools to come through the overhead guard. ...A hard hat becomes an added safety factor in this case to protect operators....

"Where construction crews or outsiders are in a facility to make repairs, management should consider allowing the use of working platforms in the hands of non-employees.... Will the non-employee have the same degree of skill? Will they use a lift platform safely?

These issues should be resolved prior to any work being done.... Contractors, as well as employees, have been known to climb upon handrailings to obtain a higher elevation from a lifting platform. This practice must be prohibited."[8]

PERSONNEL HOISTS ON CONSTRUCTION SITES

29 CFR 1926.552(c)

The OSHA standards pertaining to personnel hoists that should be verified in advance of the start of work and during a construction site safety inspection are listed below.

Properly designed personnel hoists have many safety advantages on a multistory construction site, not only for access and egress, but also for rescue purposes and transportation of injured persons. They are usually designed by a qualified engineer.

Enclosure of Hoist Towers

1926.552(c)(1)

Hoist towers outside the structure shall be enclosed for the full height on the side or sides used for entrance and exit to the structure. At the lowest landing, the enclosure on the sides not used for exit or entrance to the structure shall be enclosed to a height of at least 10 feet. Other sides of the tower adjacent to floors or scaffold platforms shall be enclosed to a height of 10 feet above the level of such floors or scaffolds.

Requirements for construction site personnel hoist

- properly enclosed
- anchored to structure every 25 ft. or less
- tie-ins and guys
- locks on doors
- overhead protection
- capacity/data plate
- emergency stop

1926.552(c)(2)

Towers inside of structures shall be enclosed on all four sides throughout the full height.

1926.552(c)(3)

Towers shall be anchored to the structure at intervals not exceeding 25 feet. In addition to tie-ins, a series of guys shall be installed. Where tie-ins are not practical the tower shall be anchored by means of guys made of wire rope at least one-half inch in diameter, securely fastened to anchorage to ensure stability.

Hoistway Doors/Gates

1926.552(c)(4)

Hoistway doors or gates shall be not less than 6 feet 6 inches high and shall be provided with mechanical locks which cannot be operated from the landing side, and shall be accessible only to persons on the car.

1926.552(c)(5)

Cars shall be permanently enclosed on all sides and the top, except sides used for entrance and exit which have car gates or doors.

1926.552(c)(6)

A door or gate shall be provided at each entrance to the car which shall protect the full width and height of the car entrance opening.

Overhead Protection

1926.552(c)(7)

Overhead protective covering of 2-inch planking, ¾-inch plywood, or other solid material of equivalent strength shall be provided on the top of every personnel hoist.

Marking of Capacity

1926.552(c)(10)

Cars shall be provided with a capacity and data plate secured in a conspicuous place on the car or crosshead.

Emergency Stop

1926.552(c)(13)

An emergency stop switch shall be provided in the car and marked "Stop."

Inspection and Testing

1926.552(c)(15)

Following assembly and erection of hoists, and before being put in service, an inspection and test of all functions and safety devices shall be made under the supervision of a competent person. A similar inspection and test is required following major alteration of an existing installation. All hoists shall be inspected and tested at not more than 3-month intervals. The employer shall prepare a certification record which includes the date the inspection and test of all functions and safety devices was performed; the signature of the person who performed the inspection and test; and a serial number, or other identifier, for the hoist that was inspected and tested. The most recent certification record shall be maintained on file.

CRANES AND DERRICKS

29 CFR 1926.550(g)

1926.550(g)(2)

General requirements. The use of a crane or derrick to hoist employees on a personnel platform is prohibited, except when the erection, use, and dismantling of conventional means of reaching the worksite, such as a personnel hoist, ladder, stairway, aerial lift, elevating work platform or scaffold, would be more hazardous or is not possible because of structural design or worksite conditions.

PERSONNEL PLATFORMS ELEVATED BY CRANES

1926.550(g)(3)(i)(A)

Hoisting of the personnel platform shall be performed in a slow, controlled, cautious manner with no sudden movements of the crane or derrick, or the platform.

Load Lines

1926.550(g)(3)(i)(B)

Load lines shall be capable of supporting, without failure, at least seven times the maximum intended load, except that where rotation resistant rope is used, the lines shall be capable of supporting without failure, at least ten times the maximum intended load. The required design factor is achieved by taking the current safety factor of 3.5 (required under 1926.550(b)(2)) and applying the 50 percent derating of the crane capacity which is required by 1926.550(g)(3)(i)(F).

Brakes

1926.550(g)(3)(i)(C)

Load and boom hoist drum brakes, swing brakes, and locking devices such as pawls or dogs shall be engaged when the occupied personnel platform is in a stationary position.

Level

1926.550(g)(3)(i)(D)

The crane shall be uniformly level within one percent of level grade and located on firm footing. Cranes equipped with outriggers shall have them all fully deployed following manufacturer's specifications, insofar as applicable, when hoisting employees.

Total Load

1926.550(g)(3)(i)(E)

The total weight of the loaded personnel platform and related rigging shall not exceed 50 percent of the rated capacity for the radius and configuration of the crane or derrick.

No Live Booms

1926.550(g)(3)(i)(F)

The use of machines having live booms (booms in which lowering is controlled by a brake without aid from other devices which slow the lowering speeds) is prohibited.

Instruments and Components

1926.550(g)(3)(ii)(A)

Cranes and derricks with variable angle booms shall be equipped with a boom angle indicator, readily visible to the operator.

1926.550(g)(3)(ii)(B)

Cranes with telescoping booms shall be equipped with a device to indicate clearly to the operator, at all times, the boom's extended length, or an accurate determination of the load radius to be used during the lift shall be made prior to hoisting personnel.

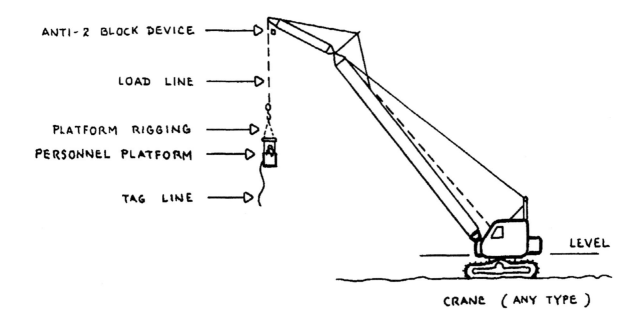

Components of the lifting system for personnel platforms elevated by cranes

1926.550(g)(3)(ii)(C)

A positive acting device shall be used which prevents contact between the load block or overhaul ball and the boom tip (anti-two-blocking device), or a system shall be used which deactivates the hoisting action before damage occurs in the event of a two-blocking situation (two-block damage prevention feature).

1926.550(g)(3)(ii)(D)

The load line hoist drum shall have a system or device on the power train, other than the load hoist brake, which regulates the lowering rate of speed of the hoist mechanism (controlled load lowering.) Free fall is prohibited.

Design of Personnel Platforms

1926.550(g)(4)(i)(A)

The personnel platform and suspension system shall be designed by a qualified engineer or a qualified person competent in structural design.

1926.550(g)(4)(i)(B)

The suspension system shall be designed to minimize tipping of the platform due to movement of employees occupying the platform.

1926.550(g)(4)(i)(C)

The personnel platform itself, except the guardrail system and personnel fall arrest system anchorages, shall be capable of supporting, without failure, its own weight and at least five times the maximum intended load. Criteria for guardrail systems and personal fall arrest system anchorages are contained in subpart M of this Part.

Platform Specifications

1926.550(g)(4)(ii)(A)

Each personnel platform shall be equipped with a guardrail system which meets the requirements of Subpart M, and shall be enclosed at least from the toeboard to mid-rail with either solid construction or expanded metal having openings no greater than ½ inch (1.27 cm).

1926.550(g)(4)(ii)(B)

A grab rail shall be installed inside the entire perimeter of the personnel platform.

Access Gates

1926.550(g)(4)(ii)(C)

Access gates, if installed, shall not swing outward during hoisting.

1926.550(g)(4)(ii)(D)

Access gates, including sliding or folding gates, shall be equipped with a restraining device to prevent accidental opening.

Overhead Protection

1926.550(g)(4)(ii)(F)

In addition to the use of hard hats, employees shall be protected by overhead protection on the personnel platform when employees are exposed to falling objects.

Capacity

1926.550(g)(4)(ii)(I)

The personnel platform shall be conspicuously posted with a plate or other permanent marking which indicates the weight of the platform, and its rated load capacity or maximum intended load.

Loading

1926.550(g)(4)(iii)(A)

The personnel platform shall not be loaded in excess of its rated load capacity, When a personnel platform does not have a rated load capacity, then the personnel platform shall not be loaded in excess of its maximum intended load.

1926.550(g)(4)(iii)(B)

The number of employees occupying the personnel platform shall not exceed the number required for the work being performed.

1926.550(g)(4)(iii)(C)

Personnel platforms shall be used only for employees, their tools, and the materials necessary to do their work, and shall not be used to hoist only materials or tools when not hoisting personnel.

1926.550(g)(4)(iii)(D)

Materials and tools for use during a personnel lift shall be secured to prevent displacement.

1926.550(g)(4)(iii)(E)

Materials and tools for use during a personnel lift shall be evenly distributed within the confines of the platform while the platform is suspended.

Rigging

1926.550(g)(4)(iv)(A)

When a wire rope bridle is used to connect the personnel platform to the load line, each bridle leg shall be connected to a master link or shackle in such a manner to ensure that the load is evenly divided among the bridle legs.

1926.550(g)(4)(iv)(B)

Hooks on overhaul ball assemblies, lower load blocks, or other attachment assemblies shall be of a type that can be closed and locked, eliminating the hook throat opening. Alternatively, an alloy anchor type shackle with a bolt, nut, and retaining pin may be used.

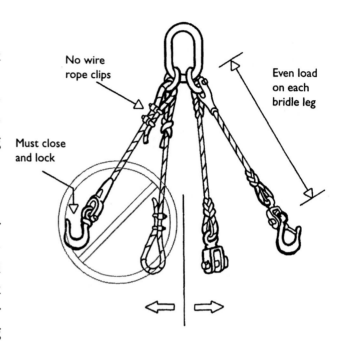

Wire rope bridle requirements

1926.550(g)(4)(iv)(C)

Wire rope, shackles, rings, master links, and other rigging hardware must be capable of supporting, without failure, at least five times the maximum intended load applied or transmitted to that component. Where rotation resistant rope is used, the slings shall be capable of supporting without failure at least ten times the maximum intended load.

1926.550(g)(4)(iv)(D)

All eyes in wire rope slings shall be fabricated with thimbles.

1926.550(g)(4)(iv)(E)

Bridles and associated rigging for attaching the personnel platform to the hoist line shall be used only for the platform and the necessary employees, their tools, and the materials necessary to do their work and shall not be used for any other purpose when not hoisting personnel.

Trial Lift, Inspections, and Proof Testing of Personnel Platform Hoisted by Crane

1926.550(g)(5)(i)

A trial lift with the unoccupied personnel platform loaded at least to the anticipated lift weight shall be made from ground level, or any other location where employees will enter the platform to each location at which the personnel platform is to be hoisted and positioned. This trial lift shall be performed immediately prior to placing personnel on the platform. The operator shall determine that all systems, controls, and safety devices are activated and functioning properly; that no interferences exist; and that all configurations necessary to reach those work locations will allow the operator to remain under the 50 percent limit of the hoist's rated capacity. Materials and tools to be used during the actual lift can be loaded in the platform, as provided in paragraphs (g)(4)(iii)(D), and (E) of this section for the trial lift. A single trial lift may be performed at one time for all locations that are to be reached from a single set up position.

1926.550(g)(5)(ii)

The trial lift shall be repeated prior to hoisting employees whenever the crane or derrick is moved and set up in a new location or returned to a previously used location. Additionally, the trial lift shall be repeated when the lift route is changed unless the operator determines that the route change is not significant (i.e., the route change would not affect the safety of hoisted employees).

1926.550(g)(5)(iii)

After the trial lift, and just prior to hoisting personnel, the platform shall be hoisted a few inches and inspected to ensure that it is secure and properly balanced. Employees shall not be hoisted unless the following conditions are determined to exist:

(A) Hoist ropes shall be free of kinks;

(B) Multiple part lines shall not be twisted around each other;

(C) The primary attachment shall be centered over the platform; and

(D) The hoisting system shall be inspected if the load rope is slack to ensure all ropes are properly stated on drums and in sheaves.

1926.550(g)(5)(iv)

A visual inspection of the crane or derrick, rigging, personnel platform, and the crane or derrick base support or ground shall be conducted by a competent person immediately after the trial lift to determine whether the testing has exposed any defect or produced any adverse effect upon any component or structure.

1926.550(g)(5)(v)

Any defects found during inspections which create a safety hazard shall be corrected before hoisting personnel.

1926.550(g)(5)(vi)

At each job site, prior to hoisting employees on the personnel platform, and after any repair or modification, the platform and rigging shall be proof tested to 125 percent of the platform's rated capacity by holding it in a suspended position for five minutes with the test load evenly distributed on the platform (this may be done concurrently with the trial lift). After proof testing, a competent person shall inspect the platform and rigging. Any deficiencies found shall be corrected and another proof test shall be conducted. Personnel hoisting shall not be conducted until the proof testing requirements are satisfied.

Safe Practices—Personnel Platform Hoisted by Crane

1926.550(g)(6)(i)

Employees shall keep all parts of the body inside the platform during raising, lowering, and positioning. This provision does not apply to an occupant of the platform performing the duties of a signal person.

1926.550(g)(6)(ii)

Before employees exit or enter a hoisted personnel platform that is not landed, the platform shall be secured to the structure where the work is to be performed, unless securing to the structure creates an unsafe situation.

1926.550(g)(6)(iii)

Tag lines shall be used unless their use creates an unsafe condition.

1926.550(g)(6)(iv)

The crane or derrick operator shall remain at the controls at all times when the crane engine is running and the platform is occupied.

1926.550(g)(6)(v)

Hoisting of employees shall be promptly discontinued upon indication of any dangerous weather conditions or other impending danger.

1926.550(g)(6)(vi)

Employees being hoisted shall remain in continuous sight of and in direct communication

PERSONAL FALL ARREST SYSTEM ANCHORAGE

GRAB RAIL

GUARDRAIL SYSTEM

Some safety requirements when hoisting personnel with a crane

- Keep all parts of the body inside
- Use tag lines unless this creates a hazard
- Crane operator must remain at controls
- Crane operator must maintain contact with hoisted personnel or use signal person
- Discontinue in dangerous weather

with the operator or signal person. In those situations where direct visual contact with the operator is not possible, and the use of a signal person would create a greater hazard for the person, direct communication alone such as by radio may be used.

1926.550(g)(6)(vii)

Except over water, employees occupying the personnel platform shall use a body belt/harness system with lanyard appropriately attached to the lower load block or overhaul ball, or to a structural member within the personnel platform capable of supporting a fall impact for employees using the anchorage. When working over water the requirements of 1926.106 shall apply.

1926.550(g)(6)(viii)

No lifts shall be made on another of the crane's or derrick's loadlines while personnel are suspended on a platform.

Crane Travel

1926.550(g)(7)(i)

Hoisting of employees while the crane is traveling is prohibited, except for portal, tower, and locomotive cranes, or where the employer demonstrates that there is no less hazardous way to perform the work.

1926.550(g)(7)(ii)

Under any circumstances where a crane would travel while hoisting personnel, the employer shall implement the following procedures to safeguard employees:

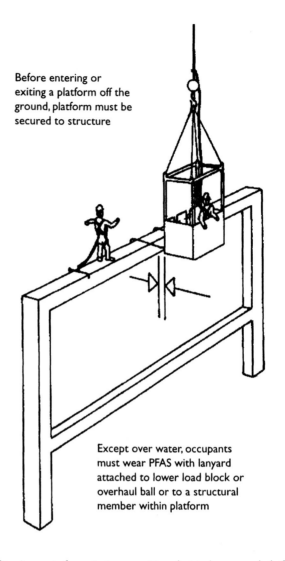

Before entering or exiting a platform off the ground, platform must be secured to structure

Except over water, occupants must wear PFAS with lanyard attached to lower load block or overhaul ball or to a structural member within platform

Requirements for entering or exiting a hoisted personnel platform

(A) Crane travel shall be restricted to a fixed track or runway;

(B) Travel shall be limited to the load radius of the boom used during the lift; and

(C) The boom must be parallel to the direction of travel.

(D) A complete trial run shall be performed to test the route of travel before employees are allowed to occupy the platform. This trial run can be performed at the same time as the trial lift required by paragraph (g)(5)(i) of this section which tests the route of the lift.

(E) If travel is done with a rubber tired-carrier, the condition and air pressure of the tires shall be checked. The chart capacity for lifts on rubber shall be used for application of the 50 percent reduction of rated capacity. Notwithstanding paragraph (g)(5)(i)(E) of this section, outriggers may be partially retracted as necessary for travel.

Pre-Lift Meeting

1926.550(g)(8)(i)

A meeting attended by the crane or derrick operator, signal person(s) (if necessary for the lift), employee(s) to be lifted, and the person responsible for the task to be performed shall be held to review the appropriate requirements of paragraph (g) of this section and the procedures to be followed.

1926.550(g)(8)(ii)

This meeting shall be held prior to the trial lift at each new work location, and shall be repeated for any employees newly assigned to the operation.

RELATIVE SAFETY OF OPTIONS

The main hazards associated with vehicle-mounted elevating and rotating equipment is overreaching, so fall protection should always be used to supplement guardrails. The use of this type of equipment is considered relatively safe, because of the many engineering design requirements manufacturers must meet.

Lift trucks that are designed to raise personnel, such as order pickers and scissor lifts, have additional requirements to maintain stability while traveling or turning, and may not

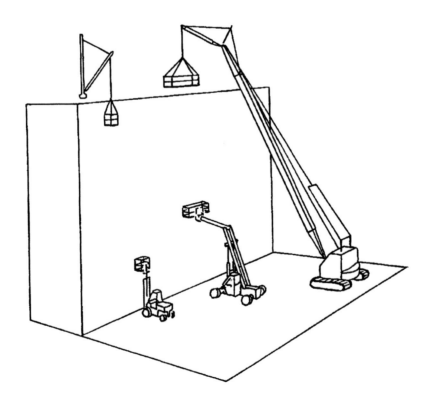

Types of personnel platform lifting and lowering equipment

be quite as safe in their design as vehicle-mounted elevating and rotating equipment. Fork-lift trucks on which personnel platforms are used have many additional requirements for employee safety.

Personnel hoists on construction sites that are properly designed are relatively safe to use unless they are misused as material hoists when not being used to lift personnel.

Platforms lifted by cranes on construction sites involve many hazards that must be controlled to protect employees. This practice is prohibited unless it is absolutely necessary, because it is relatively unsafe—lots of things can go wrong and cause an accident.

ENDNOTES

1. George Swartz, *Forklift Safety* (Rockville, MD: Government Institutes, 1997) page 230.

2. OSHA, *Fatal Facts*, No. 20.

3. Frank Schimaneck and David K. Merrifield, "Aerial Work Platforms: Safety, Liability and the Rental Center," *Professional Safety*, January 1998, page 27.

4. J. Nigel Ellis, *Introduction to Fall Protection* (Des Plaines, IL: American Society of Safety Engineers. 1993), page 69.

5. George Swartz, *Forklift Safety*, page 50.

6. *Ibid.*, page 50.

7. *Ibid.*, pages 228–229.

8. *Ibid.*, page 230.

Special Applications

ROOF ACCIDENTS

Analyze the following accidents and think about the recommendations you would make to prevent a recurrence. Record your comments. As you progress through this chapter, add to the list of recommendations any regulatory requirements or safety rules that apply that are not already listed.

Fall from Roof

"A 26-year-old Dallas man died Sunday night from injuries he sustained in a construction accident in Plano. Guadalupe Davila was injured on Dec. 8 after he fell from a roof at 8123 Ohio Drive in Plano. He was taken to Medical Center of Plano, where he remained until his death Sunday...."[1]

Recommendations to Prevent Recurrence

_____

_____

_____

_____

_____

_____

_____

_____

_____

Metal Roof Decking

"On August 9, 1996, an employee of LeMaster Steel fell 28' to his death during a metal roof decking operation. OSHA's investigation into the facility revealed that five employees were, at different times, working at the edge without fall protection. OSHA cited the company on Jan. 30, 1997, for two alleged willful violations for lack of fall protection and then referred the case to the Justice Department for possible criminal prosecution.

"The indictment alleges that LeMaster Steel, through the actions of its site foreman, obstructed justice by falsely stating to OSHA investigators that fall protection was in place prior to the accident. The company and its supervisor were charged with two counts of obstructing justice by intentionally instructing witnesses to withhold information about the lack of fall protection."[2]

Recommendations to Prevent Recurrence

_____

_____

_____

_____

_____

_____

_____

_____

WORK ON ROOFS

OSHA standards in 29 CFR 1926 Subpart M (Sections 500–503 and Appendices A–E) cover construction, alteration, and repair work on roofs and other elevated walking and working surfaces, except for steel erection or electric transmission-distribution operations, which are covered by other standards that will be reviewed in this chapter. Walking and working surfaces do not include ladders, vehicles, or trailers on which employees perform work.

For purposes of compliance with these standards, roofing work includes hoisting, storage, application, and removal of roofing materials and equipment, including insulation, sheet metal, and vapor barrier work, but _not_ including the construction of the roof deck.

Before beginning work, an employer has a duty to ensure that the walking or working surfaces are strong enough to safely support workers.

OSHA has different requirements for steep roofs and low-slope or flat roofs:

♦ A steep roof is one that has more than a 4-foot rise per 12 feet of horizontal distance.

♦ A low-slope roof has a slope less than or equal to a rise of 4 feet per 12 feet of horizontal distance.

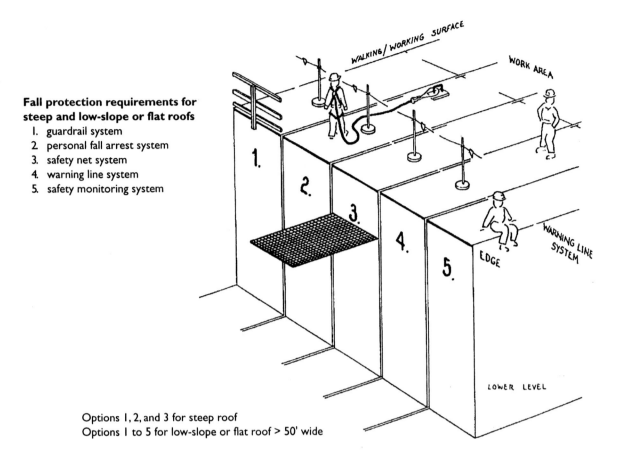

Fall protection requirements for steep and low-slope or flat roofs
1. guardrail system
2. personal fall arrest system
3. safety net system
4. warning line system
5. safety monitoring system

Options 1, 2, and 3 for steep roof
Options 1 to 5 for low-slope or flat roof > 50' wide

WORK ON LOW-SLOPE AND FLAT ROOFS

Except for personnel who are only inspecting or investigating roof conditions, personnel who are working on a low-slope or flat roof that is wider than 50 feet must be protected from falls:

♦ By a motion-stopping safety system that uses effective fall protection components or combinations of components, including guardrails, scaffolds, or platforms with guardrails, safety nets, and personal fall arrest systems; OR

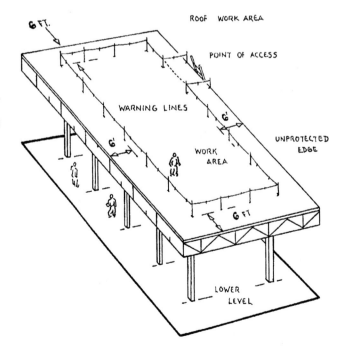

Warning line system where *no* mobile equipment is used

♦ By a warning line system erected not less than 6 feet from unprotected edges where there is a danger of personnel falling, and not less than 10 feet from edges where mobile mechanical equipment is used (except for wheel barrows and mop carts). However, if personnel are working within 6 feet of an unprotected edge, then a motion-stopping system or a safety monitoring system must be used.

Mechanical equipment may only be used in areas where employees are protected by a warning line system, guardrail system, or personal fall arrest system.

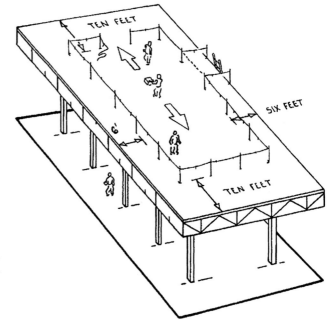

Warning line system where mobile equipment is used

Warning Line Systems

A warning line system is a barrier erected on a roof to warn employees that they are approaching an unprotected side or edge. It designates an area in which roofing work may take place without the use of guardrails, safety nets, or PFAS to protect employees in the area.

When warning lines are used, they must be erected around all sides of the roof work area. No employee is allowed in the area between a roof edge and a warning line, unless he/she is performing roofing work in that area.

Warning lines consist of ropes, wires, or chains supported by stanchions that will not tip when 16 pounds of force is applied horizontally. No tape, plastic, or metal banding may be used. The lowest point of the line must be at least 34 inches from the work surface, and the highest point, no more than 39 inches. The warning line must be attached to each stanchion or support so that pulling on one line section will not take up slack in the adjoining sections. Warning lines must be flagged at intervals of 6 feet or less with high visibility flags or materials.

An access path formed by two warning lines must be placed at

Warning line system specifications

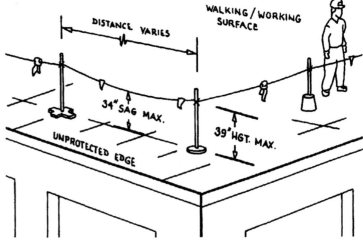

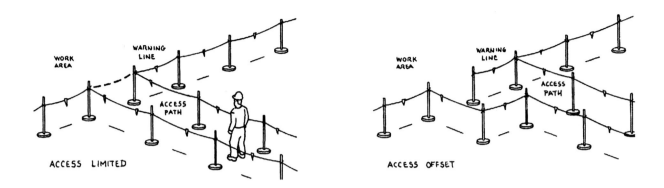

ACCESS LIMITED   ACCESS OFFSET

When the path to a point of access is not in use, a rope, wire, chain, or other barricade must be placed across the path at the point where the path intersects the warning line erected around the work area, OR the path shall be offset so that a person cannot walk directly into the work area.

all points of access, material handling areas, storage areas, and hoisting areas that are connected to the work area.

Safety Monitoring System

A safety monitoring system is a system in which a competent person monitors the safety of all employees in a roofing crew and warns them when it appears to the monitor that they are unaware of a fall hazard or are acting in an unsafe manner. The competent person must be on the same roof and within visual sight and voice communication of the other employees.

For low-slope and flat roofs that are less than or equal to 50 feet in width, the use of a safety warning system alone is permitted, without the use of a warning line, provided that OSHA guidelines for measuring the roof are followed. As a general rule, the width is measured parallel to the edge across the minimum dimension of the roof. If there are various sections of a building roof that are different sizes, the minimum dimension across each section would be used to determine the width of the roof for purposes of compliance with OSHA rules. (Refer to Appendix A of Subpart M for measurement guidelines and illustrations.)

A safety monitoring system is the least effective option for fall protec-

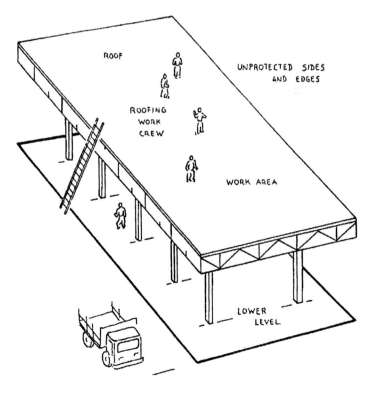

A typical safety monitoring system

tion, because there are many potential weaknesses:

- ◆ Monitor may be inattentive.

- ◆ Monitor's attention may be momentarily distracted.

- ◆ Monitor may be unable to anticipate worker's loss of balance.

- ◆ Worker may be unable to react to monitor's warning once balance has been lost.

- ◆ Background noise or hearing loss may interfere with worker's ability to hear monitor's warning.

- ◆ Monitor and worker may be deceived by appearance of roofing felt that extends over edge without being tacked or wrapped.

- ◆ Worker may react to spilled hot roofing tar in a way that could result in a fall which could not be foreseen by a monitor.

- ◆ Unexpected difficulties while handling materials at the edge of a roof may cause a worker to fall before the monitor can say anything.

LEADING EDGES AND STEEP ROOFS

Some types of roofs are constructed using metal rolls or other methods that involve what OSHA calls "leading edges." A leading edge is the edge of a floor, roof, or formwork for a floor or deck or other walking or working surface which changes location as additional sections are placed, formed, or built. A leading edge is considered unprotected when it is not actively and continuously under construction.

Sides and edges are considered "unprotected" when there is no wall or guardrail system at least 39 inches high (except for an entrance or point of access).

Each employee who is constructing a leading edge, or who is on a steep roof with unprotected sides and edges that are 6 feet or more above a lower level, must be protected from falling by one of the following methods:

- ◆ Standard guardrails with toeboards; OR

- ◆ Safety nets; OR

- ◆ A personal fall arrest system.

A lower level is any area or surface onto which an employee can fall, such as the ground, floor, platform, ramp, runway, excavation, pit, tank, water, equipment, structures, etc.

Fall Protection Plan—Leading Edge Work

If an employer can prove that the above fall protection measures are infeasible (impossible) or could create a greater hazard while performing leading edge work, there must be a formal Fall Protection Plan. (Refer to information at end of Chapter 3.)

Even when the employer has a Fall Protection Plan, other workers in the area of leading edge work who are not involved in it must be protected by guardrails, safety nets, or a personal fall arrest system. If there is a control line that separates other areas from the controlled access zone where leading edge work is being done, and other workers are not allowed access, then the control line can be considered as protection that is equivalent to a guardrail for the unprotected edge on the other side of the control line.

When control lines are used, they must be erected at least 6 feet, but not more than 25 feet, from the unprotected or leading edge (except for precast concrete work). The control line must extend along the entire length of the unprotected edge or leading edge, and must be approximately parallel to it. Each control line must have a minimum breaking strength of 200 pounds and may be made of ropes, wires, tapes, or equivalent materials. Like warning lines, control lines must be flagged at intervals of 6 feet or less with high visibility flags or materials. Although control lines are supported on stanchions like warning lines, an important difference is that a control line must be connected on each side to a guardrail system or a wall.

CONTROLLED ACCESS ZONES

A controlled access zone (CAZ) means an area in which certain work (such as overhand bricklaying or certain types of concrete construction) may take place without the use of a guardrail system, personal fall arrest system, or safety net system. However, access to the zone is limited to the employees engaged in the work.

A safety monitoring system is an option for work in a controlled access zone.

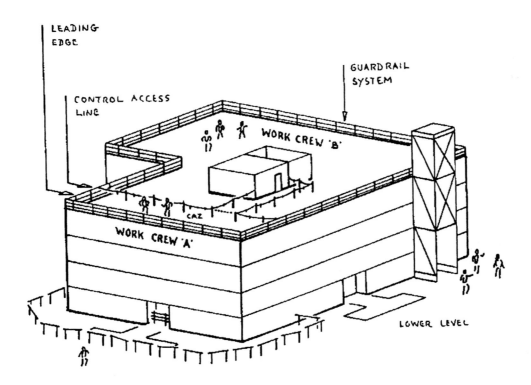

Controlled access zone (CAZ) with safety monitoring system

Overhand Bricklaying

On floors and roofs where guardrail systems are not in place prior to the beginning of overhand bricklaying operations, controlled access zones shall be enlarged, as necessary, to enclose all points of access, material handling areas, and storage areas.

On floors and roofs where guardrail systems are in place but need to be removed to allow overhand bricklaying work or leading edge work to take place, only that portion of the guardrail necessary to accomplish that day's work may be removed.

When control lines are used to control access to areas where overhand bricklaying and related work is being done, they must be placed at least 10 feet, but no more than 15 feet, from the working edge. Additional lines must be installed at each end of the work area to enclose the controlled access zone. Control lines for overhand bricklaying operations may be up to 50 inches high.

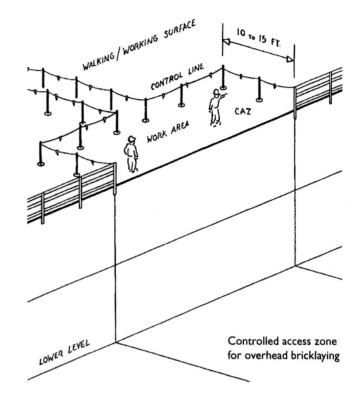

Controlled access zone for overhead bricklaying

Controlled Access Zones for Precast Concrete Members

Only employees engaged in erecting precast concrete members are allowed in the controlled access zone. When erecting precast concrete members, the distance from the control line to the leading edge must be not less than 6 feet, nor more than 60 feet, or half the length of the concrete member being erected, whichever is less.

Subpart Q of the OSHA Construction Standards covers concrete and masonry construction. There are a number of specialized requirements for concrete construction that are intended to prevent concrete beams, slabs, or panels from falling.

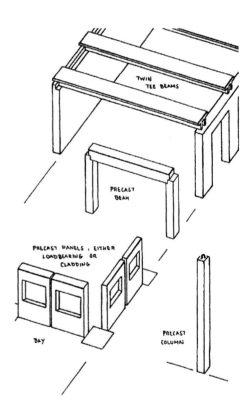

Examples of typical precast concrete members

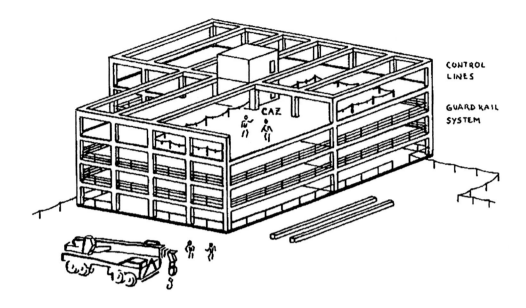

Controlled access zone for precast concrete members

Limited Access Zone for Masonry Walls

A limited access zone is required whenever a masonry wall is being constructed. The limited access zone must be equal to the height of the wall to be constructed plus four feet. It must run the entire length of the wall.

The limited access zone must be established on the side of the wall that is not scaffolded. Only employees who are actively constructing the wall are allowed in the limited access zone. It must remain in place until the wall is adequately supported to prevent overturning and to prevent collapse.

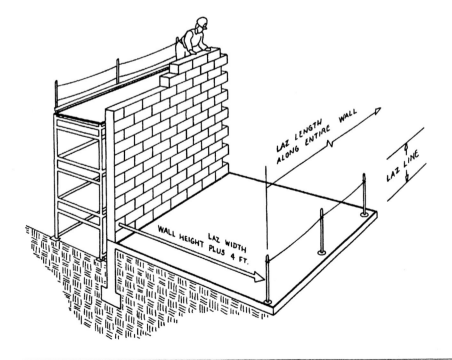

Limited access zone for masonry wall construction

STEEL ERECTION

OSHA has proposed new steel erection standards that apply to activities such as hoisting, connecting, welding, bolting, and rigging structural steel, steel joists, and metal buildings; installing metal deck, siding systems, miscellaneous metals, ornamental iron, and similar materials; and moving point-to-point while performing these activities.

Overview

An *Compliance Magazine* article by Bob Wujek and Joseph Feldstein summarized the key provisions of the proposed standards:[3]

- ◆ A 15' trigger height is established for the use of fall protection equipment.
- ◆ Fall protection may include any of the following systems:
  - A. perimeter safety cable systems;
  - B. guard rail systems;
  - C. safety net systems; and
  - D. personal fall arrest or fall restraint (work positioning) systems.

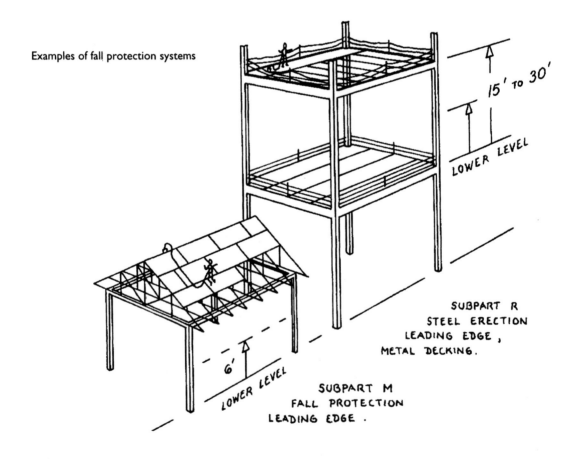

Examples of fall protection systems

15' TO 30'

LOWER LEVEL

SUBPART R
STEEL ERECTION
LEADING EDGE,
METAL DECKING.

6'

LOWER LEVEL

SUBPART M
FALL PROTECTION
LEADING EDGE.

♦ Workers performing steel connecting must be provided with fall arrest or fall restraint equipment when working at heights over 15' and up to 30' above a lower level, but they may use their judgment whether to actually tie-off under certain circumstances. The rule-making committee believes that under certain conditions, the connector is at greater risk if he or she is tied-off. For example, in the event of structural collapse, a tied-off connector could be forced to ride the structure to the ground. The committee believes that "...the connector is in the best position to determine when to tie-off, and so the connector must have the ability to choose to tie-off."

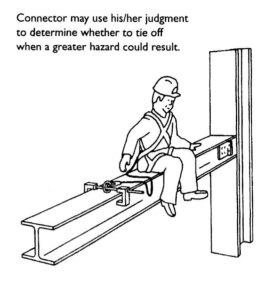

Connector may use his/her judgment to determine whether to tie off when a greater hazard could result.

♦ A controlled decking zone is defined as one in which trained workers may perform leading edge work in areas of a structure over 15' and up to 30' above a lower level without fall protection. The committee developed a combination of specification and work practice requirements to protect employees engaged in decking activities if the employer elects to establish a controlled decking zone rather than provide fall protection as otherwise required by this section.

Proposed Steel Erection Standards for Structural Steel Assembly

New provisions related to fall protection in structural steel assembly include the following:

Proposed 1926.754(b)

The following additional requirements shall apply for multi-story structures:

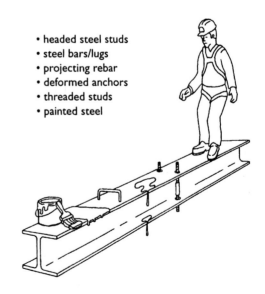

• headed steel studs
• steel bars/lugs
• projecting rebar
• deformed anchors
• threaded studs
• painted steel

(3) A fully planked or decked floor or nets shall be maintained within 2 stories or 30 feet (9.1 m), whichever is less, directly under any erection work being performed.

Proposed 1926.754(c) Walking/working surfaces

(1) **Shear connectors and other similar devices.**

    (i) **Tripping hazards.** Shear connectors (such as headed steel studs, steel bars or steel lugs), reinforcing bars, deformed anchors, or threaded studs shall not be

Tripping or slipping hazards on skeletal structural steel

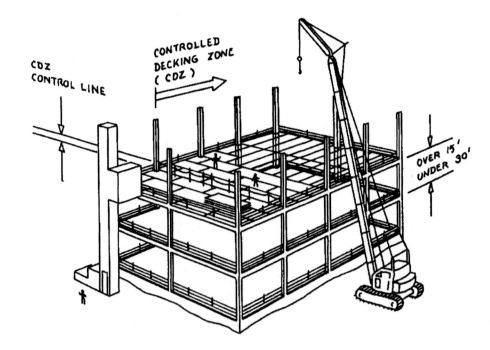

Decking requirements for multi-story structures during erection

attached to the top flanges of beams, joists or beam attachments so that they project vertically from or horizontally across the top flange of the member until after the decking, or other walking/working surface, has been installed.

(ii) **Installation of shear connectors on composite floors, roofs, and bridge decks.** When shear connectors are utilized in construction of composite floors, roofs, and bridge decks, employees shall lay out and install the shear connectors after the decking has been installed, using the deck as a working platform. Shear connectors shall not be installed from within a controlled decking zone (CDZ), as specified in Sec. 1926.760(c)(8).

(3) **Skeletal structural steel.** Workers shall not be permitted to walk the top surface of any structural steel member installed after [effective date of final rule] which has been finish-coated with paint or similar material unless documentation or certification, based on an appropriate ASTM standard test method, is provided that the finished coat has not decreased the coefficient of friction (COF) from that of the original steel before it was finish-coated. Such documentation or certification shall be available at the site and to the steel erector. (See Appendix B of this subpart.)

Proposed Steel Erection Standards for Decking

Proposed 1926.754(e) Decking

(1) **Hoisting, landing, and placing of deck bundles.**

    (i) Bundle packaging and strapping shall not be used for hoisting unless specifically designed for that purpose.

Guarding against falling material hazards

Secure loose items to bundles

(ii) If loose items such as dunnage, flashing, or other materials are placed on the top of deck bundles to be hoisted, such items shall be secured to the bundles.

(iii) Bundles of decking on joists shall be landed in accordance with Sec. 1926.757(e)(4).

(iv) Bundles shall be landed on framing members so that enough support is provided to allow the bundles to be unbanded without dislodging the bundles from the supports.

(v) At the end of the shift or when environmental or jobsite conditions require, decking shall be secured against displacement.

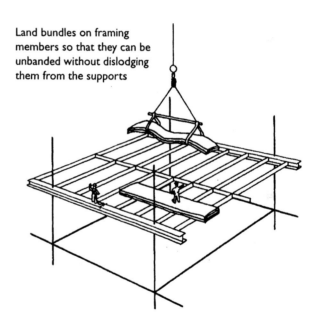

Land bundles on framing members so that they can be unbanded without dislodging them from the supports

Secure decking against displacement when wind or job site conditions require it and at the end of each shift

Proposed 1926.754(e)

(2) **Roof and floor openings.** Metal deck at roof and floor openings shall be installed as follows:

(i) Where structural design and constructability allow, framed deck openings shall have structural members turned down to allow continuous deck installation.

Proposed steel erection standards for decking

- do not cut holes until needed
- cover/protect holes immediately
- framed deck openings should have structural members turned down to allow continuous decking

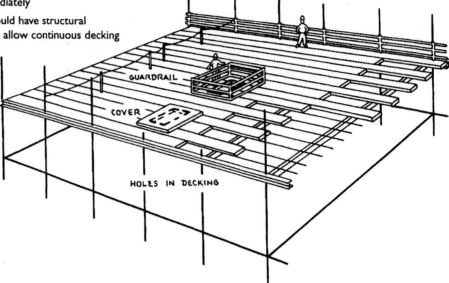

(ii) Roof and floor openings shall be covered during the decking process. Where structural design does not allow openings to be covered, they shall be protected in accordance with Sec. 1926.760(a)(2).

(iii) Decking holes and openings shall not be cut until essential to the construction process, and openings shall be protected immediately in accordance with Sec. 1926.760(d) or be otherwise permanently filled.

(3) **Space around columns.** Wire mesh, exterior plywood, or equivalent, shall be used around columns where planks or decking do not fit tightly.

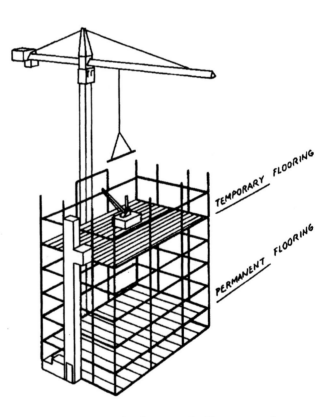

Requirements for flooring as building is erected

(4) **Floor decking.** Floor decking shall be laid tightly and secured to prevent accidental movement or displacement.

(5) Derrick floors.

(i) A derrick floor shall be fully decked and/or planked and the steel member connections completed to support the intended floor loading.

(ii) Temporary loads placed on a derrick floor shall be distributed over the underlying support members so as to prevent local overloading of the deck material.

Proposed Steel Erection Standards for Perimeter Safety Cables

Proposed 1926.756

(e) **Perimeter columns.** Perimeter columns shall extend a minimum of 48 inches (1.2 m) above the finished floor to permit installation of perimeter safety cables prior to erection of the next tier except where structural design and constructibility do not allow. (See Appendix F to this subpart.)

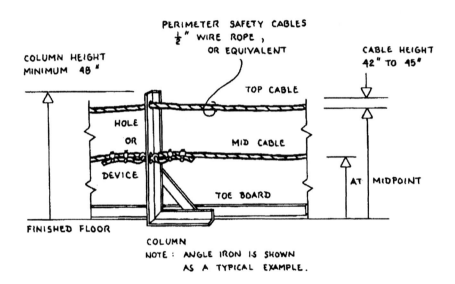

(f) **Perimeter safety cables.**

(1) Perimeter safety cables shall be installed at the perimeter during the structural steel assembly of multi-story structures.

(2) Perimeter safety cables shall consist of ½-inch wire rope or equivalent installed at 42–45 inches above the finished floor and at the midpoint between the finished floor and the top cable.

(3) Holes or other devices shall be provided by the fabricator/supplier and shall be in or attached to perimeter columns at 42–45 inches above the finished floor and the midpoint between the finished floor and the top cable to permit installation of perimeter safety cables except where structural design and constructibility allow. (See Appendix F of this subpart.)

Proposed Standards for Erection of Steel Joists

Proposed 1926.757

(c) Erection of steel joists.

(1) One end of each steel joist shall be attached to the support structure before an employee is allowed on the steel joist.

(2) On steel joists that span 40 feet (12.2 m) or less and that do not require erection bridging per Tables A and B, only one employee shall be allowed on the joist until all bridging is installed and anchored.

(3) Employees shall not be allowed on steel joists that span more than 40 feet except in accordance with Sec. 1926.757(d).

(4) When permanent bridging terminus points cannot be used during erection, additional temporary bridging terminus points are required to provide stability. (See Appendix C of this subpart.)

(d) Erection bridging.

(1) Where the span of the steel joist is equal to or greater than the span shown in Tables A and B, or in bays of 40 feet (12.2 m) through 60 feet (18.3 m), the following shall apply:

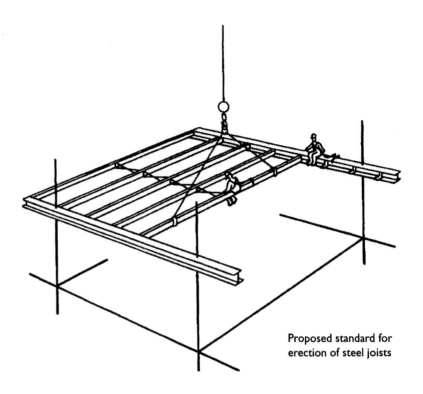

Proposed standard for erection of steel joists

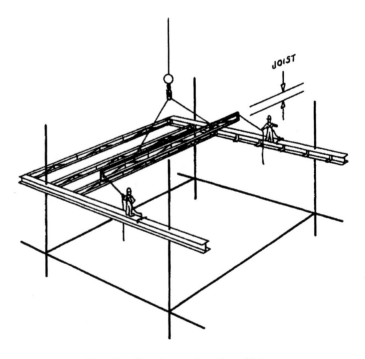

Use of tag lines in erection of steel joists

(i) The row of erection bridging nearest the midspan of the steel joist shall be bolted diagonal bridging;

(ii) Hoisting cables shall not be released until this bolted diagonal erection bridging is installed; and

(iii) No more than one employee shall be allowed on these spans until all other bridging is installed and anchored.

(2) Where the span of the steel joist is over 60 feet (18.3 m) through 100 feet (30.5 m), the following shall apply:

(i) The two rows of erection bridging nearest the third points of the steel joist shall be bolted diagonal bridging;

(ii) Hoisting cables shall not be released until this bolted diagonal erection bridging is installed; and

(iii) No more than two employees shall be allowed on these spans until all other bridging is installed and anchored.

(3) Where the span of the steel joist is over 100 feet (30.5 m) through 144 feet (43.9 m), the following shall apply:

(i) All rows of bridging shall be bolted diagonal bridging;

(ii) Hoisting cables shall not be released until all bridging is installed; and

(iii) No more than two employees shall be allowed on these spans until all bridging is installed.

Proposed Steel Erection Standards for Pre-Engineered Metal Buildings

Proposed 1926.758

(g) Purlins and girts shall not be used as an anchorage point for a fall arrest system unless written direction to do so is obtained from a qualified person.

(h) Purlins may only be used as a walking/working surface when installing safety systems, after all permanent bridging has been installed and fall protection is provided.

Definitions from proposed 1926.751

Pre-engineered metal building means a field-assembled building system consisting of framing, roof, and wall coverings, and it is generally made of steel. Typically, in a pre-engineered metal building, many of these components are cold-formed shapes. These individual parts are fabricated in one or more manufacturing facilities and shipped to the job site for assembly. Engineering design of the system is normally the responsibility of the pre-engineered metal building manufacturer.

Purlin (in pre-engineered metal buildings) means a Z- or C-shaped member formed from sheet steel spanning the primary framing and supporting roof material.

Girt (in pre-engineered metal buildings) means a Z- or C-shaped member formed from sheet steel spanning the primary framing and supporting wall material.

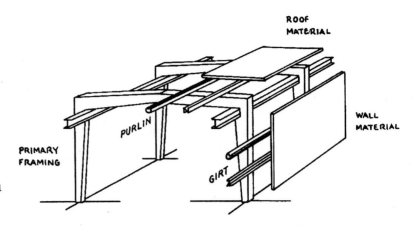

Pre-engineered metal buildings: purlin and girt

Proposed Steel Erection Standards on Falling Object Protection

Proposed 1926.759

(a) **Securing loose items aloft.** All materials, equipment, and tools, which are not in use while aloft, shall be secured against accidental displacement.

(b) **Overhead protection.** The controlling contractor shall ensure that no other construction processes take place below steel erection unless adequate overhead protection for the employees below is provided.

Proposed Steel Erection Standards—Fall Protection

Sec. 1926.760 Fall protection.

(a) **General requirements.**

(1) Except as provided by paragraph (a)(3) of this section, each employee covered by this subpart who is on a walking/working surface with an unprotected side or edge more than 15 feet (4.6 m) above a lower level shall be protected from fall hazards.

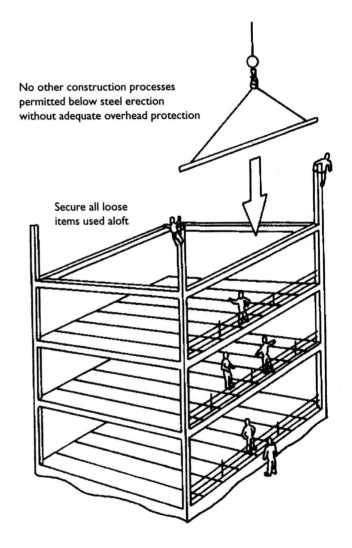

No other construction processes permitted below steel erection without adequate overhead protection

Secure all loose items used aloft

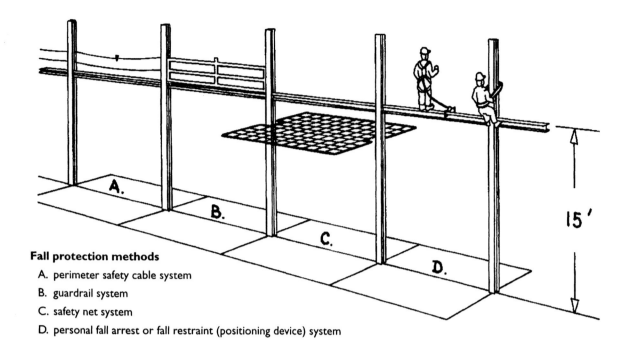

Fall protection methods

A. perimeter safety cable system

B. guardrail system

C. safety net system

D. personal fall arrest or fall restraint (positioning device) system

(2) Protection from fall hazards required by this subpart shall consist of perimeter safety cable systems, guardrail systems, safety net systems, or personal fall arrest or fall restraint (positioning device) systems. Guardrail systems, safety net systems, personal fall arrest systems and fall restraint (positioning device) systems shall conform to the criteria set forth in Sec. 1926.502.

(3) Connectors and employees working in controlled decking zones shall be protected from fall hazards as provided in paragraphs (b) and (c) of this section, respectively.

(b) **Connectors.** Each connector shall:

(1) Be protected from fall hazards of more than two stories or 30 feet (9.1 m) above a lower level, whichever is less;

(2) Have completed connector training in accordance with Sec. 1926.761; and

(3) Be provided, at heights over 15 and up to 30 feet above a lower level, with a personal fall arrest or fall restraint (positioning device) system and wear the equipment necessary to be able to be tied off; or be provided with other means of protection from fall hazards in accordance with paragraph (a)(2) of this section.

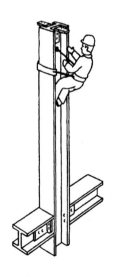

Positioning system

• connector toggle and lanyard

• work positioning belt

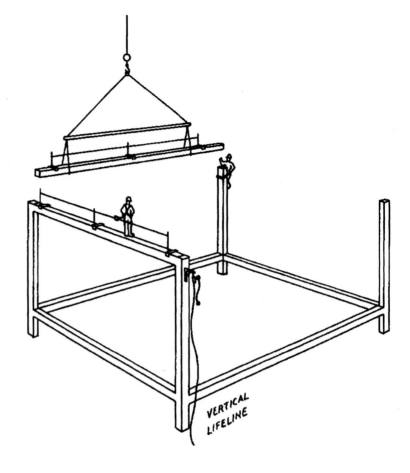

Examples of horizontal and vertical lifelines
as part of a fall protection system

VERTICAL
LIFELINE

(e) **Custody of fall protection.** Fall protection provided by the steel erector shall remain in an area to be used by other trades after the steel erection activity has been completed only if the controlling contractor or its authorized representative:

(1) Has directed the steel erector to leave the fall protection in place; and

(2) Has inspected and accepted control and responsibility of the fall protection prior to authorizing persons other than steel erectors to work in the area.

NOTE: *Climbing Rebar Assemblies*

With regard to whether paragraph 1926.501(b)(5) of the final rule on subpart M applies to employees while moving vertically and/or horizontally on the vertical face of rebar assemblies built in place, "...fall protection is not normally required when employees are moving. OSHA considers that the multiple hand holds and foot holds on rebar assemblies as providing similar protection as that provided by a fixed

Climbing rebar assembly

ladder. Similarly, no fall protection is necessary while moving point to point for heights below 24 feet."[4] However, the use of rebar chain fall protection devices should be encouraged.

Proposed Steel Erection Standards—Controlled Access Zones for Leading Edge Work

(c) **Controlled decking zone (CDZ).** A controlled decking zone may be established in that area of the structure over 15 and up to 30 feet above a lower level where metal deck is initially being installed and forms the leading edge of a work area. In each CDZ, the following shall apply:

Positioning device, rebar chain assembly

(1) Each employee working at the leading edge in a CDZ shall be protected from fall hazards of more than two stories or 30 feet (9.1 m), whichever is less.

(2) Access to a CDZ shall be limited exclusively to those employees engaged in leading edge work.

(3) The boundaries of a CDZ shall be designated and clearly marked. The CDZ shall not be more than 90 feet (27.4 m) wide and 90 feet (27.4 m) deep from any leading edge. The CDZ shall be marked by the use of control lines or the equivalent. Examples of acceptable procedures for demarcating CDZ's can be found in Appendix D to this subpart.

(4) Each employee working in a CDZ shall have completed CDZ training in accordance with Sec. 1926.761.

(5) During initial placement, deck panels shall be placed to ensure full support by structural members.

(6) Unsecured decking in a CDZ shall not exceed 3000 square feet (914.4 m²).

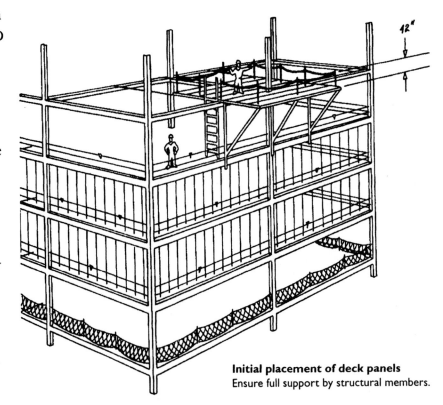

Initial placement of deck panels
Ensure full support by structural members.

**Controlled decking zone (CDZ)
general requirements**

- unsecured decking in a CDZ
  shall not exceed 3000 sq. ft.

- final deck attachments and
  shear connectors not allowed
  in CDZ

- safety deck attachments from
  leading edge back to the
  control line and ≥ 2
  attachments per panel

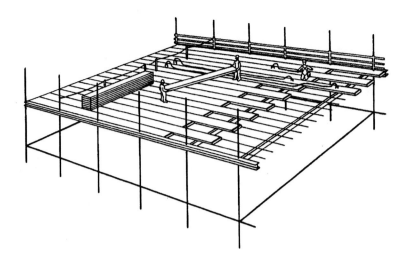

(7) Safety deck attachments shall be performed in the CDZ from the leading edge back to the control line and shall have at least two attachments per deck panel.

(8) Final deck attachments and installation of shear connectors shall not be performed in the CDZ.

Controlled decking zone (CDZ) with
control line and leading edge work

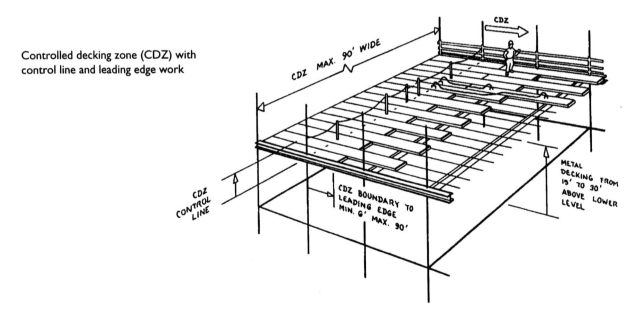

Proposed Appendix D to Subpart R

Illustration of the Use of Control Lines to Demarcate Controlled Decking Zones (CDZs): Non-Mandatory Guidelines for Complying with Sec. 1926.760(c)(3)

(1) When used to control access to areas where leading edge and initial securement of metal deck and other operations connected with leading edge work are taking place, the controlled decking zone (CDZ) is defined by a control line or by any other means that restricts access.

(i) A control line for a CDZ is erected not less than 6 feet (1.8 m) nor more than 90 feet (27.4 m) from the leading edge.

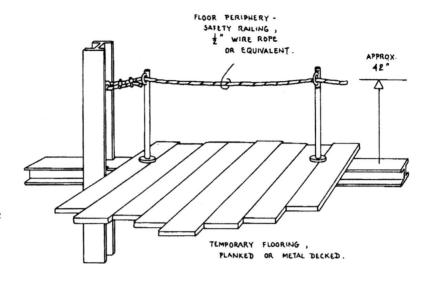

Floor periphery safety railing for all temporary flooring

(ii) Control lines extend along the entire length of the unprotected or leading edge and are approximately parallel to the unprotected or leading edge.

(iii) Control lines are connected on each side to a guardrail system, wall, stanchion or other suitable anchorage.

(2) Control lines consist of ropes, wires, tapes, or equivalent materials, and supporting stanchions as follows:

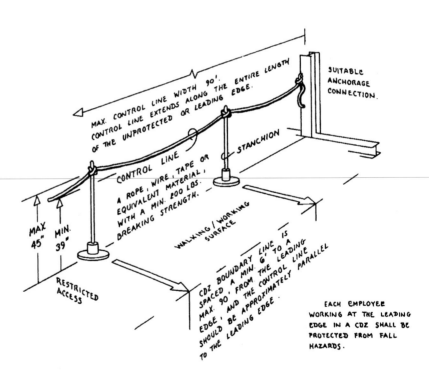

Control line specifications for controlled decking zone (CDZ)

(i) Each line is rigged and supported in such a way that its lowest point (including sag) is not less than 39 inches (1.0 m) from the walking/working surface and its highest point is not more than 45 inches (1.3 m) from the walking/working surface.

(ii) Each line has a minimum breaking strength of 200 pounds (90.8 kg).

Proposed Steel Erection Standards—Covering Roof and Floor Openings

Proposed 1926.757(d) Covering roof and floor openings.

(1) Covers for roof and floor openings required by Sec. 1926.754 (e)(2)(ii) and (e)(2)(iii) shall be capable of supporting, without failure, the greater of either:

    (i) 30 psf for roofs and 50 psf for floors; or

    (ii) twice the weight of the employees, equipment, and materials that may be imposed on the cover at any one time.

(2) All covers shall be secured when installed to prevent accidental displacement by the wind, equipment, or employees.

(3) All covers shall be painted with high-visibility paint or shall be marked with the word "HOLE" or "COVER" to provide warning of the hazard.

(4) Smoke dome or skylight fixtures, which have been installed, are not considered covers for the purpose of this section unless they meet the strength requirements of paragraph (d)(1) of this section.

ELECTRICAL TRANSMISSION AND DISTRIBUTION

29 CFR 1910.269(e)(5) and 1910.269(g)(2)

General Industry Standards for electrical transmission and distribution workers, issued in 1994, introduced the concept of a *qualified climber*, which applies to journeymen and trained linemen when weather conditions are suitable.

Fall protection is required for all trainees and when weather conditions increase the hazards associated with climbing poles and towers.

1910.269(g)(2)(v)

Fall arrest equipment, work positioning equipment, or travel restricting equipment shall be used by employees working at elevated locations more than 4 feet (1.2 m) above the ground on poles, towers, or similar structures if other fall protection has not been provided. Fall protection equipment is not required to be used by a qualified employee climbing or changing location on poles, towers, or similar structures, unless conditions, such as, but not limited to, ice, high winds, the design of the structure (for example, no provision for holding on with hands), or the presence of contaminants on the structure, could cause the employee to lose his or her grip or footing.

NOTE 1: This paragraph applies to structures that support overhead electric power generation, transmission, and distribution lines and equipment. It does not apply to portions of buildings, such as loading docks, to electric equipment, such as transformers and capacitors, nor to aerial lifts. Requirements for fall protection associated with walking and working surfaces are contained in subpart D of this Part; requirements for fall protection associated with aerial lifts are contained in 1910.67 of this Part.

NOTE 2: Employees undergoing training are not considered "qualified employees" for the purposes of this provision. Unqualified employees (including trainees) are required to use fall protection any time they are more than 4 feet (1.2 m) above the ground.

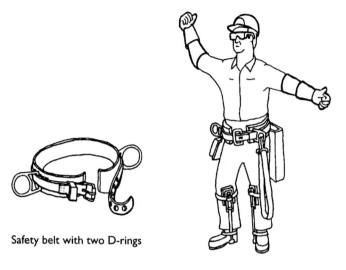

Safety belt with two D-rings

Personal protective equipment (PPE) for qualified electrical transmission or distribution worker

Removal of Covers

1910.269(e)(5)

Removal of covers. When covers are removed from enclosed spaces, the opening shall be promptly guarded by a railing, temporary cover, or other barrier intended to prevent an accidental fall through the opening and to protect employees working in the space from objects entering the space.

WHY YOU MAY NEED TO KNOW ABOUT SPECIAL TRADES

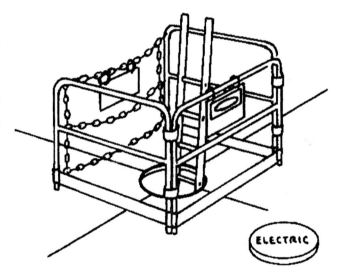

Guarding requirements for uncovered manholes

Special rules apply for specific applications as outlined in this chapter. These applications include trades that are at a high risk of falling—roofers, masons, ironworkers, and electric utility workers.

Personnel who have safety responsibilities related to coordinating, inspecting or auditing this work need to have a basic understanding of what is acceptable and what is unsafe, so that they can intervene when necessary.

ENDNOTES

1. "26-year-old dies from injuries suffered in Plano fall," *Dallas Morning News*, Tuesday, January 5, 1999, page 12A.

2. "Contractor Referred for Criminal Prosecution," *Compliance Magazine*, October 1998, page 21.

3. Bob Wujek and Joseph Feldstein, "Fall Protection: Beyond Harnesses and Lanyards," *Compliance Magazine*, January 1999, page 22.

4. OSHA Interpretation, §1926.501, "Fall protection during rebar assembly construction," December 23, 1994.

Fall Protection Workshop

EXERCISE FOR SMALL GROUPS

After dividing into small groups, participants should consider the situations outlined below in light of all the information that has been presented in this book, along with personal knowledge and experience.

Each group will be responsible for listing safety recommendations to prevent injuries caused by falls and falling objects. A spokesperson for each group should orally summarize the group's consensus.

Window Washing

"The universal problem for all suspended scaffolding window cleaning contractors is the lack of predesignated tie-backs for scaffold and independent lifelines on building roofs. ...Using air-conditioning equipment, exhaust or piping systems for rigging tie-backs and lifeline anchorage points is not realistic for safe contractor work on buildings."[1]

Questions

♦ What option for fall protection is best and what other options are acceptable?

Recommendations

_____

_____

_____

_____

_____

_____
_____
_____
_____
_____
_____
_____
_____

Tops of Trucks, Tank Trucks, or Intermodal Containers

There are many situations in which workers or contractors may have to perform some task on top of a truck, tank truck, or intermodal container.

Questions

- Describe some situations in which work must be done from the tops of trucks, tank trucks, or intermodal containers.

- Recommend fall protection measures for each situation described.

Recommendations

_____
_____
_____
_____
_____
_____
_____
_____
_____
_____
_____
_____
_____
_____

Installation of Flat Metal Roof Rolls—Leading Edge Work

Many falls have occurred during roof construction using rolls of metal roofing material.

Questions

- ◆ List fall protection measures and safe work practices that should be followed while performing this work.

- ◆ Describe any practices that you feel are so unsafe as to warrant shutting the job down.

Recommendations

_____

_____

_____

_____

_____

_____

_____

_____

_____

_____

_____

_____

_____

_____

_____

_____

_____

_____

_____

_____

_____

Repair or Replacement Involving Removal of Raised Flooring

A fall hazard, caused by removal of sections of the floor, may exist while raised flooring is being repaired or when it is being replaced.

Questions

- Describe locations at your facility where raised flooring is used. What is located under the raised flooring?

- Recommend safe work practices to prevent falls of workers and passers-by.

Recommendations

_____

_____

_____

_____

_____

_____

_____

_____

_____

_____

_____

_____

_____

_____

_____

_____

_____

_____

_____

_____

Work on Top of an Atrium

Work may occasionally be done on top of an atrium, such as washing the windows or repairs after a storm.

Question

◆ What hazards are involved in work on top of an atrium? List these hazards along with recommended controls. Concentrate on fall protection.

Recommendations

_____

_____

_____

_____

_____

_____

_____

_____

_____

_____

_____

_____

_____

_____

_____

_____

_____

_____

_____

_____

_____

_____

_____

_____

GROUP DISCUSSION

The instructor and class participants may comment on additional considerations after each group's representative has presented the group's findings. If questions remain or there are issues that cannot be resolved, the instructor will make a note of them to follow up at a later date.

ENDNOTE

1. J. Nigel Ellis, *Introduction to Fall Protection* (Des Plaines, IL: American Society of Safety Engineers, 1993), page 148.

Summary
of Key Points

CHAPTER 1—TREND ANALYSIS

Fatal Falls

♦ Falls to a lower level accounted for 8 to 11 percent of fatal job injuries in Texas from 1993 through 1997.

♦ In the construction industry, falls represent anywhere from about 28 to 33 percent of fatal injuries.

♦ An OSHA study of 99 fall-related fatalities suggests that virtually all of those deaths could have been prevented by the use of guardrails, body belts, body harnesses, safety nets, covers, or other means that would reduce employee exposure to the fall hazard.

♦ One study by the Texas Workers' Compensation Commission indicated that problem areas include falls from roofs, scaffolding, building girders or structural steel, and ladders. Many falls involve young, unskilled Hispanic laborers.

Disabling Falls

♦ Bureau of Labor Statistics data over a 3-year period indicates that a disproportionately high number of disabling falls to a lower level occur in two industries:

1. roofing, siding, and sheet metal work; and
2. masonry, stonework, and plastering.

Skylights

♦ A NIOSH survey in seven states revealed that about 22 percent of the fatal falls that were reported occurred when workers fell through skylight openings or smoke-vent skylights.

Steel Erection

◆ An in-depth study of hazards related to steel erection was done by OSHA in conjunction with the Steel Erection Negotiated Rulemaking Advisory Committee (SENRAC). The major activities that were being performed when fatal falls occurred were decking, connecting, and bolting. Two identified primary factors that contributed to fatal falls were slips and collapse. Fall protection was not provided or used in almost 88 percent of the fatalities.

OSHA Citations

◆ Violations of standards related to fall prevention and protection represent 15 out of the top 50 most frequently cited OSHA standards for the construction industry.

CHAPTER 2— OVERVIEW OF APPLICABLE REGULATORY STANDARDS

Construction Standards

Unprotected Side or Edge

◆ Before work is done in an elevated location, a competent person must inspect walking/working surfaces to ensure they are strong enough to safely support workers.

◆ When there is a 6-foot or greater drop from an unprotected side or edge, workers must be protected by a guardrail system, safety net system, or personal fall arrest system.

Fall Protection Plan

◆ When conventional fall protection measures are impossible or would create a greater hazard, there must be a formal Fall Protection Plan.

Roof/Floor Openings

◆ Each employee who could fall 6 feet or more through a hole, skylight, or other roof or floor opening must be protected by a personal fall arrest system or covers or guardails.

Access between Levels

◆ A double-cleated ladder or two or more separate ladders must be provided when ladders are the only means of access or exit from a working area for 25 or more employees, or when a ladder is to serve simultaneous two-way traffic.

◆ At least one point of access between levels must be kept clear to permit free passage of employees.

♦ When guardrail systems are employed around holes (such as ladderways) which are used as points of access, they shall be provided with a gate or be offset so that a person cannot walk directly into the hole.

♦ Unprotected sides and edges of stairway landings must have guardrails.

General Industry Standards

Guardrails

♦ Covers and/or guardrails shall be provided to protect personnel from the hazards of open pits, tanks, vats, ditches, etc.

♦ Every open-sided floor or platform 4 feet or more above the adjacent floor or ground level must have standard guardrails.

♦ Toeboards are required when persons may pass below or where there is moving machinery or equipment with which falling materials could create a hazard.

Dangerous Equipment

♦ Regardless of height, there must be standard guardrails with toeboards on walking and working surfaces adjacent to dangerous equipment.

Stairs

♦ Every flight of stairs having four or more risers must have standard stair railings.

♦ Where doors or gates open directly onto a stairway, a platform shall be provided, and the swing of the door shall not reduce the effective width to less than 20 inches.

Wall Openings

♦ Every wall opening from which there is a drop of more than 4 feet shall be guarded by a barrier such as a screen, rail, roller, picket fence, or half door.

Window Openings

♦ Every window wall opening at a stairway landing, floor, platform, or balcony, from which there is a drop of more than 4 feet, and where the bottom of the opening is less than 3 feet above the platform or landing, shall be guarded by standard slats, standard grill work, or standard rails.

STEEL ERECTION

Floor or Decking

- ◆ Where skeleton steel erection is being done, a tightly planked and substantial floor shall be maintained within two stories or 30 feet, whichever is less, below and directly under that portion of each tier of beams on which any work is being performed.

- ◆ The erection floor shall be solidly planked or decked over its entire surface except for access openings. Planking or metal decking shall be laid tight and secured to prevent movement.

- ◆ Wire mesh, exterior plywood, or the equivalent shall be used around columns where planks do not fit tightly.

Perimeter Protection

- ◆ A safety railing of ½-inch wire rope or the equivalent must be installed about 42 inches high around the perimeter of all temporary planked floors or temporary metal deck floors.

Unused Floor Openings

- ◆ All unused openings in floors, temporary or permanent, shall be completely planked over or guarded.

Safety Nets

- ◆ Safety nets must be installed whenever the potential fall distance exceeds two stories or 25 feet on buildings or structures that are not adaptable to temporary floors and where scaffolds are not used.

CHAPTER 3—PRINCIPLES OF FALL PROTECTION

- ◆ As free fall distance increases, arresting forces or forces upon impact also increase. Limiting the free fall distance to less than 2 feet is the most effective way to prevent serious injuries.

- ◆ When free fall distance cannot practically be held below 2 feet, adequate shock absorption and proper body support are of critical importance, along with rapid rescue.

- ◆ A relatively safe level for arresting forces is about 650 pounds.

Body Support Systems

- ◆ There are five main functions of body support systems which require different design features:

1. fall arrest
2. climbing protection
3. work positioning
4. fall restraint
5. rescue and retrieval

One Hundred Percent Fall Protection

♦ One hundred percent fall protection means that no exposure to an elevated fall hazard is permitted without backup protection. It means continuous protection.

♦ Exposure can be prevented by:
1. establishing walls, floors, and guardrails;
2. using work platforms and aerial lifts;
3. implementing an operational change; or
4. restricting workers' travel and erecting warning lines 6 or more feet away from an exposed edge.

Effective Program

♦ The basic steps to implement an effective fall protection program are as follows:
1. establish a fall hazard committee;
2. designate program coordinators;
3. train the workforce;
4. implement fall hazard controls; and
5. evaluate implemented controls.

Hazard Analysis

♦ A complete analysis should be done before designing or specifying fall protection for each job:
1. Identify fall hazards.
2. Plan work to eliminate exposure to falls and restrict access to areas where falls may occur.
3. Consider feasibility of guardrails.
4. Consider feasibility of scaffolding or use of manlifts, aerial lifts, or suspended platforms.
5. Select a suitable fall arrest system when above control measures are not feasible.
6. Evaluate requirements for vertical and horizontal mobility.
7. Identify anchor points.
8. Determine environmental conditions, other factors, and additional precautions.

Hierarchy of Solutions

◆ Hierarchy of fall protection solutions:
1. Eliminate fall hazards.
2. Prevent fall hazards.
3. Arrest falls.
4. Implement administrative controls (access restrictions, warning lines, safety monitors, etc.).

Hierarchy of Platforms

◆ Hierarchy of work platforms:
1. Elimination of the need for access/fall protection
2. Engineered platforms
3. Aerial platforms
4. Scaffolds (temporary platforms)
5. Work positioning using belts/seats
6. Ladders and administrative techniques

Fall Protection Program

◆ When a formal Fall Protection Program is required because conventional fall protection is not feasible, it must be prepared, implemented, and kept up to date by a qualified person, and it must apply specifically to the site.

CHAPTER 4—PREVENTION OF FALLS AND FALLING OBJECTS

Notes on Guardrails

◆ Guardrail systems are generally considered to be the most effective means of preventing falls and should be an option that receives preferential consideration.

◆ Do not step on, climb, or straddle guardrails.

◆ Do not lean over or lean through guardrails.

◆ Do not use guardrails as anchor points for a fall arrest system.

Preventing Injuries Caused by Falling Objects

◆ Wear hard hats on construction sites.

◆ Install toeboards, screens, or guardrail systems that will prevent objects from falling from higher levels.

Comparison of Guardrail Specifications

Parameter	Construction	General Industry
Top rail	42" ± 3" high	42" high
Midrail	≥ 21" high	Halfway to floor
Ends of rails*	—— should not overhang posts ——	
Strength of guardrails	≥ 200 lbs. on top rail without failure	
Spacing of 2" x 4" posts	≤ 8 feet	≤ 6 feet
Wood top rail, mid rail	2" x 4"; 1" x 6"	both 2" x 4"
Pipe rails*	≥ 1.5" nominal diameter at ≤ 8 ft. apart	
Structural steel*	≥ 2" x 2" x ⅜" angles at ≤ 8 ft. apart	
Perimeter cables	flags every 6' 42" to 45" high	not specified
Toeboards	≥ 3.5" high ≤ ¼" clearance	4" high ≤ ¼" clearance

* Same specifications for both construction and general industry.

◆ Erect a canopy or debris net or barricade the area below.

◆ Keep objects far enough from the edge to prevent them from falling.

Stored Materials

◆ Material stored inside buildings under construction shall not be placed within 6 feet of any hoistway or inside floor openings, nor within 10 feet of an exterior wall which does not extend above the top of the material stored.

◆ Employees required to work on stored material in silos, hoppers, tanks, and similar storage areas shall use personal fall arrest equipment.

◆ Materials shall not be stored on scaffolds or runways in excess of supplies needed for immediate operations.

◆ Materials and equipment shall not be stored within 6 feet of a roof edge unless guard-rails are erected at the edge.

CHAPTER 5—FALL PROTECTION

- If a fall cannot be prevented by guardrails or other barriers, then a personal fall arrest system should be used.
  - The user must have a rescue plan and the means at hand to implement it should a fall occur.
  - Rescue options may include a basket stretcher with a lifting bridle, availability of an aerial lift, or systems that include features for self-rescue or controlled descent.

Primary vs. Backup Protection

- A personal positioning system or a suspension system (primary protection) should be used in combination with a personal fall arrest system (backup protection). All equipment must be inspected prior to each use.

Compatible Components

- The anchor point, harness, and connecting means must be compatible and designed for the specific application.

Connecting Means

- Connecting means include lanyards and lifelines and associated hardware.
  - Locking snap hooks are required.
  - Always visually check that each snap hook freely engages the D-ring or anchor point and that its keeper is completely closed.
  - Do not attach two snap hooks into one D-ring.
  - Fall protection connecting devices should be attached to the back D-ring of a full body harness or body belt.
  - Side, front, and chest D-rings should be used for positioning only.
  - Shoulder D-rings should be used for retrieval only.
  - Do not attach multiple lanyards together or attach a lanyard back onto itself.
  - Avoid working where your connecting subsystem may cross or tangle with that of another worker.
  - Do not allow connectors to pass under arms or between legs.

Distance and Path of Potential Fall

♦ The length of a lanyard must limit a fall to no more than 6 feet. Lanyards with shock absorbers can elongate up to 3.5 feet. A 100-foot nylon rope will stretch several feet in a fall.

○ Always check to be sure the potential fall path is clear of obstructions.

Lifelines

♦ Lifelines must not be used for any purpose other than fall protection.

♦ Personnel who install lifelines must be protected from falls at all times by using retractable lifelines or by tying off to structural steel or other approved anchor points.

♦ Horizontal lifelines should be used for sideways movement so that fall arrest will occur in a vertical plane.

○ Horizontal lifelines in skeletal steel structures shall be ⅜" cable or larger and shall be secured on each end by at least two cable clamps.

○ Horizontal lifelines must not be used by workers to support their balance or weight at any time.

○ Horizontal lifelines should be attached to body harnesses at waist level or higher.

○ Permanent horizontal lifelines should be ¼" x 2" rigid rail or adequately strong cable that allows a light-weight trolley to slide easily with the worker (one trolley per attached worker).

♦ When vertical lifelines are used, each person must be provided with a separate lifeline.

♦ Static rope lifelines with rope grabs are required for personnel working from two-point suspension scaffolds and are recommended for other operations where tie-off points are limited and vertical mobility is required, such as during the erection of scaffolds and structural steel.

○ Sliding rope grabs, approved for the size rope in use, must be employed to secure a safety lanyard to a vertical lifeline.

○ Rope grabs should be positioned on the lifeline above shoulder level or higher.

♦ Retractable lifeline devices must be secured by means of shackles and wire rope chokers or synthetic slings. Miller Equipment specifies using a locking carabiner or Miller tripods, Quad Pods, davit systems, or wall mounts.

○ A retractable lifeline should be equipped with a rope (¼" synthetic fiber) tag line extending from the reel to lower elevations or to the ground, as applicable.

○ Test retraction and braking mechanism prior to use.

○ Connecting a lanyard to a self-retracting lifeline is *not* recommended.

- ◆ An anchor point must support a dead weight of 5,400 pounds or 5,000 pounds per attached employee or 3,600 pounds when certified by an engineer or qualified professional.
  - ○ It should be independent of the work surface.
- ◆ The strength of an eye-bolt is rated along the axis of the bolt and is greatly reduced if the force is applied at an angle to this axis.
- ◆ Minimum recommended sizes for anchor points:
  - ○ 2" schedule 10 carbon steel or nickel pipe or 2" schedule 10 stainless steel
  - ○ 3" metal pipe or larger if in good condition and if pipe length is continuous for at least two supports on either side of the attachment
  - ○ Span between pipe supports must be 20 feet or less for any size pipe
  - ○ Structural steel, 2.5" x 2.5" x ⅜" angle, if span is 20 feet or less

Anchorages

- ◆ An anchor point for a harness-lanyard combination should be at shoulder level and overhead for lifelines or fall arrest devices.
- ◆ Connector toggles are devices that lock into structural steel bolt holes to provide an attachment point for a lanyard. These devices should be used by structural iron connectors and bolt-up personnel during steel erection.
- ◆ Concrete form tie-offs are devices that attach to patented concrete forms to provide an attachment point for lanyards. They should be used when placing concrete forms at elevations where a fall exposure exists.

Components Stressed in a Fall

- ◆ Any lifeline, safety belt, harness, or lanyard actually subjected to in-service loading (as in a fall) shall be immediately removed from service and shall not be used again for employee safeguarding.

CHAPTER 6—SCAFFOLDS

General Rules for Scaffolds

- ◆ Fall protection requirements are triggered at a 10-foot height for scaffolds.
- ◆ Scaffolds must be inspected by a competent person before each shift and after any event that could affect its structural integrity.

Suppported Scaffolds

◆ Fall protection for supported scaffolds usually consists of guardrails. However, there may be some unique situations in which a properly anchored personal fall arrest system may be necessary.

◆ Poles, legs, posts, frames, and uprights must be plumb and braced to prevent swaying and displacement. Guys, ties, and braces must be installed at each end of the scaffold and at horizontal intervals of 30 feet or less.

◆ Vertical and horizontal tie-ins are required on all supported scaffolds with a height-to-base ratio of more than four times the minimum base width.

   ○ If the scaffold is 3 feet wide or less, it must be tied in at vertical intervals of 20 feet or less.

   ○ If the scaffold is wider than 3 feet, it must be tied in at vertical intervals of 26 feet.

◆ An unbalanced load will require additional bracing to prevent tipping.

◆ Both base plates and mud sills or other adequate firm foundations (e.g., concrete slab) are required.

Access and Change of Direction

◆ Direct access to a supported scaffold must be less than 24 inches away vertically and less than 14 inches away horizontally.

◆ Workers are not allowed to climb cross bracing to access or descend a scaffold.

◆ At all points where the scaffold platform changes direction, the part that rests on a bearer at an angle must be laid first, and platforms that rest at right angles shall be laid on top.

Mobile Ladder Stand and Scaffolds

◆ Occupied mobile ladders shall not be moved.

◆ Mobile ladders shall only be used on level surfaces.

Suspended Scaffolds

Fall Arrest Systems

◆ Some types of suspended scaffolds (such as single-point or two-point adjustable suspension scaffolds) must have both a guardrail system and personal fall arrest system.

◆ On some types of scaffolds, only a personal fall arrest system is required (catenary, float and needle beam scaffolds, boatswain's chairs, roof bracket scaffolds and ladder jack scaffolds).

♦ Attach personal fall arrest systems by lanyard to a vertical lifeline, horizontal lifeline, or scaffold structural member. If lanyards are conected to horizontal lifelines or structural members on single-point or two-point adjustable suspension scaffolds, the scaffold must have additional independent support lines and automatic locking devices to stop the fall of the scaffold.

♦ Vertical lifelines, independent support lines, and suspension ropes must *not* be attached to each other, nor to the same anchor points, nor to the same point on the scaffold or personal fall arrest system.

♦ Fall protection is required when employees install support systems for suspended scaffolds.

Counterbalancing and Securing a Suspended Scaffold

♦ A suspended scaffold should be counterbalanced by at least four times the rated load of the hoist. Flowable materials are not allowed to be used as counterweights.

♦ Two-point and multi-point suspension scaffolds must be tied or secured to prevent swaying. Window cleaner's anchors are not allowed to be used for this purpose.

Hoist Ropes on Suspended Scaffold

♦ There must be no less than 4 wraps of wire rope left on the drum of winding drum hoists at the lowest point of scaffold travel.

♦ A hoist rope must be replaced if it has any physical damage, kinks, 6 broken wires in one lay, or 3 broken wires in one strand in one lay, loss of one-third of its diameter, heat damage, or evidence of engagement of rope by the secondary brake during an overspeed condition.

♦ When wire rope clips are used, there must be a minimum of 3 clips and they must be spaced a minimum of 6 rope diameters apart. The U-bolt must be over the dead end.

Powered Platforms for Building Maintenance

♦ A written emergency plan is required for powered platforms for building maintenance that are permanent installations.

♦ A roof powered platform must have an emergency electric operating device in a secured compartment near the hoisting machine, with a label that provides instructions for use in emergencies.

♦ Winding drum type hoists on fixed installations shall have at least three wraps of the suspension wire rope on the drum when the unit has reached the lowest possible point of vertical travel.

♦ Powered platforms installed in buildings for maintenance shall not be used when wind velocity exceeds 25 miles per hour.

♦ A personal fall arrest system is required for employees who work on powered platforms installed in buildings for maintenance.

CHAPTER 7—LADDERS

Inspection of Ladders

♦ Ladders shall be inspected by a competent person for visible defects on a periodic basis and after any occurrence that could affect their safe use.

♦ Defective ladders must be marked, tagged, or blocked to prevent use and shall be removed from service until repaired.

♦ Ladders must be have skid-resistant rungs or steps and must be kept free of mud or grease.

♦ Wood ladders shall not be painted or coated with an opaque covering.

Safe Use of Ladders

♦ Face the ladder when climbing or descending. Use at least one hand to grasp the ladder when climbing up or down. Do not carry any object or load that could cause you to lose your balance and fall.

♦ The top or top step of a stepladder shall not be used as a step.

♦ Place the foot of a portable straight ladder at a distance from the wall or structure equal to about one-fourth the working length of the ladder.

♦ A ladder must have safety feet or be secured on slippery surfaces such as flat metal or concrete.

♦ When climbing a straight or extension ladder, another person must hold the ladder at its base until the ladder has been secured at the top. Another person must also hold the ladder once it has been untied and the worker is climbing down.

Preventing Falls from Ladders

♦ Secure the ladder to prevent displacement when the ladder could be moved by work activities or when placed in passageways, doorways, or driveways.

♦ When work will be done from a ladder, the worker must first secure his or her safety lanyard after climbing to the work position and shall then secure the ladder by tying it off.

♦ Keep the area around the top and bottom of the ladder clear.

◆ The side rails of a straight ladder must extend at least 3 feet above the upper landing surface. For fixed ladders, this distance is 42 inches.

◆ A retractable lifeline should be placed at the top of temporary construction ladders used for repeated access.

Fixed Ladders

◆ Fixed ladders shall be provided with cages, wells, ladder safety devices that limit a fall to 2 feet or less, or self-retracting lifelines where the length of climb is less than 24 feet, but the top of the ladder is at a distance greater than 24 feet above lower levels.

◆ When the total length of a climb equals or exceeds 24 feet, fixed ladders must have ladder safety devices that limit a fall to 2 feet or less OR self retracting lifelines AND rest platforms at intervals not to exceed 150 feet, OR a cage or well AND offset multiple ladder sections that are 50 feet or less in length.

CHAPTER 8—ELEVATING PERSONNEL

Manlifts and Aerial Lifts

◆ Whenever personnel use manlifts or aerial lifts for work positioning, fall protection is needed, because workers tend to reach outside the guardrails or aerial basket.

　○ Personnel in an aerial basket must wear a body harness with a lanyard that is no longer than 4 feet and is connected to an approved anchor point.

　○ When leaving an aerial basket or manlift platform to perform work at a height of 10 feet or more, fall protection must be provided.

Stock Pickers

◆ Follow manufacturer's recommendations for fall protection on stock pickers. Retractable lines are preferable to lanyards.

　○ Employees on stock pickers should not step across an opening of more than 12 inches.

　○ Employees should not stand or place their whole weight on a rack.

Scissor Lifts

◆ Areas where scissor lifts are used should be blocked off.

◆ Scissor lifts can be top heavy and can be hazardous while traveling. A scissor lift must not make turns while elevated.

Personnel Platform on a Forklift

♦ When a forklift is used to elevate an approved lifting cage or properly designed personnel platform:
  ○ There must be an effective means of securing the platform to the mast of the lift truck.
  ○ There must be a means to allow personnel on the platform to shut off the power to the truck.
  ○ Workers should not be carried to the work site while on the platform.
  ○ Communication must be maintained between the forklift operator and the elevated worker.
  ○ At no time should the operator leave the lift truck while a person is elevated.

Personnel Hoists on Construction Sites

♦ Personnel hoists on construction sites must be properly designed by a qualified engineer.

♦ Personnel hoist must have a securely attached plate that describes its load capacity and other important data.

♦ A personnel hoist must be inspected and tested prior to being placed in service, following major alterations or repairs, and at intervals of 3 months or less. Records must be kept.

Personnel Platform Lifted by a Crane or Derrick

♦ The use of a crane or derrick to hoist employees on a personnel platform is prohibited, except when the erection, use, and dismantling of conventional means of reaching the work site would be more hazardous or when conventional means are not possible because of structural design or work site conditions.

♦ Hoisting of a personnel platform shall be performed in a slow, controlled, cautious manner with no sudden movements of the crane or derrick or the platform.

♦ The crane must be uniformly level and located on firm footing. If the crane has outriggers, they must be used.

♦ The total weight of the loaded personnel platform and rigging shall not exceed 50 percent of the rated capacity for the radius and configuration of the crane or derrick.

♦ The personnel platform and suspension system shall be designed by a qualified engineer or a qualified person competent in structural design.

♦ Personnel platforms shall be used only for employees, their tools, and the materials necessary to do their work.
  ○ They shall not be used to hoist only materials or tools when not hoisting personnel.

♦ Materials and tools for use during a personnel lift shall be secured to prevent displacement.

♦ A trial lift must be conducted with the unoccupied personnel platform loaded at least to the anticipated lift weight. The trial lift should take the platform from ground level to each location where it will be hoisted and positioned in actual use.

○ The trial lift shall be done immediately prior to placing personnel on the platform.

○ An inspection by a competent person must take place immediately afterwards and before hoisting personnel.

○ The trial lift and subsequent inspection by a competent person must be repeated prior to hoisting employees each time the crane or derrick is moved.

♦ Tag lines must be used unless their use creates an unsafe condition.

♦ Except over water, employees occupying the personnel platform shall use a body belt/harness system with lanyard appropriately attached to the lower load block or overhaul ball, or to a structural member within the personnel platform capable of supporting a fall impact.

CHAPTER 9—SPECIAL APPLICATIONS

Working on Flat Roof More Than 50 Feet Wide

♦ Personnel must be protected from falls from flat roofs that are more than 50 feet wide by a motion-stopping system (which could include guardrails, scaffolds, platforms with guardrails, safety nets, and PAFS) OR by a warning line system erected not less than 6 feet from unprotected edges where there is a danger of personnel falling and not less than 10 feet from edges where mobile mechanical equipment is used (except wheel barrows and mop carts).

○ If a warning line system is used and personnel are within 6 feet of an unprotected edge, then a motion-stopping system or safety monitoring system must be used.

○ A safety monitoring system is considered the least effective option for fall protection.

Overhand Bricklaying

♦ A controlled access zone (CAZ) may be used without a motion-stopping system; however, access to the zone must be limited to the employees engaged in the work, and a safety monitoring system should be in place.

♦ Where guardrail systems are in place but have to be removed for overhand bricklaying work, only that portion of the guardrail may be removed that interferes with the day's work.

Steel Erection—Proposed Standards

♦ A 15-foot height triggers fall protection requirements for steel erection work.

  ○ Workers performing steel connecting may use their judgment whether to actually tie-off under certain circumstances where the connector could be at greater risk.

♦ Fall protection may include a perimeter safety cable system, guardrail systems, safety net systems, and/or PAFS or fall retraint (work positioning) systems.

♦ A controlled decking zone (CDZ) is an area where trained workers may perform leading edge work without fall protection, even though there is a fall exposure over 15 feet and up to 30 feet.

♦ All materials, equipment, and tools which are not in use while aloft must be secured against accidental displacement.

Electrical Transmission and Distribution Work

♦ Fall arrest equipment, work positioning equipment, or travel restricting equipment shall be used by employees working at elevated locations more than 4 feet above the ground on poles, towers, or similar structures if other fall protection has not been provided.

  ○ Fall protection equipment is not required for a qualified employee who is climbing or changing locations on poles, towers, or similar structures, unless weather conditions or contaminants on the structure make such equipment necessary for all personnel.

♦ When covers are removed from enclosed spaces (such as manholes or utility vaults), the opening shall be promptly guarded by a railing, temporary cover, or other barrier.

Books and Publications

American National Standard ANSI A14.7-1991, "Safety Requirements for Mobile Ladder Stands and Mobile Ladder Stand Platforms."

Bureau of Labor Statistics, U.S. DOL, *Occupational Injuries and Illnesses: Counts, Rates, and Characteristics*, published for the years 1994, 1995, and 1996 (Washington, D.C.: USGPO).

J. Nigel Ellis, Ph.D., CSP, P.E., *Introduction to Fall Protection*, 2nd ed. (Des Plaines, IL: American Society of Safety Engineers, 1993), 228 pages.

George Swartz, CSP, *Forklift Safety* (Rockville, MD: Government Institutes, 1997), 358 pages.

Texas Workers' Compensation Commission, *Fatal Occupational Injuries in Texas 1997* (Austin, TX: TWCC), and same title for 1996, 1995, 1994, and 1993.

Texas Workers' Compensation Commission, *Occupational Injuries and Illnesses in Texas 1996* (Austin, TX: TWCC), and same title for 1995, 1994, 1993, and 1992.

OSHA's Construction Standards

Fall Protection, 29 CFR 1926 Subpart M (§500 to 503 and Appendices A–E).

Safety Belts, Lifelines, and Lanyards, 29 CFR 1926.104.

Safety Nets, 29 CFR 1926.105.

Stairways and Ladders, 29 CFR 1926 Subpart X (§1050 to 1060 and Appendix A).

Personnel Hoists, 29 CFR 1926.552(c).

Cranes and Derricks, 29 CFR 1926.550(g).

Steel Erection, 29 CFR 1926.750(b) and 1926.752(e)–(k).

Proposed Safety Standards for Steel Erection, published on August 13, 1998 in the *Federal Register*, 63:43451-43513.

General Requirements for Storage, 29 CFR 1926.250(b).

OSHA's General Industry Standards

Walking-Working Surfaces, 29 CFR 1910 Subpart D (§21 to 32).

Powered Platforms, Manlifts, and Vehicle-Mounted Work Platforms, 29 CFR 1910 Subpart F (§66, Appendices A–D, §67 to 70).

Electrical Transmission and Distribution, 29 CFR 1910.269(e)(5) removal of covers, and 1910.269(g)(2) fall arrest equipment.

OSHA Compliance Directives and Standards Interpretations

Subpart M Interpretations and Clarifications—"Fall Protection" (http://www.osha-slc.gov/Publications/Const_Res_Man/1926m_interps.html).

Interpretation Letter, 1926.501, "Fall protection during rebar assembly construction" (http://www.osha-slc.gov/OshDoc/Interp_data/19941223.html).

Interpretation Letter, 1926.104, 105, 107, and 750, "Fall Protection in Steel Erection" (http://www.osha-slc.gov/OshDoc/Interp_data_/19950710A.html).

OSHA Directive 99-1 (CPL 2-1)—"Steel Erection" (http://www.osha-slc.gov/OshDoc/Directive_data/99-1_CPL_2-1.html).

OSHA Directive STD 3.1—"Interim Fall Protection Compliance Guidelines for Residential Construction" (http://www.osha-slc.gov/OshDoc/Directive_data/STD_3_1.html).

OSHA Directive STD 3-6.1—1926.250(b)(1), "Material Storage—as related to interim storage of temporary flooring used in steel erection" (http://www.osha-slc.gov/OshDoc/Directive_data/STD_3-6_1.html).

OSHA Directive CPL 2-1.23—"Inspection Procedures for Enforcing Subpart L, Scaffolds Used in Construction" (http://www.osha-slc.gov/OshDoc/Directive_data/CPL_2-1_23.html).

OSHA Directive STD 3-10.2—29 CFR 1926.451(i)(8), "Multistage Suspension Scaffolds" (http://www.osha-slc.gov/OshDoc/Directive_data/STD_3-10.2.html).

OSHA Directive STD 3-10.3—29 CFR 1926.451(a)(5), "Scaffolding, General Requirements, Guardrails" (http://www.osha-slc.gov/OshDoc/Directive_data/STD_3-10.3.html).

OSHA Directive STD 3-10.4—29 CFR 1926.451, "Scaffolding" (http://www.osha-slc.gov/OshDoc/Directive_data/STD_3-10.4.html).

OSHA Directive CPL-2-1.27, "Focused Inspection Program for Intermodal Container Top Fall Protection" (http://www.osha-slc.gov/OshDoc/Directive_data/CPL_2-1_27.html).

OSHA—Miscellaneous References

"Fall Protection in Construction," OSHA Publication No. 3146-1995.

Preamble to Fall Protection Standards, Section 2, "Hazards Involved" (http://www.osha-slc.gov/Preamble/Fall_data/Fall_100003.html).

Preamble to Scaffolds Standards, Section 2, "Hazards Involved" (http://www.osha-slc.gov/Preamble/Scaffold_data/Scaffold_100003.html).

Construction Resource Manual, Appendix B, "50 Most Frequently Cited Standards, January 1, 1990–April 1, 1996 Aggregated Data" (http://www.osha-slc.gov/Publications/Const_Res_Man/AppendixB.html).

OSHA National News Release, USDL: 95-499, "Consensus Reached on Draft Proposal for OSHA Steel Erection Standard" (http://www.osha.gov/media/oshnews/dec95/osha95499.html).

OSHA Regional News Release, BOS 99-020, "OSHA Concludes Investigation of Quincy, Mass., Scaffolding Collapse Which Took the Lives of Two Young Irish Workers; Proposes Penalties Totaling Over $313,000 for Willful and Serious Safety Violations by Massachusetts Contractors" (http://www.osha.gov/media/oshnews/feb99/reg1_99020.html).

OSHA Regional News Release, BOS 99-022, "OSHA Proposes Over One-Third of a Million Dollars in Penalties Against Contractor Following Scaffold Failure and Worker Death at Cutler, Maine, Naval Air Station" (http://www.osha.gov/media/oshnews/feb99/reg1_99022.html).

OSHA, *Fatal Facts.* Numbers 1, 6, 8, 12, 14, 16, 20, 21, 23, 24, 26, 27, 29, 32, 42, 43, 46, 47, 54, 56, 58, 62, 64, 66, 68, and 70 (http://www.osha-slc.gov/OshDoc/toc_FatalFacts.html).

NIOSH Publications

"Preventing Worker Deaths and Injuries from Falls through Skylights and Roof Openings," NIOSH Publication No. 90-100.

"Request for Assistance in Preventing Worker Injuries and Deaths Caused by Falls from Suspension Scaffolds," NIOSH Publication No. 92-108.

Magazine Articles and Published Reports

American Insurance Services Group, Inc., "Fall Management Program," *Construction Management Report,* No. 75.00, (New York, NY, September 1995).

Consumer Benefits of America, "Home Repairs and Ladder Falls," *Forum,* Vol. 11, No. 2, June/July 1998, page 3.

Robert J. Derocher, "Safe Scaffolding," *Safety & Health,* March 1999, pages 56–60.

J. Nigel Ellis, Ph.D., CSP, PE, "Reviewing Fall Protection in General Industry," *Compliance Magazine*, September 1998, pages 22–24.

Tom Kabaker, "Step Up to Ladder Safety," *Safety & Health*, January 1999 (Itasca, IL: National Safety Council) pages 60–63.

David May, "Rise and Fall," *Occupational Health & Safety*, February 1999, 40–43.

Barrett Miller, "Safe Ladder Management," *Professional Safety*, November 1997, 30–32.

Charles E. Paulson, M.S., "Fall Protection: Constructive Change," *Professional Safety*, December 1995, 37–40.

Michael R. Roop, "Rewriting the Rules of Rescue," *Occupational Health & Safety*, February 1999, 32–39.

Key Sandow,"Up on the Roof," *Occupational Health & Safety*, October 1998, 170–171.

Frank Schimaneck and David K. Merrifield, "Aerial Work Platforms: Safety, Liability and the Rental Center," *Professional Safety*, January 1998, 25–28.

Steve Spotts, "Higher Ground," *Occupational Health & Safety*, March 1998, 55–56.

Janet Willen, "How to Prevent Falls in the Workplace," *eNSC*, August 1998 (Itasca, IL: National Safety Council).

Sarah Wortham, "How to Pitch Rooftop Safety," *Safety & Health*, April 1997 (Itasca, IL: National Safety Council), 56–59.

Bob Wujek and Joseph Feldman, "Fall Protection: Beyond Harnesses and Lanyards," *Compliance Magazine*, January 1999, 20–22.

Renee Houston Zemanski, "Don't Fall for It! Wear Your Body Harness," *eNSC*, January 1999 (Itasca, IL: National Safety Council).

Manufacturer's Instruction Manuals

DBI/SALA, "User Instruction Manual: Full Body Harnesses," (Red Wing, MN: D.B. Industries, 19__), 30 pages.

DBI/SALA, "User Instruction Manual for Self Retracting Lifelines," (Red Wing, MN: D.B. Industries, 1994), 20 pages.

DBI/SALA, "User Instruction Manual for Web and Rope Lanyards Used in Personal Restraint, Work Positioning, Suspension, and Rescue Systems," (Red Wing, MN: D.B. Industries, 19__), 6 pages.

Miller Equipment, "Instruction and Warning Information," (Franklin, PA: Dalloz Fall Protection, 1999), 23 pages.

Miller Equipment, "Miller Series 52/55 Operation and Maintenance Manual," (Franklin, PA: Dalloz Fall Protection, 1999), 23 pages.

News Articles

"Study examines construction deaths in Texas," *Dallas Morning News*, Monday, December 2, 1996, pages 8D–9D.

"Man falls 100 feet to his death from scaffolding," *Dallas Morning News*, Thursday, July 11, 1996, page 26A.

"Contractor Referred for Criminal Prosecution," *Compliance Magazine*, October 1998, page 21.

"Actor injured in fall," *Dallas Morning News*, October 12, 1998, page 25A.

"26-year old dies from injuries suffered in Plano fall," *Dallas Morning News*, Tuesday, January 5, 1999, page 12A.

"Disney World worker falls 40 feet, dies," *Dallas Morning News*, Monday, February 15, 1999, page 7A.

FOR MORE INFORMATION

Additional information may be found on the OSHA web site located at www.osha.gov.

P

R

Government Institutes Mini-Catalog

PC #		ENVIRONMENTAL TITLES	Pub Date	Price
629		ABCs of Environmental Regulation: Understanding the Fed Regs	1998	$49
627		ABCs of Environmental Science	1998	$39
672		Book of Lists for Regulated Hazardous Substances, 9th Edition	1999	$79
579		Brownfields Redevelopment	1998	$79
4100	💿	CFR Chemical Lists on CD ROM, 1998 Edition	1997	$125
4089	💾	Chemical Data for Workplace Sampling & Analysis, Single User Disk	1997	$125
512		Clean Water Handbook, 2nd Edition	1996	$89
581		EH&S Auditing Made Easy	1997	$79
673		E H & S CFR Training Requirements, 4th Edition	1999	$89
4082	💿	EMMI-Envl Monitoring Methods Index for Windows-Network	1997	$537
4082	💿	EMMI-Envl Monitoring Methods Index for Windows-Single User	1997	$179
525		Environmental Audits, 7th Edition	1996	$79
548		Environmental Engineering and Science: An Introduction	1997	$79
643		Environmental Guide to the Internet, 4rd Edition	1998	$59
650		Environmental Law Handbook, 15th Edition	1999	$89
353		Environmental Regulatory Glossary, 6th Edition	1993	$79
652		Environmental Statutes, 1999 Edition	1999	$79
4097	💿	OSHA CFRs Made Easy (29 CFRs)/CD ROM	1998	$129
4102	💿	1999 Title 21 Food & Drug CFRs on CD ROM-Single User	1999	$325
4099	💿	Environmental Statutes on CD ROM for Windows-Single User	1999	$139
570		Environmentalism at the Crossroads	1995	$39
536		ESAs Made Easy	1996	$59
515		Industrial Environmental Management: A Practical Approach	1996	$79
510		ISO 14000: Understanding Environmental Standards	1996	$69
551		ISO 14001: An Executive Report	1996	$55
588		International Environmental Auditing	1998	$149
518		Lead Regulation Handbook	1996	$79
554		Property Rights: Understanding Government Takings	1997	$79
582		Recycling & Waste Mgmt Guide to the Internet	1997	$49
615		Risk Management Planning Handbook	1998	$89
603		Superfund Manual, 6th Edition	1997	$115
566		TSCA Handbook, 3rd Edition	1997	$95
534		Wetland Mitigation: Mitigation Banking and Other Strategies	1997	$75

PC #	SAFETY and HEALTH TITLES	Pub Date	Price
547	Construction Safety Handbook	1996	$79
553	Cumulative Trauma Disorders	1997	$59
663	Forklift Safety, 2nd Edition	1999	$69
539	Fundamentals of Occupational Safety & Health	1996	$49
612	HAZWOPER Incident Command	1998	$59
535	Making Sense of OSHA Compliance	1997	$59
589	Managing Fatigue in Transportation, ATA Conference	1997	$75
558	PPE Made Easy	1998	$79
598	Project Mgmt for E H & S Professionals	1997	$59
552	Safety & Health in Agriculture, Forestry and Fisheries	1997	$125
669	Safety & Health on the Internet, 4th Edition	1999	$59
597	Safety Is A People Business	1997	$49
668	Safety Made Easy, 2nd	1999	$59
590	Your Company Safety and Health Manual	1997	$79

Government Institutes

4 Research Place, Suite 200 • Rockville, MD 20850-3226
Tel. (301) 921-2323 • FAX (301) 921-0264
Email: giinfo@govinst.com • Internet: http://www.govinst.com

Please call our customer service department at (301) 921-2323 for a free publications catalog.

CFRs now available online. Call (301) 921-2355 for info.

Government Institutes Order Form

4 Research Place, Suite 200 • Rockville, MD 20850-3226
Tel (301) 921-2323 • Fax (301) 921-0264
Internet: http://www.govinst.com • E-mail: giinfo@govinst.com

4 EASY WAYS TO ORDER

1. Tel: **(301) 921-2323**
Have your credit card ready when you call.

2. Fax: **(301) 921-0264**
Fax this completed order form with your company
purchase order or credit card information.

3. Mail: **Government Institutes Division**
ABS Group Inc.
P.O. Box 846304
Dallas, TX 75284-6304   USA

Mail this completed order form with a check, company purchase
order, or credit card information.

4. Online: Visit http://www.govinst.com

PAYMENT OPTIONS

❏ **Check** *(payable in US dollars to **ABS Group Inc. Government Institutes Division**)*

❏ **Purchase Order** *(This order form must be attached to your company P.O. Note: All International orders must be prepaid.)*

❏ **Credit Card** ☐ *VISA* ☐ *MasterCard* ☐ *American Express*

Exp. ___ / ____

Credit Card No. _____

Signature _____

(Government Institutes' Federal I.D.# is 13-2695912)

CUSTOMER INFORMATION

Ship To: (Please attach your purchase order)

Name _____

GI Account # *(7 digits on mailing label)* _____

Company/Institution _____

Address _____
(Please supply street address for UPS shipping)
_____

City _____ State/Province _____

Zip/Postal Code _____ Country _____

Tel ( ) _____

Fax ( ) _____

Email Address _____

Bill To: (if different from ship-to address)

Name _____

Title/Position _____

Company/Institution _____

Address _____
(Please supply street address for UPS shipping)
_____

City _____ State/Province _____

Zip/Postal Code _____ Country _____

Tel ( ) _____

Fax ( ) _____

Email Address _____

Qty.	Product Code	Title	Price

❏ **New Edition No Obligation Standing Order Program**
Please enroll me in this program for the products I have ordered.
Government Institutes will notify me of new editions by sending me an
invoice. I understand that there is no obligation to purchase the product.
This invoice is simply my reminder that a new edition has been released.

15 DAY MONEY-BACK GUARANTEE
If you're not completely satisfied with any product, return it undamaged
within 15 days for a full and immediate refund on the price of the product.

SOURCE CODE: BP01

Subtotal _____
MD Residents add 5% Sales Tax _____
Shipping and Handling (see box below) _____
Total Payment Enclosed _____

Shipping and Handling	Sales Tax
Within U.S: 1-4 products: $6/product 5 or more: $4/product **Outside U.S:** Add $15 for each item (Global)	Maryland .... 5% Tennessee .... 6% Texas .... 8.25% Virginia 4.5%